JANE DUNKELD is a Lecturer at the University of Edinburgh. She was awarded a Ph.D in 1979 and has worked in the University's Departments of Psychiatry and Psychology since then. She has researched cerebral palsy, Down's Syndrome and child development as well as eating disorders and dieting. She is married, with four sons, and lives in Edinburgh.

GW00361220

The

GOOD DIET GUIDE

Jane Dunkeld

MA, Ph.D, C. Psychol.

ROBINSON

LONDON

Robinson Publishing Ltd
7 Kensington Church Court
London W8 4SP

First published in Great Britain
by Robinson Publishing Ltd 1995

A copy of the British Library Cataloguing in
Publication Data for this title is available from the
British Library.

ISBN 1–85487–393–8

Note
This book is not a substitute for your doctor's or
health professional's advice, and the publishers and
author cannot accept liability for any injury or loss to
any person acting or refraining from action as a result
of the material in this book. Before commencing any
health treatment, always consult your doctor.

Printed and bound in EC

Acknowledgements

With thanks for help and advice, although all errors remain my own, to Dr Peter Alston, Linda Alston, Margaret Anstis, Richard Blackwell, Professor Peter Cooper, Maud Dunkeld, Lydia Flannigan, Joseph Goodman, Professor Robert Grieve, Dr Nadine Harrison, Dr Mike Hunter, Dr Sue Llewelyn, Shrivana McConnell, Helen Murphy, Dr Anne Payne, Angela Rew, Peter Savage, Dr Jennifer Wishart and Dr Peter Wright. I am grateful to those diet manufacturers and authors who freely shared with me information about their products, books, users and results, and to the staff of the University of Edinburgh Library, the Erskine Medical Library, the National Library of Scotland, the Western General Hospital Library, and the Queen Margaret College Library. The staff of the Boots and John Menzies stores on Princes Street, Edinburgh, were unfailingly courteous and informative. I am grateful to Gillian Bromley and Elfreda Powell for their copy-editing and to everyone at Robinson Publishing, and most of all to the ex- and present dieters who shared their experiences with me.

Contents

Contents

Contents

Contents

Dieting is now part of normal behaviour. In Britain, in the USA and Europe, millions of adults are on a diet or considering dieting at any one time. But plenty of people still think that diets are bad news. They argue that dieting makes you fat, or doesn't work, or ruins your health, or is a waste of time and money because any weight loss won't last in the long term. They claim that social and media pressures make normal people want to lose weight unnecessarily, because we ought to be happy with our bodies the way they are.

So what are people who are truly unhappy about their weight supposed to do? It is very worrying to think that you may be wasting your time and money if you diet. It is frightening to think that you may be ruining your health. It is just as upsetting to be told that the answer to your unhappiness about your weight is to stop being unhappy about your weight.

Some claims made by diet manufacturers may not be reliable. Some books promoting particular diets are based on mistaken assumptions about how the body works. Not all methods of weight control are unreliable: many of them *do* offer good advice and support, but the question is, which ones?

People need information which allows them to make sensible decisions. Anyone who wants to lose weight has to make a host of personal choices: whether to diet, when to diet, what diet to go on, how best to stick to a diet, how to keep the pounds off permanently. A non-technical overview of dietary methods hasn't been available before.

In this book I have tried to present an objective and informative guide to the diets and dietary products currently on the market in Britain. By the time you read it, some of the diets I've covered may no longer be for sale and new ones will have appeared; but as you will see, any new diet is usually just an old diet in a new form.

Jane Dunkeld
Edinburgh
January, 1995

Chapter 1

The Big Issues in Dieting

Where to start?

There's nothing new about wanting to lose weight. But what's the best way to go about it? It is over a hundred years since the first diet book was published. Since then there have been thousands of others, each one supposedly based on the latest scientific thinking – whether the diets are low fat, high fat, low carbohydrate, no carbohydrate, no alcohol or two bottles of champagne a day. Before 1900 methods of weight control included applying electricity to yourself, pummelling yourself, taking 'miracle fat-reducing' pills and potions, appetite-suppressing herbs and drugs, reduced-calorie diets, having enemas, sweating off fat, having your blood let, hypnosis and taking more exercise.

All these methods have their modern counterparts. There are still pills, based on seaweed or some other miracle ingredient, filling foods full of fibre to suppress appetite, mouth sprays supposed to do the same, bodywraps which help you sweat off weight, reduced-calorie diets, enemas (now known as 'colonic irrigation' – it sounds so much nicer), electric pads you apply to yourself, health farms where they do the pummelling for you, having your fat sucked out ('liposuction'), audiotapes you can hypnotize yourself with and personal trainers to help you exercise.

Reduced-calorie diets have expanded to include diets where you can't eat certain foods, diets where you have to eat certain foods, diets where you have to eat certain foods in certain combinations and diets where you just eat diet foods. The description in the book or packet often goes on about letting you into 'secrets' that are only now being revealed to the world or about wonderful 'new' products, to persuade you that it's not just the same old stuff repackaged or the same old advice. Too often, it is.

Poor Twiggy gets a lot of stick for starting the thin craze in the   **1**

1960s, but it was Coco Chanel who said, 'I hate fat' and designed her clothes to look best on thin people. The model figure in the 1920s was even thinner than it is now. Since the sixties we have seen the rise of commercial slimming clubs, 1970s macrobiotic food diets, 1980s very-low-calorie and high-fibre diets, and every kind of pill and potion in between. They are all designed to take the pounds off you, in money if not in weight. In the 1990s there has been no let-up in the development of slimming aids. As most diet plans now come with a height/weight scale, exercise routines and a chart on which to record your progress, new angles are needed to tempt the consumer. These include videos, massage creams and aromatherapy patches.

The big commercial dieting companies are updating their wares, too. There are new ranges of low-calorie or 'healthy' meals and new varieties of meal replacements. Diet books are becoming harder to tell apart, because nearly all promote the same thing: a low-fat, high-carbohydrate diet which is, as the author invariably says, 'recommended by nutritionists'.

Drugs supposed to help weight loss have been sold for hundreds of years. Every so often, someone promises that the Holy Grail of Slimming is just round the corner: a slimming pill *with no side-effects* that really works. Drugs can be used to interfere with the processes of digestion, so that less energy is absorbed by the body; they can increase energy output, or they can interfere with appetite, either for all kinds of foods or for specific foods. Biochemists all over the world are testing such drugs now. Fat-blockers which prevent fat being absorbed are under development; safe metabolism-boosters are being researched.

However, there isn't much point in getting excited about slimming cures like these in the near future. Even if swallowing a pill every time you fancy an ice-cream appeals to you, safety-testing of these drugs (if they prove to be effective) will take many years. In the meantime, those who want to lose weight are presented with a cornucopia of slimming aids – or a minefield.

Who goes on diets?
No one knows how many people go on a diet during their lifetime, because a proper survey has never been carried out. Statistics about the proportion of people dieting at any one time are frequently exaggerated.

One survey found that 32 per cent of respondents were trying to slim at the time, but *trying* doesn't mean they were actually eating any less or taking more exercise. The British Nutritional Survey reported in 1990 that 12 per cent of women and 4 per cent of men were dieting when they carried out their research. Men were dieting for ten weeks and women for an average of about six weeks. These people were genuinely dieting; their calorie consumption was less than average, by about 300−400 calories per day.

The best estimate is that 30 per cent of all adults attempt to slim each year, though any estimate of this kind is unreliable. People have such different ideas about what being on a diet means. Some associate 'eating sensibly' with being on a diet. Those who 'watch what they eat' may not call that dieting. For some young people, dieting is not much more than cutting out a second bar of chocolate; for some adults it means having low-calorie mixers in their drinks, or reading diet magazines, or not eating cakes.

The word 'diet' comes from the Latin *dieta*, which originally meant 'a mode of life'. It then came to mean what you eat, but now the word is really taken to mean a reducing diet. Throughout this book, I have used 'diet' to mean actually trying to lose weight by altering food intake, with or without other aids like exercise or food supplements (but excluding surgical treatments). This book is for the average dieter, who is truly overweight and knows it, who wants to lose weight but who also wants to know how to do so safely and healthily. As we shall see, given the vast number of dieting methods now available, it is not surprising that estimates of how many people are really dieting, and not just saying so, vary so much.

The trouble with doctors

Some doctors are very helpful to the would-be slimmer and some are not. You know your doctor best. If you are very overweight (see the discussion on page 32) you *must* consult your doctor before dieting.

The medical world is sharply divided about dieting. Some doctors believe that it is fine to offer overweight people dietary advice, because of the potential health and psychological benefits. But many others, perhaps the majority, think that until effective methods of inducing long-term weight loss have been found it is wrong to tell people that they should pursue expensive dieting methods that are all too likely to fail. Surveys have shown that doctors are just as prejudiced as the rest of the population about overweight people, believing them to be ugly, lacking in will-power and eating to compensate for emotional problems, none of which is necessarily true.

In a survey of doctors' knowledge of nutrition carried out by the Consumer's Association, the ignorance of more than half those interviewed was described as 'appalling'. Doctors are not taught much about obesity at medical school. Much of what they learn after graduation is likely to come from representatives of commercial organizations or the food industry.

If you decide to discuss a weight problem with your doctor, bear in mind that doctors have different ideas from the rest of us about when, how and why people should diet.

- Doctors are interested in weight reduction to improve your health, not your appearance.
- Doctors often disapprove of what they call 'cosmetic' dieting. Over one-third of people worried about their weight found their doctor unhelpful, according to a Consumer's Association survey. This was especially so if the people were intending to diet to improve their looks.
- Doctors tend to be more sympathetic to male dieters, because men are biologically better at losing weight than women. As most doctors are men this siding with their own sex is understandable, but there is no evidence that men who embark on a diet are more likely to stick to it than women. In fact, in the general population, men are much more likely to be overweight than women.

The British government wants to reduce the number of people who are extremely overweight by the year 2005. Not all of them will be able to do so with their doctor's advice, unless attitudes change and new resources are given to the problem. Doctors are now encouraged to identify patients whose obesity could lead to health problems, and to advise them. Alternatively, a practice nurse may be able to help you. The Consumer's Association survey into doctors' knowledge of nutrition rated as excellent the advice given by two out of three practice nurses. Some doctors run weight-loss clinics, and if you are very heavy your doctor may refer you to a hospital-run obesity clinic.

Legislation

'Always read the small print' applies particularly to slimming aids.

In 1993 the US government banned 111 ingredients in over-the-counter diet products, because the manufacturers couldn't prove they worked. A number of other products were also banned because they were shown to be potentially lethal. In Britain, the position is not so clear-cut, partly because the government has not yet responded to calls from organizations like Diet Breakers to have claims made by some diet manufacturers challenged. However, a company was prosecuted in 1992 for making false claims, and several newspapers were reprimanded for accepting advertisements for ineffective slimming aids.

One problem is that in Britain many over-the-counter products are classed as foods, not as medicines. This means that they don't come under the Medicines Act, and so do not have to be 'safe, efficacious and of good quality', as medicines do. It seems silly that a bottle of tablets or liquid is classified as a food, but essentially if something isn't a licensed medicine then by default it's a food. In addition, when the Medicines Act was passed certain substances were excluded. If the substance had been around for a long time and was generally considered safe, for example a herb like dandelion, then it wasn't required to be licensed and is legally a food.

This rather unsatisfactory state of affairs is changing, though slowly. In Britain, new European Community laws were planned to come into effect in 1995 requiring anyone who manufactures a herbal product to obtain a licence for it. But after long discussions with the producers, the government decided that these items could continue to be sold on the old basis because they were not 'industrially produced'. Even so, EC legislation is under consideration to control slimming foods and foods used for medical purposes.

Draft EC legislation has also been drawn up to control the labelling and contents of meal replacement products, both those used only once or twice a day and those intended to replace all your meals (these are usually known as very-low-calorie diets, or VLCDs, and are covered in Chapter 6). This is expected to become law in 1995.

In Britain, new nutrition labelling requirements from March 1995 require manufacturers to detail the amount of energy (calories), protein, carbohydrate and fat in any product for which a claim (e.g., that it is a slimming food) is made. If the product makes any claims about minerals or vitamins, these have to be listed with the amount present. Unfortunately, the rules don't say how big the labelling has to be. Although slimming aids are becoming much more tightly regulated, you may still need to take a magnifying glass down to the supermarket to read the minuscule writing on the backs of some packets and cans.

Is it bad for you to be overweight, physically?

Yes, according to the British government. They believe that 'obesity is a hazard to health and a detriment to well-being – it is one of the most important medical and public health problems of our time'.

The effects of obesity on health are studied by very long-term investigations of large numbers of people. These do show that very overweight people are more likely to suffer from high blood-pressure, kidney disease, gallbladder disease, heart disease, diabetes, some forms of cancer and menstrual irregularity.

Most of the health problems associated with obesity are reversible if you lose the excess weight, provided you keep the weight off. However, it isn't necessarily bad for you to be slightly overweight. Actuaries have found that those who are tend to live longer.

Is it bad for you to be overweight, socially?

Yes, unfortunately. Studies have shown that fat people are thought of as inferior to thin people in every way, from brain power to beauty. This holds good for people of both sexes in most cultures today. There is absolutely no evidence that fat people are intellectually or physically inferior, but if you are seriously overweight then it is highly likely that you will encounter discrimination at school, at work, in the home and even from complete strangers in the street. Some American doctors have argued that very overweight people should be able to claim the same rights as disabled people, because they face similar problems – getting on and off buses, into cinemas and so forth. But some Americans are proud to be fat, and want the world to stop treating them as if they were disabled!

Is it bad for you to be overweight, psychologically?

As most of us are brought up to regard fat people with derision, it is hardly surprising that the seriously overweight can suffer from low self-esteem. Psychiatrists and psychologists have searched long and hard for proof that fat people are different from thin people in psychological make-up or personality, but there is none to be found. Plenty of large people are perfectly happy with the way they are. There are lots of magazines for the bigger woman now, devoted to fighting back against discrimination, improving self-image, and providing beauty tips and advice. Some overweight people *are* very unhappy, but they might be just as unhappy if they were thin. There is no evidence that thin people are happier in general than fat people, any more than that fat people are jollier than thin ones.

Is fat a feminist issue?

Yes, if it means that women feel pressured to diet. Feminists argue that women must insist on being accepted for themselves whatever their size. *Fat is a Feminist Issue*, Susie Orbach's bestseller, aimed to liberate women from the tyranny of dieting, by showing how compulsive eating was a way of coping with the inequalities between men and women in society.

Most people probably never think of dieting as part of the battle between the sexes. They are entirely governed by slimming for personal motives such as health and wanting to look good. There is no doubt that for some of us dieting is an enjoyable hobby – attending classes and exercises with friends, exchanging recipes and comparing notes on success can be fun. Reading diet books and daydreaming about what you will do when you are thin is not a crime. But don't mistake the dream for the reality! Being thin is not going to solve all your problems, and the cycle of perpetually trying and failing to lose weight can be miserable. Worrying about your weight can sometimes lead to illness, whether 'compulsive eating' or 'binge-eating disorder' (if you

7

are fat) or 'sub-clinical eating disorder' (if you are thin). If your work or social life is impaired or you are abusing drink or drugs because of your concern about your weight, put this book aside and consult your doctor.

Food Fact File

British people's principles of eating are:

- You should have one good meal a day. This 'proper' meal should have meat or fish, with vegetables and potato.
- You should eat what you like; everyone is different and taste is all-important.
- Variety is the spice of life. Variety makes foods more interesting and therefore enjoyable.
- Moderation in all things. You can eat what you like so long as you do it in moderation.
- If you feel fine, your diet is all right. If you feel well and you aren't putting on weight then you must be eating the right things.

Chapter 2

You and Your Weight

Sorry, there is no magic cure

It is estimated that 20 million people in Britain are overweight, 6 million of them to the extent that their obesity is life-threatening. Many are desperate for a quick solution to their problem. There isn't one. If you diet drastically and lose 42 lb (19.1 kg) in a month, as a British man did recently, you may very well die suddenly (he did). You can lose weight only if you reduce the amount of calories that you eat or increase the rate at which you use them up, or both.

- Any slimming regime offering a novel cure is conning you. Although a small weight loss occurs if, say, you wrap yourself in cling film for hours or drink pints of diuretic herbal teas, this is just a temporary effect of dehydration and will not last. Allegedly miraculous pills or indeed any other method won't work unless you also reduce your intake of food or increase your output of energy.
- Cosmetic surgery is not a long-term fix. You can have your fat sucked out, and you will lose a little weight that way, but unless you change your eating habits the fat will come back.
- Exercise isn't particularly effective as a method of losing weight, unless you also decrease your calorie intake. To lose 1 lb (450 g) in weight through exercise you would need to do 20 000 sit ups, and the body doesn't start to burn fat until you have been exercising for at least 20 minutes. It has been calculated that one of the hardest cross-country ski races in the world, a ten-hour, 49-mile slog up and down mountains in thick snow, uses up only 2 lb (900 g) of body fat.

The pros and cons of working out

Although prolonged and vigorous exercise releases chemicals into the brain which produce a natural 'high', stretching and bending in front of the TV is not going to produce the kind of euphoria experienced by professional athletes. Comparisons of dieters who exercise with dieters who don't exercise show no differences in overall happiness as a result of working out. So what's the point, if it doesn't make you cheery and it's not very effective as a method of losing weight? Well, there are many bonuses:

- Exercise will greatly improve your general health. Even gentle exercise that doesn't burn up many extra calories can help to tone up your muscles and improve your appearance.
- Exercise always increases the amount of energy you expend, and the more you exercise the more you can eat without gaining weight. So if you take up exercise while dieting, you can eat a bit more than if you weren't exercising.
- Exercise can allow you to lose a little weight without much long-term effort. If you just walk up and down two flights of stairs a day instead of using a lift, you will lose 6 lb (2.7 kg) or more in a year.
- Exercise can be useful during weight loss in that it can help to increase the proportion of lean tissue to body fat. The more lean tissue you have, the higher your metabolic rate (the rate at which you burn up energy). This tends to fall during dieting, so if you take up exercise you can reduce the extent of this fall.
- Exercise is very important if you do succeed in losing weight, because people who exercise are less likely to put the weight back on than those who don't.

The facts of fat

Humans are naturally fat – very few animals carry so high a proportion of fat in their bodies. But the facts about fat and human biology aren't all that they seem.

- Most of our fat is an energy store, in contrast to many animals whose fat is designed to keep them warm.
- Women store more fat than men, typically about 22 per cent of their body-weight. This takes the form of an extraordinary number of fat cells – some 35 billion – called adipocytes. Men have 28 billion fat cells, and their ideal percentage of fat is about 15 per cent. Nothing can change this. It is a

fundamental aspect of our biology, just as men have beards and women have babies.

- Women need their fat stores for reproduction, and even if you have no intention of reproducing in the near future your body doesn't know that. It keeps reserves in case they are needed. Girls don't begin to menstruate until at least 17 per cent of their body-weight is fat. Athletes, dancers and anorexics find that their periods stop if they allow their fat stores to fall too low.

- It's not just how fat you are, it's where it is that makes a difference. Women tend to store fat on their hips and thighs, while men tend to do so round their middles. Hip and thigh fat is under-the-skin fat and not trunk fat. Trunk fat, which is fat inside the abdominal wall, is related to chronic disease and is much more dangerous to health.

- Some women do lay down fat round their middles, as some men do on their hips. Where you lay down fat is probably genetically determined, but how much you lay down is more to do with what and how much you eat.

- The bigger your waist in relation to your hips the greater your chance of developing diabetes and heart disease. Apple-shaped people are more likely to develop these diseases than pear-shaped people, but pear-shaped people are more likely to suffer from varicose veins and have problems with their joints.

- If you divide your waist measurement by your hip measurement, you can find out your **waist-to-hip ratio**. If it is over 0.8 in a woman or 0.95 in a man, there is a higher risk of weight-related problems. Men have a far greater chance of contracting heart disease than do women, possibly as a consequence of the way they lay down fat.

- Men and women not only store fat differently but arrange their fat cells in a different way. The cells run vertically in men and horizontally in women. If you are a woman and overweight, then as you age your largest fat cells may squeeze through the connecting tissues and you end up with what people trying to take money from you call 'cellulite'. As English-speaking doctors never tire of telling us, this is just the French word for fat. If you take some 'cellulite' out of a thigh and some fat out of an arm, under the microscope they look exactly the same, because they are exactly the same. A *Which?* survey of anti-cellulite creams concluded that while they couldn't be doing much good, massaging your thighs probably helped them look better. You can do this with any cheap moisturizer.

What your body needs

To maintain an average weight of around 10 st (63.5 kg) a woman who doesn't take much exercise needs to eat about 1900 calories a day. A man of 11 st (69.9 kg) needs about 2400 per day. This is only an average: what people actually eat and how many calories they use up varies from day to day.

The food we eat is made up of various chemical building blocks, each of which affects the body in different ways. These are carbohydrates, protein, fat, fibre, and minerals and vitamins.

Carbohydrates are the main source of energy in people's diets. These come in two forms: sugars and starches. Sugars, sometimes called simple carbohydrates, are converted to glucose, which is the main fuel used by the body. They are found mainly in fruits and plant juices. The sugars glucose, sucrose, fructose, maltose and lactose are commonly found as sweeteners in many foods. These provide energy without any nutrients. There are other sweeteners, like sorbitol and mannitol, which are related to sugars and have the same calorific value, while artificial sweeteners such as saccharin and aspartame are not sugars and have no calorific value.

The other common form of carbohydrate is starch, known as complex carbohydrate, which is also converted to glucose in the body but provides a fibre residue as well. Starch is found in the roots, seeds and leaves of plants, so bread, pasta, potatoes, pulses and cereals are all good sources of starch. These are filling and inexpensive foods, generally, and provide other nutrients apart from glucose – potatoes, for example, also provide vitamin C, while pulses are a good source of protein. The Department of Health suggests that adults aim to increase their carbohydrate intake, especially of complex carbohydrates, until it provides 50 per cent of all calories from food. Currently adults eat about 7–10 oz (200–300 g) per day.

12

Protein is an essential part of any diet. Amino acids are needed for growth, repair and maintenance of the body, and some of these, the essential amino acids, cannot be made by the body and must be present in food. Protein consists of chains of amino acids, and is found in meat, fish, eggs, cheese, cereals, nuts and pulses. Protein deficiency is almost unknown in Britain; the Department of Health recommends that adults should eat between 1½ and 2 oz (45–56 g) per day.

Fat is essential to good health. Vegetable oils and oily fish contain 'essential fatty acids', essential because they are an important part of many hormones, and fat also provides an energy store. Fat makes food smoother and tastier. Fat is obviously present in butter, fats and oils, but there is 'invisible' fat in milk, nuts, meat and other foods.

The Department of Health is encouraging everyone to eat less fat; at present the average Briton eats about 3–4 oz (90–110 g) per day. Current medical opinion suggests that we should reduce fat intake by about a quarter, so that it contributes no more than 30 per cent or so of total daily calorie intake. It's particularly important for health to reduce the amount of 'saturated' fat, which is associated with the development of heart disease. Saturated fat is found, for example, in meat and butter; it is recommended we switch to mono- and poly-unsaturated fats, such as olive oil and margarine.

The health message is the same, however; whatever kinds of fat you use, reduce the amount.

Fibre intake contributes to overall health, in that it is believed to help avoid constipation, piles and diverticular disease, and to reduce cholesterol levels and the risk of certain cancers. It is the parts of a plant which the human stomach can't digest; until fibre reaches the intestine it is almost unchanged from when eaten. It comes in two forms: one can be absorbed in the intestine, but the other (which is known as 'roughage') is not soluble and leaves the body unchanged.

There have been recent improvements in the way in which the fibre content of foods is measured. Nutritionists now use the term 'NSP', which stands for 'non-starch polysaccharides', **13** instead of 'fibre', and the recommended daily intake has changed to just under $\frac{1}{2}$ oz(15 g) from 1 oz(28 g) per day.

Vitamins are made from carbon compounds, and include such well-known substances as vitamin A (essential for good vision) vitamin B2 (needed for healthy skin and eyes) and vitamin D (required for bone repair).

Minerals come from non-carbon compounds, basically things found in the earth, and are equally important for good health. Calcium and phosphorus, for example, are needed as constituents of bones and teeth; sodium and potassium help control bodily fluids; iron prevents anaemia.

Trace elements are minerals of which you need only a small amount per day, but are still very important to health; zinc, for example, helps with the healing of wounds.

Vitamins, minerals and trace elements are found in a wide variety of different foods. About £250 million per year is spent on vitamin supplements in Britain, but vitamin deficiencies are extremely unusual in someone following a normal diet. Recommended intakes are shown in Appendix I.

What does all this mean for dieters?
It is clear that a dieter should cut down on sugars as much as possible, and fill up on carbohydrate. If sugar provides only 'empty' calories, it would be better to eat something with more nutrients in it. The number of calories per gram of carbohydrate is the same as that from protein (4), but they are less 'calorifically-dense', meaning that a huge mound of boiled rice or pasta and one small chicken breast both have the same calorific value. So it would be sensible to eat more carbohydrate and less protein.

Of course, some protein is essential, but it doesn't have to come from meat and dairy produce. Cereals and pulses can provide high levels of protein and low levels of fat with the benefits of being high in fibre (and cheaper) as well.

Fat, at 9 calories per gram, is obviously not the dieter's friend. That doesn't mean that all fat should be cut from the diet. Don't overdo it: if you cut down on fat too much, you **14** might consume too few calories and a vitamin deficiency could result – some fat is essential to health. It is important to look at the labels of whatever ready-prepared foods you buy; you will be astonished to see how much fat is contained in processed foods.

Many reducing diets provide more than the recommended daily rates of fibre intake, as it is believed that a high-fibre diet not only contributes to health but actually reduces hunger. The evidence for this is rather mixed (see page 71). The point is that high-fibre foods tend to be carbohydrates, and eating carbohydrates can allow the dieter to eat more for the same calorific input as fat.

If you go on a calorie-reduced diet, you will be taking in a reduced quantity of minerals and vitamins. Many women are low in iron anyway in Britain, and nutritionists recommend that when following a diet plan they do so carefully, making sure that they don't miss out on any of the foods supplying iron. It would be sensible to choose a breakfast cereal fortified with iron, for example.

For the same reason, some nutritionists would recommend anyone going on a diet to take a multivitamin/mineral supplement – combined tablets are just as good as the ones supplying individual vitamins, and much cheaper. However, avoid any very high-dose preparations as it is possible to have too much of a good thing.

A warning note: Professor Tom Sanders, a dieting expert, has advised that young women who change to low-fat dairy products can become deficient in vitamin A, and that all very low-fat diets, particularly those which insist that you cut out oily fish, are potentially deficient in vitamins E and D.

How do you know if something is good for you?
Easy – there is no such thing as food that is bad for you, unless it's poisonous. Junk food isn't bad for you. Crisps, for example, contain lots of fibre. Chips contain vitamin C. Sugar isn't bad for you (if you brush your teeth regularly) and it makes food taste nice. Burgers have lots of protein. Nutritionists are quite clear that eating a *variety* of foods is most likely to lead to good health, however, so eating just a few kinds of food won't give you all the nutrients you require.

Even so, nutritionists have lost credibility by changing their minds every few years about what a healthy diet actually is. Fifteen years ago they used to promote high-protein, low-carbohydrate diets; these are now Bad for You. Low-protein, high-carbohydrate diets with lots of fibre are now Good for You, the ideal being the traditional foods eaten around the Mediterranean. Unfortunately a Mediterranean diet doesn't fit most people's habits, or pockets, in northern Europe.

It's often not easy to tell from the packet what you're going to get, though, particularly with regard to the amount of sugar and salt shovelled into processed foods. There isn't a standard for most food labels. Usually, 'reduced calorie' foods have 25 per cent fewer calories than the real thing; 'low calorie' means there are fewer than 40 calories per 100 grams of food. 'Calorie counted' means just that; the calories have been added up.

In Britain, the government's latest recommendations on healthy eating were published in 1994, in a report from the Department of Health's Committee on Medical Aspects of Food Policy (COMA). Many people thought the report was ludicrous because it seemed to suggest that people should reduce their consumption to strange and unappetizing amounts, like 1.9 sugar lumps or three-quarters of a Mars Bar. In fact the report's recommendations are very sensible. It suggests that in order to reduce or avoid obesity and therefore reduce the risk of cardio-vascular disease, people should:

- Eat at least two portions of fish per week, of which one should be an oily fish like mackerel.
- Use reduced-fat dairy products or spreads rather than the full-fat versions.
- Eat 50 per cent more fruit, vegetables, potatoes and bread. This works out per day as two portions of fruit and four of vegetables; two portions of potatoes, rice or pasta; and four slices of bread.
- Cut down on cakes and biscuits, from an average of four biscuits a day to two.
- Cut down on sugar intake by 5 per cent.
- Try to switch to lean meat, and reduce consumption of meat products by 50 per cent a week.

- Eat less chocolate (down from an average of one bar a week to three-quarters of a bar).
- Reduce the amount of salt in food by half. This won't affect obesity but will help to reduce the incidence of high blood pressure in older people.

Of course, for any individual food some people will eat more and some less, depending on their age, sex and level of physical activity. These are general guidelines about amounts eaten. But for optimum health, and to avoid obesity, the report recommends that no more than 35 per cent of our total daily calories should come from fat (all kinds of fats) and no more than 10 per cent of all calories from saturated fat. Carbohydrate should account for 50 per cent of our daily calories. Overall, this is the classic high-fibre, low-fat, low-salt and low-sugar diet.

Processed or organic?

Many foods must be prepared or cooked or otherwise processed before eating, and most of the methods used involve some loss of nutrients, which is why nutritionists recommend that we eat more fresh fruit and vegetables. A completely unprocessed food is something like a banana, which is just the same when you eat it as it was when picked from the tree. 'Processed' peas have been picked from the pod, but they are then boiled and canned in liquid; a method of preserving them. White sugar is processed *and* 'refined'. Sugar-cane is cut, and then processes of crushing the cane and boiling the residue begin, but the sugar is also clarified, before the processes of condensing and crystallizing it. This clarification, where the impurities in the sugar are removed, is what's meant by 'refining' — it basically means cleaning or improving. White sugar isn't better for you than brown — it's just cleaner.

Brown bread is better for you than white, however. Wheat grains have an outer husk and an inner part, the endosperm, which contains within it the tiny wheat germ. Bread is processed — mills crush the grain which is combined with yeast and water, minerals, vitamins and additives to improve its appearance and keeping qualities. Wholemeal bread, however, retains the whole of the wheat grain, whereas white bread is 'refined' by removing the bran (the husks) and germ of the wheat, leaving only the **17** endosperm. In refining the bread some fibre is lost, which is why nutritionists recommend eating wholemeal bread and pasta and using wholemeal flour, rather than white.

It's sometimes suggested that fruit and vegetables contain fewer 'toxins' than meat and fish, but in fact raw vegetables are higher in naturally occuring toxins than meat or fish. This isn't something you need worry about, because our bodies are very efficient at breaking down and eliminating such toxins. Organically grown foods haven't been shown to contain any more nutrients than those grown conventionally; they aren't better for you, though they may be better for the environment!

How much should we eat?

A brief digression for a technical note. Nutrient levels – how much you should eat of what – are calculated in different ways. The Estimated Average Requirements (EAR) for an adult man or woman's intake of protein, fat, fibre and carbohydrate are shown in Appendix I (see page 417). If you are above or below an average size, you will need to eat more or less of them.

The table in Appendix I also shows what the Department of Health calls the Reference Nutrient Intake (RNI), the amount of a vitamin or mineral which is estimated to be enough for 97 per cent of the population. That is more than enough for most people.

To complicate matters, slimming products usually refer to the Recommended Daily Amount or RDA, which is yet another way of indicating the suggested levels of vitamins and minerals. In some cases the RNI level will be lower than the RDA, in others higher.

Fortunately, there is no real need to pay too much attention to these technical terms. It is extremely unlikely that you will suffer from a vitamin or mineral deficiency if you follow a mixed diet.

The why of eating and drinking

Why do we eat in the first place? The answer seems simple – because we are hungry. But how we experience hunger varies from person to person and has nothing to do with our weight. Some people claim never to feel hungry, others to have actual pains when they are hungry. The workings of hunger are not well understood – doctors don't know exactly how changes in body chemistry are related to feelings of hunger or, for that matter, of satiety, that is, of feeling full.

It has been suggested that very overweight people have something wrong with their perception of hunger. They don't seem to recognize when they are hungry or when they are full, perhaps because their body chemistry is different and fails to send them the right signals. Tests have indicated that some fat people respond differently to the sugar content in food, but there is no real evidence that fat and thin people differ in any way in their perception of hunger and feeling full.

So if 'feeling hungry' and 'feeling full' are poor indicators of how much we eat, perhaps the body just *knows* how much to eat, in a way we have yet to discover? Perhaps it simply calculates the calorific value of the food taken in and then the brain sends out a 'stop eating' message. This intriguing idea hasn't yet been proved, and it doesn't account for the huge variation in how much we can weigh. Some individuals weigh as little as 100 lb (45.4 kg), others up to six times that.

Yet another theory is that how much we eat is ruled by the amount of energy we expend, and that for fat people the balance between the two has somehow gone awry. The appeal of this idea is that it is self-evident: most people must be balancing intake and expenditure of energy, because most people aren't fat. But this theory, like the others, has yet to be shown to be true.

If the body and brain aren't necessarily controlling the intake of food, is anything else? Because human beings are such complex creatures, there are, of course, other influences at work on what we eat. Time and again, tests have shown that variety and taste are very important in whether or not a person eats more food, but these influences are extremely hard to quantify. You don't need a Ph.D to know that if people are presented with an abundant variety of delicious foods, they are likely to eat more of them. That's a fact of life. It may also help to explain why obesity has become such a problem in the West. Each year, stores and supermarkets offer an ever more tempting array of treats, available at every season of the year through improved methods of preservation. Winters are no longer the boring routine of potatoes, carrots and apples I remember in **19** childhood; baby corn cobs, tomatoes, peppers and exotic tropical fruits can be bought all year round.

Consuming culture

What we eat is largely determined by the culture in which we are brought up. We learn to accept certain foods as 'normal' and others as foreign and nasty. There are marked differences in cuisine even among cultural and climatic neighbours. There will be foods which you are allowed to eat and those which you are not supposed to eat, and items in the second category will be perceived as less desirable. Britons don't eat horse meat, and most of them would gag at the prospect, but the French do and they enjoy it. On the other hand Britons eat swede, which the French consider a food fit only for pigs.

France and Britain are only a few miles from each other, but not surprisingly differences in what people eat and what they don't are greater where geographical distance and climatic difference increase. Few people in Western Europe would eat seal blubber, grubs or rotted fish, all considered to be delicacies somewhere else in the world.

Another factor that affects food choice is novelty. People generally don't like completely new foods, even though they like variety. If something is similar to a known foodstuff it will be eaten, but it is very hard to get people to change their eating habits if new foods aren't thought tasty and pleasant. In Britain, with its traditions of meat, bread and fried foods, plenty of campaigns to persuade people to eat more fresh fruit and vegetables have failed for this reason.

Even though what we eat, or won't eat, is influenced by culture, eating habits all over the world still share a few things in common. Everyone can distinguish sourness, saltiness and bitterness, and people like all these tastes in different combinations (again, according to their culture). In addition, everyone in the world likes the taste of sugar. Breast milk is sweet, and babies everywhere like sweet-tasting foods; only recently has the appalling high level of sugar in foods for babies been reduced. There isn't any evidence, though, that fat people like sugar more than others do.

The appearance of a food, its texture, smell and temperature **20** are also an important part of what we do and don't like.

Supermarkets introduced bakeries into their premises because the aroma of baking bread encouraged people to splash out on more groceries. Processed foods are very big business indeed, and to keep consumers happy manufacturers produce them in ever-changing varieties, using powerful advertising techniques to persuade us to buy them.

Food and society

Food is very important for social cohesion and for forming and maintaining relationships. Almost everywhere in the world offering food is seen as a sign of love, affection or friendship. Withholding food is a punishment or a sign of anger, whether sending children to bed without anything to eat or making prisoners live on bread and water. Refusing an offer of food or drink is seen as a sign of rejection.

Food is also crucial to family cohesion: eating together in a group may be the only time family members actually talk to each other and share experiences, which is why favourite family dishes can evoke pleasant memories and happy feelings. Food is shared at all major social and religious occasions. Preparing and eating food together is a cue for celebration and solemnity, whether christening parties, wedding breakfasts or funeral wakes. The major religious festivals were originally known as feast days for just that purpose, even if now we think of them as merely secular public holidays. The nature of the food we eat is invariably specific to the occasion. A birthday wouldn't be a birthday without a birthday cake, and we don't eat hot cross buns at Christmas or mince pies at Easter.

Take-aways, restaurant meals and even convenience foods are used as rewards for ourselves when we want to celebrate or just cheer ourselves up. Two-thirds of the £11.3 billion that Britain spends on catering each year is now spent on fast foods.

Food and mood

The jury is still out on the connection between what we eat and how we feel. For example, it has been suggested that eating carbohydrate makes you feel better, because carbohydrate increases the levels of a neuro-transmitter, serotonin, in the brain. Although prescribing serotonin-increasing drugs to depressed people has been shown to improve their depression, **21** there isn't any hard evidence that people in good mental health who eat lots of carbohydrate will feel happier.

In fact people do use food to change their moods, but they tend to do so in complex ways. Some women are prone to eating carbohydrate before a period, and this has been interpreted as an effort to cheer themselves up. Actually, a woman's energy intake tends to rise by up to 17 per cent in the two weeks before a period, so you may find yourself eating more pasta and potatoes simply because you are hungrier at this time.

Similarly, many women crave sugar during PMT, but this is not necessarily a question of mood. Women who crave sugar do so before, during and after feeling depressed, so there is no simple relation between feeling miserable and having a bar of chocolate. For every person who expresses a desire for more sugar or carbohydrate when they are emotionally under the weather, someone else finds that if they stop eating sweets or lay off potatoes they actually feel better. The picture isn't at all easy to understand.

If food doesn't seem to affect mood in general, does it do so specifically through the day? In many studies scientists have experimented with the composition of breakfasts and lunches to determine how different foods may affect mood (relatively few studies have included evening meals – neither diners nor scientists want to hang about laboratories till late at night). So far, the answers aren't straightforward. Eating a breakfast or lunch rich in carbohydrate but poor in protein seems to make women more sleepy and lethargic, but the effects aren't so clear for men, the elderly or young people.

Why do we pile on the pounds?

Medical textbooks always insist that 'the causes of obesity are not well understood', but certain facts about fat are well established. Professor John Garrow, Britain's leading expert in this field, believes that obesity develops as a consequence of genetic, cultural, social and psychological factors. Put another way, it's a combination of who you are, where you live, and who your parents are.

Our genes: Human beings have probably spent the last 10 000 years eating as much as possible when food was available, but only people with an ability to store food as fat would have been able to survive the inevitable famines and crop failures which occurred.

For most of human history there simply wasn't enough food around for people to become obese. Even when there was plenty of it, an incredible amount of energy was required to obtain it. If you have to grow your own food, you have to put in *real* effort. Planting, weeding, watering, harvesting, threshing, winnowing and grinding corn, hauling firewood, fetching water, finding salt and then cooking dough uses up a lot more calories than nipping down to the shops for a loaf of bread. In those societies that still live by hunting and gathering there are no fat people. Even in this century, people in agricultural societies tended to put on weight in the summer and lose it in the winter.

This implies that the ability to lay down fat stores is a consequence of natural selection. Those who couldn't do so were less likely to survive lean times or at least produce children. During the terrible drought and famine in the Sahel in the early 1980s, women lost and then regained 50 per cent of their fat each year, depending on food supply; for them their fat stores were still acting for the purpose for which they were intended.

Over thousands of years, therefore, genes that gave individuals a superior ability to store fat in lean times and use it when required could have established themselves among our ancestors. Those who had genes which performed well in this respect were more likely to have children, and those children were likely to inherit the same ability. It is known that the children of very heavy people are more likely than the children of thinner people to be heavy themselves when they grow up, which suggests there is a genetic component to fatness.

Race is another genetic component which may affect how fat we are. Asian women, for example, are more likely to be apple-shaped than European women and are more prone to heart disease. Their BMIs (see page 423) are lower than those of European women, even when they are fatter, because they tend to lay down fat differently. But while there is strong evidence of a genetic component to the ability to store fat, social and cultural factors still play a part in just how fat we get and choose to remain. Some people may have a genetic tendency to get **23** fat, but whether they do or not depends on their other circumstances.

Genetics wholly and completely determines the general shape of your body; on the instant of conception, when your mother's egg met your father's sperm, your adult height, the length and size of your bones, and the sites for distribution of fat on your body were fixed forever. Each of us is born to be the shape we are and no diet can change that.

Social influences: Lifestyles today don't demand so much energy as they used to, which may be why on average consumption is decreasing in the West. Women in Britain are eating about 250 calories a day less than they did in 1979 and men about 600. Fewer men and women work at such demanding jobs as mining and agricultural labour. Sitting in front of a computer terminal all day, taking something out of the freezer and sticking it into the microwave at night, and then settling down for the evening with the remote control would have sounded like paradise to our grandparents, but it is making us fat.

Just how fat depends on social class, at least in developed countries, especially so for women and to a lesser extent for men and children. The higher your social class, the less likely you are to be overweight. Three reasons are usually put forward to explain these findings.

- Fat people are discriminated against because they are fat. As a result, they may not get as good an education or job as thinner people, and so tend to move into a lower social class.
- People in jobs carrying a higher status *have* to be thin because it is less acceptable to be fat in the higher social classes. Such people also have the nutritional know-how, the leisure time and the money to develop a trimmer figure.
- Genes and heredity may influence both social class and degree of fatness.

No one knows the answers yet. What can be said is that poorer people have been accused of preferring less nutritious diets through feckless laziness for hundreds of years, but all the evidence shows that where good food is available at reasonable prices they will always take advantage of it.

24   Although the children of very heavy parents are more likely to be heavy than the children of thinner parents, the reason isn't necessarily *only* genetic. It has been argued that they are overweight because they share the same lifestyle as their parents. They may learn to prefer high-fat foods and dislike exercise, and so end up piling on the pounds. They may also learn different eating styles from their parents, styles different from those adopted by thinner people. For example, there is evidence that *some* fat people chew their food less thoroughly, and take bigger bites, even if they don't necessarily take more bites. Fatter children tend to watch more TV than thinner children. This may contribute to their fatness because their metabolic rate is not so high slumped in front of the TV as it would be if they were running about, or because watching TV is often associated with snacking on crisps, chocolate and ice-cream.

How fat you can be before others start to think you are fat varies all over the world. With very few exceptions, all societies prefer men to be physically large but not actually fat (Japan's Sumo wrestlers are an obvious exception). Women, on the other hand, are thinner or fatter depending on the era and culture – Marilyn Monroe, who was a size 16, might well be considered too large to be a star these days. In general a pleasant plumpness seems to have been the usual standard. It may have been recognized from earliest times that very thin women are unlikely to produce babies.

As it happens, slimness is presently in vogue. Some people argue that this is because in the past only the rich could afford to be fat, and so obesity was an obvious sign of superiority over poor people. Now virtually everyone in developed countries can afford to be fat, the rich emphasize the attractions of slimness instead. It is a way of showing that they have access to better foods and more expensive leisure pursuits than their poorer neighbours.

A weight on the mind: The psychological factors that may contribute to obesity aren't clear-cut. Some people's appetite is affected by emotional events, but not everyone's. Even where appetite is affected, some people eat more when upset, while others eat less. What is clear is that those individuals who tend to eat when distressed are far more likely to put on excess weight. And these days, as every corner shop and supermarket **25**

groans with tempting new delights, they have every opportunity to try to eat the blues away.

The way that people eat all over the world is extraordinarily different. We regard our three meals a day as the normal pattern, but it is far from universal and isn't even very old. It seems to have developed as a consequence of the demands of the Industrial Revolution, when factory bosses demanded that their workers took regular breaks for food. Elsewhere in the world people eat once or twice a day, or three or four times, or all day off-and-on.

The point is that people learn to eat when it's time for a meal, not when they are hungry. When a society changes to such an extent that it's apparently always time for a meal, you can afford to snack all day and there's no one to tell you not to eat between meals, then you are more likely to get fat. It is estimated that every hour between 7 a.m. and 12 midnight one-third of the population of Britain has something to eat or drink.

Do fat people eat more than thin people?

Fat people do eat more calories than thin people who take the same amount of exercise, otherwise they would lose weight. A fat body needs more calories than a thin one just to keep going. The problem is that it can be very hard to keep count of consumption. When asked to report what they'd had to eat, overweight people in one survey consistently underestimated their real calorific input, claiming that they ate about 1000 calories a day less than they actually did. They also overestimated their physical activity, by about 50 per cent. A similar group of lean people also underestimated what they ate, but by a much smaller margin.

When these statistics were first produced, they appeared to confirm the prejudices of many doctors who had listened for years to obese people telling them that they couldn't lose weight on what it takes to feed a sparrow. But the doctors were wrong. The real problem is that many of us don't have the slightest idea what a normal diet is or how many calories we eat. One researcher, surveying a group of people who thought they were on a low-fat diet, found that half were in fact on a very-low-fat diet and half on a very-high-fat diet. We all like to think we eat a healthy diet whether we do or not.

Calorie counting is a very inexact science for most of us. We don't weigh our food precisely, and there is no general definition of a normal-sized portion of anything. Who – except perhaps a trading inspector – goes to the butcher asking for a 'normal' sausage?

You and your metabolism

Your metabolic rate is the rate at which your body uses up oxygen. Basal Metabolic Rate (BMR) is the rate at which you use up energy when, for example, you are just lying in bed. Even while resting your body needs energy to keep breathing, digesting, repairing cells, pumping blood. There is a very clear relationship between BMR and weight; the more you weigh, the higher your BMR will tend to be. The metabolic rate of very fat women is 25 per cent higher than that of thin women.

BMR can vary between persons of the same weight, probably for genetic reasons. It also varies with your age and sex. BMR is much greater in childhood than in adulthood, and declines up to the age of about 20, though the fall for girls is more rapid than for boys, reaching adult levels by about 15.

Some of the differences in BMR between one person and another are because their bodies contain different ratios of FFM (fat free mass) to BFM (body fat mass). Fat doesn't use up a lot of energy to keep itself going, but muscle does, so the more muscle you have in relation to fat the higher your BMR. Male, and younger people have more FFM, and so their metabolic rates tend to be higher than those of female, and older people of the same height and weight.

There is a special kind of fat, brown fat, which may explain other puzzling differences between people. It is different from ordinary white fat in that it is metabolically very active, so the more brown fat you have the higher your metabolic rate. There is a lot of controversy about whether or not we can stimulate the growth of brown fat cells, but there is some evidence that people who spend a lot of time outdoors in cold weather do have more brown fat than those who cower inside by the radiator. Special new clothes which are designed to burn off brown fat have come on the market, but as yet there is no evidence that wearing them causes any metabolic change (they are hardly fashion accessories, with gaping bits at armpit and back).

It is estimated that about 1 per cent of an adult's body-weight is brown fat, but its effectiveness as a mechanism for burning off unwanted calories decreases with age. This might help to explain why we tend to get fatter as we get older. Even in countries where food is not plentiful and just living requires serious physical effort, never mind aerobics, people do tend to gain weight as they age.

So what should your BMR be? As a very rough guide, if you are just lying in bed, it is about ½ a calorie per pound of body-weight per hour, so if you weigh 10 st (63.5 kg) you will use up approximately 70 calories an hour or 1680 calories per day doing nothing except living. If you weigh 14 st (89 kg), you will need 2352 calories per day to keep on going at that weight.

In the real world we all have to get up, and BMR accounts for only about 60–70 per cent of energy expenditure. Another 10 per cent or so is taken up by what is called the thermic effects of food. It has been known for hundreds of years that when humans and animals eat their oxygen consumption increases (i.e., their metabolic rate goes up) and they burn excess calories as heat. How and why this happens is not well understood. Stimulants like caffeine, alcohol, chilli and mustard increase metabolic rate, although not by much.

It has been suggested that eating more meals per day increases metabolic rate. It seems to be true that people who eat a hearty breakfast have slightly higher metabolic rates, by about 5 per cent, than those who don't. Other studies have shown that eating breakfast increases mental performance until lunchtime, but not afterwards; for some people, drinking coffee improves mood and performance all day. It's all terribly complicated, but it doesn't mean that starting to eat breakfast if you haven't done so before will necessarily increase your metabolic rate or your brain power. It may mean that the kind of people who eat breakfast have higher metabolic rates for some reason as yet unknown.

The thermic effect of food, at only 10 per cent of total output, means that it's not really that important. Based on the daily nutritional requirement for the average woman it is only about 190 calories, and eating your food cold, drinking lots of coffee or dowsing everything with chilli won't make very much difference.

The last component of total energy expenditure is the amount of exercise you take. This is not necessarily aerobics or swimming but just the total level of physical activity, which could be knitting, taking the dog out or bathing the children. Exercise causes you to expend energy, but you have to exercise pretty vigorously to expend very much. Gentle walking uses up about 100 calories per hour, only a little more than just resting at approximately 60 per hour, whereas really brisk walking could use up 300 calories per hour.

It had been thought that prolonged exercise raised the metabolic rate even after the exercise period was over. The present consensus seems to be that this may be true for highly trained athletes, but not for ordinary people. In fact, *prolonged* exercise and a *very* low calorie diet seems to accelerate the decline in metabolic rate which is inevitable with a reduction in food intake.

Despite all the research, how our metabolism works is not well understood. Even if the differences could be put down to the genes we inherit, these shouldn't be enough to make people fat. Humans can adjust their intake to suit their output – most people, after all, are not obese – but some people don't. Why is so far a mystery.

Less weight, lower metabolic rate

When you lose weight your metabolic rate changes. As you don't have to use so much energy to keep a small body going, your resting rate is reduced; your thermic effect is reduced, because you aren't eating as much food; and your exercise output is reduced, as it takes less energy to walk a thin body to the shops than a fat one. There may well also be a physiological mechanism developed over thousands of years of human history whereby a drop in food intake tells the body that this might be the beginning of a famine. The body responds by conserving its stocks of fat and reducing metabolic rate. In fact, BMR doesn't change all that much even when a person loses an enormous amount of weight. It has been estimated that the maximum reduction possible is 25 per cent.

Concerns were expressed in the 1980s that dieting could permanently alter your metabolism. It is true that there is an *inevitable* drop in metabolic rate when you diet, but when you stop dieting your body gradually adjusts to a new metabolic rate right for your new weight, body composition and food intake. **29**

Can you speed up your metabolism?

Many diets claim to increase metabolic rate through special fat-burning exercises or dietary changes. In fact your metabolic rate will *fall* if you embark on a diet and start to shed excess pounds, for the reasons just given. You may be able to reduce the extent of that falling by increased exercise or simply by eating more (at the risk of putting the weight back on), but all this means is that your metabolic rate won't fall as far as it otherwise would have done. There is no evidence whatsoever that your metabolic rate will be higher than it was before you dieted.

Energy expenditure during physical activity is very closely related to weight: it takes more calories to do anything with a heavier body. The thinner you are, the more exercise you need to take to burn off a given weight. So how would vigorous exercise combined with a diet affect your metabolism? There is some evidence that exercising while dieting doesn't increase the amount of weight you lose. What exercise will do is preserve more of your lean body tissue. The higher your proportion of lean body tissue, the higher your metabolic rate.

Other methods of trying to increase metabolism are not recommended:

- Eating food cold, because this uses up more calories than eating it hot. The difference between having a plate of chips hot and having it cold is only 6 calories' worth of expenditure, and I know which I'd rather have.
- As temperature decreases, metabolic rate increases, but to bring about any significant change in your metabolic rate you would have to be so cold that you were shivering. Poking your head into the freezer is not an effective method of increasing metabolic rate.
- Smoking and drinking alcohol or caffeine can affect metabolic rate, but the results are hard to evaluate. Women (but not men) who drink more than ten units of alcohol per week are thinner than women who don't drink that much, but some of those not drinking will be doing so in order to lose weight. Although smoking seems to increase metabolic rate in men, it doesn't do so to any great effect in women (see the section on smoking, page 413). Caffeine does increase metabolic rate, but only very slightly. All this is aside from the

other effects of abusing these substances: terrible hangovers, lung cancer and frequent visits to the lavatory.

I am afraid that it is not possible to blame your metabolism for obesity, except in the rare cases of serious metabolic illness. Your metabolism certainly has an effect on how much you weigh, but the real reasons lie elsewhere.

How much should you weigh?

How much a person should weigh used to be calculated from the charts published by the American Metropolitan Life Insurance Company. These showed the lowest mortality associated with a particular weight for a given height, the 'ideal' weight. Those who didn't make the ideal weight faced reassessed insurance premiums.

By 1924, according to the company's charts, half of all Americans were overweight. As people got heavier and heavier in the 1920s, the ideal weights in the tables were scaled down. The scales were in any case unrepresentative – there had been hardly any women in the original sample (hardly any women had life insurance in those days). So the ideal weight for women went up between 1943 and 1959, but not for men. In 1983 the company put up the weights again for both men and women, further complicating the situation.

Some slimming aids still show the very old Metropolitan Life tables, which had ideal weights for different 'frame sizes' (i.e., body shapes). Frame-size allowances for weight were eventually dropped because people often decided themselves what frame they were and wrote it on the insurance form. Frame sizes have never been agreed on by doctors, let alone anyone else. I have never met anyone who was overweight and described themselves as having a small frame!

Calculating how much you should weigh

There are various ways to calculate whether or not a person's body shape or weight is indicative of a health risk. It is possible to measure how fat a person is by comparing the amount of Fat Free Mass (FFM) – bones, muscle, organs, etc. – with the amount of Body Fat Mass (BFM), or fat, but the only methods available are not ones you can use at home. They involve being

31

weighed underwater, using special kinds of tongs to measure skinfold thickness, or having the electrical conductivity or impedance of various parts of your body measured.

Alternatively, you can calculate the ratio of waist-to-hip size (see page 11). This will show you how your body fat is distributed – whether it is mainly abdominal or mainly on the hips, which carry different health risks – but it is not a very satisfactory index of overall fatness.

The most commonly used method today is known as Body Mass Index (BMI). This is calculated by dividing your weight in kilograms by your height in metres squared (or by multiplying your weight in pounds by 705 and dividing the result by your height in inches squared). This is incredibly difficult for those of us who failed arithmetic and can't use a calculator, so the tables on page 423 show you how to calculate your BMI whether in centimetres and kilos or pounds and inches. (You must ignore these tables completely if you are under 18; if you don't know whether or not you are fat, ask your friends. If they say you aren't fat, you aren't.)

The optimum BMIs associated with the lowest risks of mortality from all causes vary from country to country and study to study. Looking at the biggest studies, involving nearly one million people, it seems that

- The optimum BMI for women is 18.8 to 23.4
- The optimum BMI for men is 19.8 to 24.
- The optimum BMI for adults in general is 20–25.
- A BMI of 25–30 is considered mildly obese.
- Anyone with a BMI of more than 27 is putting themselves at risk of developing the diseases associated with obesity such as diabetes and high blood pressure.
- Anyone with a BMI of over 30 is technically classed as moderately obese.
- If your BMI is 40 or more, you are morbidly obese. If you haven't done so already, you must see a doctor at once for specialist advice.
- Don't think you are super-healthy if your BMI is much below 19. For women especially, this can be associated with health risks.
- The average height of a woman in Britain is 5 ft 4 in (1.63 m).

At this height the optimum BMI of 20–25 is a weight of 8 st 4 lb to 10 st 8 lb (52.7–67 kg). There is no risk to health until she reaches a BMI of 27, about 11 st 3 lb (71.3 kg). Still, very few women would not be considered overweight if seen naked at this weight, by other women if not by doctors.

Although a perfect method of calculating healthy weight has yet to be found, BMI is the best so far, because it is closely related to the percentage of body tissue which is actually fat.

A problem with BMI as a measure of ideal weight is that it is the sum of fat, bones, organs and muscle. You can have two people, one fat and one thin, who are exactly the same height and weight, for two reasons. The first is that lean muscle weighs more than fat, so if one person is a complete couch potato and the other is a highly trained athlete they may well weigh the same. The second reason is that bone is lighter than body tissue. So if you have short legs and a long trunk you will have a higher BMI than someone of the same height with long legs and a short trunk. I think you may well have noticed the shape of your body by now. You can allow yourself a few pounds of leeway if you think you've got short legs.

How fast should you lose weight?
Health professionals insist that losing 1–2 lb (450–900 g) per week is the most healthy rate and the one most likely to be maintained in terms of long-term weight loss. You may well lose more than this in the first two weeks of a diet, but this loss is always regained as it is simply a depletion of the body's essential stores of glycogen (see page 34).

What happens when you lose weight?
Losing weight should be simple. It takes a depletion of 3500 calories to shed 1 lb (450 g) of fat, so if you cut out 500 calories a day you would lose 1 lb a week.

So far so good, but there are complications. There is a decrease in metabolic rate within 24–48 hours if you go on a very-low-calorie diet. In addition, when you start to diet, some doctors believe that the subsequent weight loss activates the gene responsible for an enzyme called lipoprotein lipase (LPL), which helps store calories as fat. There are differences in the **33** activity of this enzyme, too, which depend on sex. In women the fat cells in the hips, thighs and breasts secrete LPL, while in men it tends to be fat cells round the middle. Fat cells in the abdomen release their contents for quick energy, while hip and thigh cells are intended for long-term stores. So, it is often easier for a man to shed the excess pounds round the tum than it is for a woman round her bum. This is why men are said to be better at losing weight than women.

The body keeps stores of its fuel, glucose, in the liver. The glucose is bound up in water to make glycogen. When you restrict your calorie intake, the body releases the glucose from the liver. This means that the water holding the glucose must be released as urine if the stores are to be used up. The result is that at the start of a restrictive diet you are likely to lose 3–4 lb (1.4–1.8 kg) in weight, because you lose 3–4 pints (1.7–2.3 l) of water from your tissues, and a pint of water weighs about 1 lb (450 g). This is not fat – the body hasn't started to burn fat yet – but it is going to make you think the diet is working. The moment you stop dieting these stores will come back, because you need them for long-term health.

For many women, this inevitable increase in weight just after a diet, combined with the vagaries in weight associated with menstruation, leads them to believe that all their efforts have been in vain. Suddenly, they have put on 7 lb (3.2 kg) or so in a week. The importance of a diet which encourages you to return to a 'normal' diet *gradually*, and which allows for apparent weight increases, cannot be overemphasized.

Of course, you don't only lose fat when you diet. You lose muscle as well, and if you are very heavy even bone. This is to be expected: you need more muscle and more bone to carry about a heavy body than a lighter one. Providing you don't embark on an idiotic crash diet, the amount of fat and lean tissue lost should be in the right proportion and won't cause any health problems.

Are you fat because your clothes don't fit?

If you think you are fat because standard-sized clothes don't seem to fit you, that could be because the usual dress sizes for women – 12, 14, 16, 18 and so on – are based on measurements of 18–60 year-old women taken in the early 1950s. These women had been through food rationing during the Second World War, and a recent survey has shown that their body shapes were completely different from those of women today. Now, women between the ages of 19 and 90 have fuller upper arms, their busts are larger and lower, their ribcages are larger, their waists are larger, their stomachs are more rounded and their upper hips larger than was the case 40 years ago. Today's natural shape is less like the traditional 'hour glass' and is more rounded.

It is assumed that these changes are the result of better nutrition and perhaps also because of the contraceptive pill. It's high time that clothing manufacturers paid attention to the fact that women's bodies have changed, and it would be helpful if they standardized sizes, too – one store's size 12 can be another's 16. If your clothes don't fit, it may not be because you are fat.

Do you want to be more attractive to men?

In all societies the epitome of sexual beauty is a fit and healthy young adult; extreme obesity is not generally valued in any society. But if you want to look more attractive to men, be warned: studies have shown they can't tell the difference between 'before' and 'after' photographs of women who have lost up to 18 lb (8.2 kg) in weight. So there isn't much point in trying to lose a small amount of weight in order to look more attractive on the beach. The chances are no one will notice except you. In any case, women tend to think that men prefer thinner bodies than in fact they do.

Beautiful fantasies

Supermodels attract a lot of criticism for being too thin. It's said that their quite unreal, wafer-thin image causes eating disorders in young girls. But many supermodels never diet and eat what they like apparently. So, they're lucky: they've been born with shapes we happen to find attractive and it isn't their fault if their looks are valued. The media tend to follow public opinion rather than form it in matters of the body beautiful. Ballet companies, to take another example, increasingly prefer the thinnest dancers because they say that's what the ballet-going public want.

It would be wrong to encourage little girls to think that supermodel looks are the ideal, or that they could ever be **35** attained by more than a very few individuals. Photographs of women in advertisements and magazines aren't to be trusted anyway. They are usually 'cleaned up' electronically: with the touch of a computer light-pen on a screen a model's teeth are made whiter, tiny imperfections are removed from her skin, her legs are lengthened to unnatural proportions, her bust increased or reduced. Barbie Doll's bodily dimensions could only be achieved by a woman over 8 ft (2.4 m) tall. All children have fantasies of attaining unattainable goals, but it is important to give them a sense of perspective, and to reassure them that they are loved and valued for themselves.

Whenever some film star needs publicity they give interviews about their eating problems and how they've managed to overcome them while remaining pin-thin on their personal chef's *sushi* diet or whatever. Leave that kind of talk strictly to glossy magazines. If you have emotional problems which you think may be affecting your eating patterns, please talk to your doctor and ask to be referred to a specialist.

Food Fact File

The more obviously feminine a woman looks the less likely she is to be judged as a potential manager, or as a competent person; the larger her bust, the less likely she is to be judged as intelligent.

Chapter 3

The Dangers of Dieting

Don't even think about dieting if . . .

You must *never* go on a diet without your doctor's advice if

- You are pregnant.
- You are breast-feeding a baby.
- You are under 18 years of age.
- You have or have had any kind of serious medical problems.
- Your BMI is below 20.
- Your BMI is above 30.
- You are taking any kind of prescribed medication.
- You have or suspect you have an eating disorder.

Dieting and your body

Extreme dieting can be very dangerous, which is why doctors do not recommend anyone to go on a diet of less than 1000 calories per day without medical advice. When you lose weight you lose muscle and other tissue as well as fat. Lose too much weight too fast and you may lose too much heart muscle – there have been many deaths attributed to heart failure as a result of extreme dieting.

'Yo-yo' dieting means going on a diet, losing weight, regaining the weight and going on a diet again, repeatedly. For many years this was thought to be particularly harmful. It was believed that metabolic rate was permanently slowed, that every time you dieted you put on a greater proportion of fat than you had had before, that it became progressively more difficult to lose weight the more often you dieted, and that yo-yo dieters were prone to binge-eating disorders.

Recent research has shown this not to be true. No matter how many times you diet, your body will react as if you had never dieted before, so there is no need to feel guilty and think you have ruined your health because previous diets haven't worked. Bigger people and thinner people put on and lose weight at the rates appropriate for their different body sizes. Previous dieting attempts do not affect the ability to gain or lose weight in any way.

All the great religions of the world advise their followers to fast for short periods of time, and each year millions of people do so without ill-effect. But going on a long fast in order to lose weight can be very dangerous and potentially lethal.

Dieting and your mind

People often feel happier and less anxious while dieting, particularly if they work on bad habits at the same time. Just feeling healthier is likely to improve your mood: if your thighs don't get sore from rubbing together when you walk and your knees stop hurting, then you are going to feel happier. On the other hand, the pressures of eating less, of feeling hungry, can be very frustrating, so it is not all a one-way street.

Doctors have noted improvements in self-esteem, assertiveness and self-confidence as a result of significant weight loss. If you feel you can face the world in a swimsuit you are more likely to be confident enough to go on holiday with your friends; if people start to compliment you on your appearance and pay obviously sexual attentions, self-esteem may rise.

There is a downside to improved self-esteem, however. Your family, friends and particularly your partner may not like the new you as much as the passive, self-deprecating person you may have been. Jealousy and suspicion can lead to serious relationship problems, and some people find it much easier just to put on weight again.

If you have got used to blaming all your ills on your weight – you can't find a partner, or settle in a job – and then lose weight but find that your circumstances don't change, you will have to face the fact that there are underlying problems which have nothing to do with how fat you are. The first step to feeling better is to realize that being thin is not necessarily going to make you happier.

Other factors that may affect your mood when on a diet include:

Alertness: A diet can make you feel stressed, and an extreme
diet could mean that you aren't taking enough nutrients to keep

your brain in top gear. For this reason it is not a good idea to diet while taking exams.

Carbohydrate levels: There is some evidence that carbohydrate affects mood. If your diet calls for a high carbohydrate intake which you weren't eating before, then you might feel more cheerful, but how carbohydrate works on the brain is poorly understood (see page 22). For every woman who thinks that bingeing on carbohydrate makes you fat and lethargic, another of us feels that it's only the big bar of chocolate that prevents us taking a hatchet to our loved ones at certain times of the month.

Hunger: If you cut down the amount you are used to eating then you are likely to feel hungry. However, there is no evidence that going on a particular diet will lead anyone to *crave* certain foods. A comparison of people on a very-low-calorie diet, of lean meat only and those on a low-calorie diet with all foods allowed in moderation showed no difference in increase in food cravings between them, even in those who lost the most weight. Cravings seem to be more to do with mood than with hunger.

Boredom: Allow your weight to take over all your thoughts, and you'll become a crashing bore. Worrying about a few pounds either way or counting calories obsessively is a tragic waste of time you could be enjoying.

Dieting and eating disorders

No one knows why more and more women and men have come forward with eating disorders in recent years. Although many people diet, the number with eating disorders is very low. Experts consider that dieting may possibly be a predisposing factor in the development of bulimia nervosa, but not anorexia nervosa.

Anorexia seems first to have been described in 1694, but as a problem it stretches way back into history. Many early Christian saints, like Saint Catherine of Siena, fasted for most of their lives (which were short) and induced vomiting when forced to eat. St Veronica apparently ate only bread and water for five years, **39** though other nuns claimed to have seen her binge-eating in the convent kitchen. Many bulimic patients report never having been on a diet.

Eating disorders are psychiatric illnesses which cause sufferers great distress. Where food is avoided above the barest minimum, the person is likely to have anorexia. Where food is avoided as much as possible, and then eaten hastily and in huge amounts, the person is likely to suffer from binge-eating. If food is avoided as much as possible, then eaten hastily in huge amounts, and self-induced vomiting, laxative or diuretic abuse takes place to prevent weight gain, the person is likely to be suffering from bulimia.

In all these conditions there is great shame and secrecy, a feeling of being out of control, and a strong desire to be thin, even where the person is already very thin. If you think that any of these symptoms applies to you, have a talk with your doctor and above all don't embark on a diet.

Dieting and children

There has been an alarming increase in the number of children who say they are dieting. Perhaps they are just *saying* so, because they think it's grown-up, in order to impress the person who is talking to them. Unfortunately this isn't always true: some of the children who say they are dieting *are* actually eating less. This is very bad news. Healthy eating is especially important for children, and reducing intake could interfere with their growth and development.

Don't feel it's all your fault if your child is concerned about her or his shape; there are other influences at work on children apart from the home and family. Children learn society's prejudicial attitudes towards fat people at a very early age. But next time you are at Mothers and Toddlers, resist the temptation to tell your friends that you 'hate' your thighs and bum, or how you were 'bad' and felt 'guilty' because you ate ice-cream or chocolate or whatever. Little pitchers have big ears, and it is better to keep such conversations well away from them.

Children *should not diet* except at the instigation of doctors, but there is no need for them to eat unhealthily and get fat
either. Common problems include:

Chips with everything: Reassure your child that healthy eaters don't get fat, and provide healthy meals at home. Make sure there are lots of filling and nutritious foods for a packed lunch, or badger the school into providing healthy foods if she or he takes school lunches. If all the pals are going down to the chip shop at lunchtime, check out healthier options like sandwich shops. Failing that, join up with other parents and try to persuade the chip shop to provide healthy alternatives.

Growing pains: If your pre-teen child is getting fatter, remember that it is very common for children to put on weight before their adolescent growth spurt starts. As long as she or he is happy and eating healthy foods, don't worry. Children nearly always regain their slim proportions when they have finished growing.

Fat is fat: If your child is really and truly fat and is unhappy, see your doctor. After a thorough check-up, the doctor will recommend a healthy diet for all the family, as a first step. It doesn't matter if some family members miss their sweets and biscuits; they can eat them out of the house, if they want to. It's not much of a sacrifice. The doctor will also suggest more exercise.

The sweet run: Most children buy sweets on their way home from school. It isn't fair to try to stop your child from joining in with everyone else. But you can suggest healthier options like low-fat crisps or fruit juice.

Exercise: Although children nowadays consume fewer calories, they weigh the same as they did sixty years ago, probably because their levels of physical activity are so much lower. Walk with your child to school, take him or her swimming or whatever you like doing. Research has shown that if a reducing diet is combined with exercise, overweight children lose 10 per cent more weight than if they are just on a diet alone.

Babies: Children under two *should not* be given low-fat milk products, ever. Babies need more fat and less fibre than adults. The recent COMA report (see page 16) recommended that after the age of five children eat the same kind of diet as that suggested for adults (in appropriate amounts).

41

'Mummy, they say I'm fat': Don't *ever* criticize your child's appearance or tease them about their weight. It is never helpful and is likely to make them unhappy and prone to eat more. If people do make horrible remarks to them, explain that it's because of the fat, not because they are in some way bad.

The terrible teens: It's all a lot easier when children are small. Teenage girls who will not eat are a terrible trial to their parents, though fortunately very, very few of them will develop an eating disorder. Refusing food is a common way for girls to express their increasing independence, and you can't beat it for getting your mother into a lather of hysteria. Stay calm, mothers. Find out in a peaceful moment what she will eat. Give it to her. Find something else she can argue with you about – there are usually plenty of options. What time she should come in or the state of her room could keep you going for a while.

If your teenage daughter (or more unusually son) loses a lot of weight suddenly, becomes very depressed or withdrawn, then you must seek a doctor's advice. The sooner eating disorders are recognized and treated, the better the chances of a full recovery.

Dieting and your purse

In Britain, the total slimming products market for 1992 was estimated at £1.6 billion. That doesn't include diet books or magazines. Most of this – about £1 billion – was spent on low-calorie soft drinks. About £80 million was spent on slimming aids. Companies spent nearly £8 million advertising and promoting slimming products.

The market is growing all the time. Meal replacements increased sales by 167 per cent between 1986 and 1992, while appetite suppressants, pills and potions went up by 20 per cent in the same period. In the United States 50 million dieters spend $33 billion a year on diet products and programmes.

So are you wasting your money on useless remedies? Some people are very dissatisfied with what they get for their hard-earned cash, as you will see later in this book. I have spoken to women who have spent a lifetime and thousands of pounds failing to control their weight, and to others who decided to cut down on sweets, lost weight and saved money.

If you find that you are buying every new diet that comes out, read this book carefully. Some new diets are just old diets in new packets with new names. Others describe their very ordinary ingredients using long Latin names, so check the Food Labelling section at the end of this book (pages 419–21) next time you are tempted to buy some exotic-sounding concoction. Sensible, scientifically proven and reasonably priced slimming aids are available: don't be conned.

Food Fact File

The worst diet I've ever encountered, nutritionally the pits and without doubt one of the most expensive, is the 'champagne and grapefruit' diet. Essentially this consists of seven glasses of champagne, for elevenses, lunch, early afternoon, late afternoon, early evening, dinner and before going to bed – with three grapefruits and three spoons of sugar as well. You are supposed to lose 2½ lb (1.1 kg) a day on this diet which, if you've read this far, you will know is preposterous.

Chapter 4

Is Long-Term Weight Loss Possible?

Do diets work?

There is one foolproof way to ensure that you lose weight. You have yourself confined to a locked room on a diet of 1000 calories a day, and you make absolutely sure that your minders don't give you anything else to eat. Call your doctor by all means, and he or she will tell you that you will definitely come out thinner than when you went in – *yes, every time!*

In the real world, this isn't an option. But bear it in mind the next time you moan about having eaten practically nothing but rabbit food for months and not lost any weight.

Secrets of successful slimming

Several studies have been conducted into the differences between successful and unsuccessful slimmers. In general they show that people are more likely to lose weight if

- They lose weight in the first week of the diet. In other words, they see immediate results.
- They have tried dieting before.
- They are aiming for a high monthly weight-loss.

It doesn't take genius to realize that the main secret of successful dieting is serious determination. Other characteristics of successful slimmers include

- Encouragement and support from friends and partners.
- Keeping a food diary.
- Taking more exercise.
- Cutting down on fatty foods.

People who diet successfully were found in one study to be more likely to have a normal-weight partner than an overweight one, but divorce isn't necessarily the answer to your problems! When an overweight person diets, their overweight partner tends to lose weight as well.

Who sticks to diets?

The drop-out rate for most forms of dieting is very high. There's some evidence that people who overeat for emotional reasons are more likely to drop out of treatment for obesity (in a medical setting) than those who don't. If you find that you frequently overeat when you feel anxious, or unhappy or simply when you've had a bad day, it may be better to consider dieting when you have resolved your emotional problems. Dieting is not necessarily going to help, and failing to stick to a diet may make you feel even worse than before.

How diets work

All successful diets work by reducing input, increasing output, or both.

None of this is anything new. In fact, it's basic common sense. To reduce input a diet may suggest that you eat new or unusual foods, perhaps in specific places or circumstances, or prepared in new ways. A diet may suggest, for example, that you avoid cold or fried foods, or that you should eat or drink special items before meals, or that you keep a close count of calories or a food diary. All of these methods are likely to reduce your calorie intake. Alternatively you can take drugs which act on the brain to reduce appetite, and therefore you eat fewer calories.

If you reduce your calorie intake below what you need to keep your body functioning, the extra resources must come first from stored carbohydrate (see page 34) and then from the breakdown of fat and some lean tissue. That is the only way any diet works. Increased exercise will speed weight loss, because you are increasing output, but it is a slow process if you only increase output without decreasing input.

There are as yet no drugs which safely increase metabolic rate, and therefore output. A few people abuse thyroid medicines in the hope of losing weight, but at the price of risking their health for nothing in terms of weight loss. Some of the fattest people in America, where this is more common, are thyroid-drug abusers.

45

Keeping it off once you've lost it

Even when dieting by themselves, people will agree that diets work, in that they lose weight while they are following them. But the key question is whether it is possible to keep off the pounds permanently. Most doctors would look over a period of five years to see whether a particular method had worked, or at the very least one year, but 98 per cent of ordinary people don't keep their weight to within a few pounds either way over a year anyway. When I asked people if different diets had worked for them, their time-scales for success or failure were much shorter. They had kept the weight off until they got married, went on holiday or whatever, and then admitted to going back to their bad old ways.

Statistics about the percentage of all dieters who regain weight are bandied about without any scientific justification. The most commonly quoted is that 98 per cent of dieters regain all the weight lost within five years. This figure is taken from a 1960 review of studies of treatments for obesity. It included statistics for treatments such as high-fat diets, hypnotism and milk diets, in studies dating back to 1908.

The only large-scale study of ordinary dieters – people who want to lose only a stone or so – found that 35 per cent maintained their initial weight loss for four years. Another study in which ordinary people were asked about how much weight they had lost found that after going on a diet 54 per cent had managed to maintain their weight loss, some for many years. In a *Which?* survey, 64 per cent of successful slimmers had maintained their weight loss for a year or more.

So where do all the gloom and doom figures come from? One problem is that most people do not consult their doctor every time they go on a diet or tell eminent dietary experts about how much weight they have lost. Surveys of thousands of American men and women concluded that successful weight control was more common in dieters who did so without professional help than in people who attended specialist clinics or were admitted to hospital.

Another reason for the apparently high failure rate is that for many people reading diet books is as good as going on a diet, just as reading cookery books is as good as cooking the dishes. There are plenty of self-confessed 'diet junkies' who like nothing better than reading new diet books, buying new wonder pills and thinking 'this time it will work'. No one knows how many people actually follow the diets described in books and magazines, as opposed to starting on a Monday morning and giving up by teatime.

Some diets don't work, of course, because they are absolutely useless, but there is no doubt that particular diets work very well for some people. One study showed that 61 per cent of those who had combined a very-low-calorie diet, nutritional education and behaviour therapy kept off 50 per cent of the average of a stone or so they had lost 12–18 months later.

So what are the best ways of ensuring that lost weight stays off? There are four golden rules:

- Steer clear of fatty foods. Don't go back to bad old ways of sausages and chips after you have finished dieting.
- Keep taking exercise, especially if you were taking more exercise while on the diet. Make up a weekly timetable you feel sure you can accomplish and stick to it.
- Choose a diet with a maintenance programme. This has been shown to increase the chances of keeping off the pounds in the long term.
- If you want to maintain weight loss, you can never go back to eating as many calories as you did before you dieted. Remember that once you lose weight your resting metabolic rate falls, so you need fewer calories than you did before. As a rough guide, for every pound of weight lost, you need to eat ten fewer calories per day. So, supposing you lost 14 lb (6.3 kg) on a diet, in order to maintain the weight loss you would need to consume 140 calories per day less than you did before the diet.

Questions to ask yourself before choosing a diet

It makes sense to decide why you want to diet and how you want to do it, because all the evidence suggests that motivation is a crucial aspect of successful slimming. The diet that will work for you is the one that suits your lifestyle, your food preferences and you.

The first and crucial question to ask yourself is, 'Am I overweight?' If your BMI is less than 25, you don't need to diet **47** because you are overweight (you aren't). Between a BMI of 25 and 30, there is an increasing risk that obesity could damage your health. If your BMI is above 30, you are seriously overweight and a DIY diet is not the solution to your problems. Go and see your doctor; this book is not for you.

Other factors to take into account before embarking on any diet include the following:

- Be sceptical of any method which claims to be easy, effortless, guaranteed, miraculous, magical, a breakthrough, a new discovery, mysterious, exotic, secret, exclusive or ancient (as in 'an ancient Chinese cure').
- Are there potential health risks? Read the labelling closely.
- Can you find any evidence that the diet works?
- What does the diet say about keeping off weight in the long-term? If it sounds like a quick fix, be sceptical.
- How much does the diet cost?
- Are there any hidden 'extras' that will add to the cost? A long-term weight-maintenance programme should be included in the basic price.
- How much support is given, or do you want to diet by yourself?
- Can you meet the diet's requirements? See whether it calls for sharp skills with a calculator and scales.
- Does the diet fit your lifestyle? Do you live on your own, have four ravenous teenagers to feed or live with a man who won't eat vegetables? Perhaps you are on a strict budget that precludes expensive slimming foods?
- How independent are you? Some diets are quite bossy and assume that you like a regimented existence. Others are more free-wheeling.
- What is your food style? Do you
     Nibble all day.
     Eat lots of high-fat snacks.
     'Taste' so often when cooking that you're not hungry by the time the food is ready.
     Prefer three proper meals a day.
     Like convenience foods.
     Live on biscuits, coffee and cigarettes.
     Throw nothing out.

Keep stuff in for the kids and eat it yourself.
Starve all day and binge at night.
- How do you react to food generally? Do you
  Not mind dieting in the week but must eat and drink at weekends.
  Like or dislike cooking.
  Enjoy eating new things.
  Not mind weighing everything.
  Refuse to give up the things you like.

Look at your answers carefully. Have you told yourself the truth? Are you dieting for yourself or for others? Remember, people are usually more successful if they are self-motivated, and doing something because someone else wants you to is not a recipe for success. Make sure that you decide to diet only when *you* want to. Are you being realistic? No one is going to love you more just because you're slimmer, and there is no quick fix – any weight you lose on a crash diet is going to go straight back on afterwards, probably leaving you feeling worse than before.

To help you choose a diet that will fit in with your lifestyle, the diets in this book are flagged with a 'guideline box' with ticks (yes) or crosses (no) to indicate their key aspects. The important factors to consider here are:

Cost: The first consideration is cost. If you're fabulously wealthy, you can trip off to a health farm and lose weight while having a holiday, but most of us will never be able to afford that. Any slimming club costs money; you pay to join and to attend each week, and you may have travel expenses as well. On the other hand, many people swear that handing over their hard-earned cash is what makes them more motivated to lose weight. But if you want to diet for only a short time to lose a small amount of weight, then a slimming club would be too expensive (and they probably wouldn't have you anyway).

Meal replacements and slimming foods can be useful for a short time, but they're not something you can use for the rest of your life. It would be too expensive, and these items don't provide a healthy long-term eating plan. They aren't for the long-term slimmer who has a lot of weight to lose. **49**

Having laid out the original money, there is then the cost of the diet itself to consider. If it calls for expensive ingredients you can't afford, don't buy it. All the evidence suggests that people are most likely to succeed in losing weight when the diet is closest to what they are used to eating every day. (Slimming clubs and books offer the greatest range of dietary plans.) Books seem cheaper because the initial outlay is low, but again if unusual or expensive ingredients are required then the diet itself can be dear.

Personal circumstances: The next thing to decide is whether you want to be told exactly what to eat each day or whether you want to choose from a range of foods. Review your personal circumstances: do you just have yourself to feed, or a partner or family too? If you have a family, are you the sort of dieter who likes to eat separately while dieting, or do you want to find a diet the whole family can go on, with modifications?

Can you be bothered to provide separately for yourself? Some dieters just can't stand watching others eat more than them, whereas others don't mind. If you don't want to have separate food then you must choose a diet that gives you guidance about the needs of non-dieting family members.

Restrictions: If you like convenience foods, or the odd drink, or meat, the chances are that a diet which forbids these is not going to be one you can stick to for very long. If you're a vegetarian, you'll be restricted from some menu options (grilled chicken, steamed fish etc., often appear).

Menu plans: Do you like cooking, and if so, do you prefer old favourites or cooking new dishes? Check the diet's menu plans before you buy; many books now have both simple and more elaborate dishes. It is pointless to choose a diet that needs a lot of fancy cooking if you don't usually have time and the family won't put up with it.

Sharing: Would you rather share your experience with others or diet in secret? There is evidence that the support of family and friends may be a factor in successful dieting, but if you have **50** failed time and again it's hard to face the groans when you announce yet another diet. It may be more sensible to wait until you have lost a bit of weight, and can then show you have been successful this time, before you tell your partner or friends.

Counting up: Should you choose a diet where you have to count calories and weigh amounts, weigh amounts but not count calories, or neither? Different diets have different solutions to the problems of people who don't want to weigh or count the calories in their food, and one of them may suit you.

Exercise: With all diets, you should also take more exercise, a little at a time. If you really can't face it, promise yourself that you will start after you lose a certain amount of weight. It is sometimes easier to exercise when you weigh less, and often not nearly as embarrassing.

Keeping off the pounds: After going through the pain of losing weight, you want to make sure that it stays off. A good diet will have a maintenance plan, to make sure that you don't go straight back to eating the way you did before. The plan should gradually reintroduce you to a wider variety or greater amount of foods. Make sure that any diet you use has a detailed weight-loss maintenance plan. Any plan which doesn't promote healthy eating in the long term, and which doesn't allow a variety of foods to be eaten, isn't likely to be effective over time.

You know best which strategy will work for you.

Chapter 5

How This Guide Works

Every year thousands of articles and hundreds of books are published about everything to do with diets and dieting. In compiling this guide I have used the most up-to-date scientific reports from the most respected sources and searched all the relevant computer databases for facts and figures. I have read most of the diet books currently in print and, of course, I have dieted.

The weight-loss methods I have covered are those widely available, including diets for sale in chemist's shops, health food shops and supermarkets, and dietary methods advertised in women's and health magazines. I have also included diets available from slimming clubs and books describing particular diets.

The essential criteria for judging a diet are

- Is the theory scientifically sound?
- Is the diet nutritionally adequate?
- Does the diet promote long-term healthy eating, a change in eating habits and an increase in exercise?
- Is there evidence of maintaining weight loss in the long term?
- Is the diet physically and psychologically safe?

Professionals concerned with nutrition, dietetics, psychology, psychiatry, biology, pharmacy and pharmacology and general practice have advised me, and hundreds of past or present dieters have told me of their experiences. All the personal quotes are verbatim.

The judgements made of the diets are a condensation of all of these sources of information.

The criteria
In deciding whether or not a diet was scientifically sound I looked for published evidence that it worked, or that the theory on which it was based was known to be correct.

A typical day from each diet was analysed using a computer programme. A nutritionist advised me on the basis of this analysis and a reading of the general principles of the diet on whether or not it was nutritionally adequate. (I worked out the calorie count when this wasn't given.)

Long-term healthy eating is defined as the kind of dietary regime which would conform to the current guidelines issued by the government's advisers. These suggest that for long-term health a wide variety of foods should be eaten; fat should be reduced, and fruit, vegetable and carbohydrate intake increased.

Learning new habits is considered essential if weight loss is to be maintained. If a diet simply suggests eating from a smaller plate, that's not in my view sufficient. (Of course, the space on tablets and packets is limited, and there may not be room for further information.)

You don't *have* to exercise to lose weight, but it is supposed to make it easier. Where products do give exercise plans these should be clearly laid out and easy to understand, to minimize the risk of injury.

Published reports have been used to judge how successful users of a particular diet have been in maintaining weight loss, and in assessing the known physical and psychological problems associated with any diet.

The chapters

Each chapter covers a particular category of diet – therapies, appetite suppressants, slimming clubs and so on. I have assessed diets or weight-loss methods individually under set headings, but I have begun with a general assessment of the diets in each chapter in terms of their scientific credibility, the ease with which you can stick to them, known psychological and physical problems and evidence of weight loss in the long term. Note, though, that any weight loss carries the potential for physical or psychological damage, so before embarking on a diet read Chapter 3, 'The Dangers of Dieting'.

At the end of each chapter there is an 'Overview' of the diets just covered with some comparisons between them. Obviously, comparisons can only be of like with like. It is easy to compare the sugar content of different meal replacements, for example,

but there's no point in doing that for pills. For ease of reference,
I have sorted the comparisons into tables.

The diets

I have classified each diet or dietary method by type: meal
replacement, high-fibre, low-fat, reduced-calorie and so on.

To help you to compare one diet with another, I have assessed
each diet under headings, which are expanded below. These
include:

What is it? Including a diet's history, ingredients and
flavours, details on where you can obtain it and its cost.

How does it work? Including the theory behind the diet,
the diet itself, recipes and variations.

A typical day's diet This provides an example of a typical
day's eating from the leaflet or book under discussion. If
the diet includes a choice of plans, I have chosen a day that
would be suitable for the average dieter – a woman of
average height with 1–2 st (6.3–12.7 kg) to lose. Where
applicable, a calorie count, and an estimate of the daily
cost, is also shown.

Exercise and **Learning new habits** These sections are
described if a diet includes them.

Who shouldn't use it? This tells you who the diet is not
suitable for, according to the manufacturers.

Side-effects: Unless there are unusual or specific side-effects
I haven't listed under each diet all the side-effects described
by the manufacturer if a full and complete list is given.

Additional information This describes height/weight charts,
nutritional information, helpful hints, charts to record
achievements or other material which may be included with
the diet.

Expected weight loss This tells you how much weight you
can expect to lose each week.

Keeping off the pounds If a diet includes a weight-loss
maintenance plan, this is described here.

They say What manufacturer's or author's claims are.

You say Comments from people who have tried the diet.

We say My own and others' views on the diet as a whole.

In Britain, the Advertising Standards Authority insists that the promoters of any weight-reducing programme should be able to prove any claims they make about the effectiveness of their product, and believes that treatments for obesity should not be offered to the general public. All diet aids must make clear how they work and must state that they cannot aid slimming except as part of a calorie-controlled diet. The ASA also stipulates that in advertisements claims about expected weight loss should not state that specific amounts can be lost within a stated period, or suggest that larger amounts of weight can be lost than are consistent with medical and nutritional practice.

Naturally I agree with all the points the ASA makes. But in addition I believe that all diet programmes, books, supplements and so on should indicate who can't use them; not simply use a standard phrase – 'go and see your doctor before starting a diet' – but make it absolutely clear as a matter of course that pregnant women, nursing mothers, children and those with specific medical problems shouldn't ever diet.

I don't think that a diet need necessarily come with height/weight charts, but if it does they should be accurate and indicate that a BMI of 20–25 is considered optimum for health. Similarly, a steady weight loss of 1–2 lb (450–900 g) is believed by doctors to be safest and most likely to lead to success in the long term, so if an expected weight loss is mentioned, that in my view should be the amount indicated.

Each kind of weight-loss method has particular features, so at the end of every individual diet you'll find a table which compares its characteristics with those of similar diets. For example, some particular types of diet may have certain side-effects – reduced-calorie and meal replacement diets, for example, could lead to dehydration. So, where such a method is used the advice to drink plenty of water should be given, and the table will tell you whether it is or not. For some diets you can be advised personally about health and diet at point of sale, with others there are forbidden foods, some diets don't require

55

weighing of food, some do; the table will show the important features about that diet.

Advice given in the books and diet plans may, of course, have been altered, and the ingredients and varieties of pills, supplements and meal replacements changed, since going to press.

The cost of dieting

I have calculated the cost of a diet per week on the direct cost of the diet itself (food supplies, supplements, treatments, membership fees and so on). Where a diet is an alteration of a normal diet, I have used the figure given by the Family Expenditure Survey for average expenditure per week in British households in 1992 (the latest available) as the basis of the calculation. At present the usual amount spent is around £25 per person per week. So *on average* people spend £3.57 per day on food eaten at home.

Where a particular diet stipulates one or more ordinary meals per day to be taken in addition to the dietary product, I have calculated each of these at one-third of daily cost, which is £1.19 (£3.57 divided by 3). For example, if a diet called for two food supplements per day and one 'normal' meal, the cost per day would be calculated as the price of two supplements plus £1.19.

Some diets call for relatively expensive and exotic ingredients such as tropical fruits or organic vegetables. But spending on other foods that *are* often eaten, like cakes, crisps and sweets, is reduced at the same time. So where a diet involves a change of normal eating pattern – less fat, more fibre and so on – I have calculated the cost as the average per day of £3.57.

I have not included an allowance for magazines, travel to a slimming club and the like, as this varies so much from one person to another. For diets out of books, no additional charge for the purchase of the book has been made to the usual daily expenditure. (You can buy a book, or you can borrow it from a friend or a library for nothing, so it's pointless to add such a notional item to daily food costs.)

Weights and measures

I understand the old imperial measures of length and mass, that

is, feet and inches, stones, pounds and ounces. Only a few times in my life has anyone told me their weight or height in metric terms. I don't know what a gram is, and nor do the shop assistants or supermarket staff where I buy my food. 'I'll have 400 grams of Cheddar, please' invites odd looks; they can cut half a pound by eye. You may be more up to date than I am and so may your shop assistants. I have therefore given both imperial and metric measures throughout this book.

A few of the recipes employ American cups (about 8 fl oz or 225 ml by volume), which I have not tried to change. I have also followed the recipes in their use of the familiar *tbsp* for tablespoon and *tsp* for teaspoon.

It is not easy to decipher the information about ingredients on most diet products. Normally they abbreviate a gram (about 0.035 of an ounce) as *g*; a milligram, which is one-thousandth of a gram, as *mg*; and a microgram, which is a thousandth of a milligram, as *µg*. These are the abbreviations I have used here. Other abbreviations you may come across, both in this book and in diet books and diet products are, in imperial measures, *st* for stone, *lb* for pound, *oz* for ounce, *pt* for pint, *fl oz* for fluid ounce, *ft* for foot and *in* for inch; and in metric measures *kg* for kilogram, *m* for metre, *cm* for centimetre, *l* for litre and *ml* for millilitre.

Under European law, the familiar calorie – in fact it is properly called the kilo-calorie – will soon be giving way to a new unit of measurement, the joule, on food labelling; 1 kilo-calorie equals about 4 kilo-joules, or four-thousandths of a joule. This change was first suggested nearly 50 years ago, so it's taken some time to implement (Britain decided to adopt metric measures as long ago as 1864, and we are still waiting). However, as hardly anyone knows what a joule or kilo-joule is, I have used the term calorie throughout this book.

Food Fact File

A typical Indian take-away – onion bhaji, samosa, chicken korma, rice, nan, dahl and cucumber raita – is over 2000 calories.

Chapter 6

Very-Low-Calorie Diets

What's the theory?

Very-low-calorie diets (VLCDs) are designed to enable you to lose more weight, faster, than low-calorie diets. They are given in a form that completely replaces normal meals, and so there is no need to count calories or measure portions; at the same time the recommended daily allowance (see page 417) of minerals, vitamins and other nutrients, though not calories, is guaranteed. This is believed to be safer than devising a very-low-calorie diet for yourself.

The first very-low-calorie diets were produced in the 1920s as an alternative to fasting, which until then had been the medically preferred treatment for very overweight people. When a body fasts, it loses not only fat but also muscle, and if the muscle in question is the heart, the consequences can be dangerous, even lethal. In the 1970s VLCDs, marketed as 'liquid protein diets', were discovered to have been made from cowhide, water and sweetening. Several deaths were blamed on the use of these diets, which were nutritionally valueless.

Current VLCDs have been formulated to provide essential nutrients and high quality protein. Even so, they have proved extremely controversial. After great success in the late 1980s their sales are now declining rapidly, with the value of the market falling from over £40 million to under £4 million in five years; the Healthcrafts Five Day Diet Plan ceased production very recently, and other VLCDs available from specialized sources have also disappeared.

The latest review of the safety of the VLCDs by the United States National Task Force on the Prevention and Treatment of Obesity concluded that they were generally safe when medically supervised, but should be used only for people who are 20 per cent or more overweight (i.e., whose BMI is greater than 30). In the USA moves have been made to restrict VLCDs to doctor's prescription only; in Canada this is already law and, in addition, no low-calorie diet (i.e., less than 900 calories a day) is allowed to be advertised to the general public.

In Britain a report by the Committee on Medical Aspects of Food Policy (COMA) on the use of very-low-calorie diets recommended in 1987 that VLCDs contain a minimum of 400 calories per day including 40 g (about 1½ oz) protein for women. For men and tall women (over 5 ft 8 in, 1.73 m) the recommended minimum was 500 calories, including 50 g (nearly 2 oz) of protein. VLCDs must be supplemented with vitamins and minerals, particularly potassium.

A draft EC directive recommends that VLCDs' labelling state if the product has a laxative effect, emphasize the importance of an adequate fluid intake, and stress the need to follow instructions properly, making clear that use for longer than three weeks is not recommended, unless under medical supervision.

Do these diets work?

A review of many studies of VLCDs shows that 90 per cent of patients treated with VLCDs lost 20 lb (9.1 kg) or more (the people taking part in these studies were very overweight to start with), so it is clear that they do work when medically supervised. It seems, however, that people find a diet like this very hard to stick to for any length of time when using it by themselves. In one study 45 per cent of people dropped out before the end of the 12-week treatment. A British study of users of a VLCD, whose diet costs were paid for them, found that only 19 per cent fully complied with the diet for even two weeks.

How much fibre there is in a VLCD seems to affect how easy it is to stick to. Men who had additional fibre (30 g, just over 1 oz) in their VLCD diets lost the same amount of weight as other men who didn't have the extra fibre, but they said they found them easier to stick to.

Keeping off the pounds

If unsupervised, most people who have followed a VLCD regain most of the weight lost within a year after completing the diet, studies show. This is less likely if an exercise plan is kept up, and where advice about changes in habits and lifestyle are combined with the diet.

Any problems?

Anyone with a history of heart, gall-bladder, liver or kidney disease, stroke, hypertension (high blood-pressure), diabetes or psychiatric disorder, or who is pregnant, should not use a VLCD. A doctor's advice should be sought before use by children, breast-feeding women and the elderly.

It is likely that you will feel hungry and irritable in the evenings of the first week of a VLCD. Without medical supervision, short-term complications can include fatigue, dizziness, muscle cramping, headache, gastro-intestinal complaints and feeling the cold. The symptoms will not be very severe, and will go away when you stop using the VLCD. These side-effects are less likely if you drink enough fluid.

Although metabolic rate is depressed during the course of a VLCD, it returns to the correct level for the newly thin body at the end of the diet.

Combined with changing your habits, the diet can in fact lessen depression – this is probably because losing weight will make you feel less depressed than you were when you were overweight.

Diet type
A supervised, very-low-calorie diet.

What is it?
All meals are replaced by separate meal sachets of powder, which you mix with water to make a drink or a soup. There are also chocolate-coated meal bars.

Varieties: Drinks: chocolate, strawberry, vanilla, banana, chocolate mint and butterscotch (137 calories). Soups: vegetable and chicken with mushroom (132 calories). Bars: caramel, malt toffee, chocolate, orange (167 calories).

Ingredients: Drinks and soups: skimmed milk powder, soya flour, soya protein, minerals and vitamins, with different flavourings and colourings. Bars: oats, yoghurt, sugar and skimmed milk powder with minerals and vitamins.

The Cambridge Diet (now part of the Cambridge Health Plan) was introduced in 1984 and reformulated in 1989 to provide the calories and protein recommended by the COMA report (see page 59). It has been used by 15 million people worldwide and is now the most popular very-low-calorie diet in Britain. It is distributed only by trained counsellors and you can't buy it in shops. There are press advertisements which tell you where you can get the product, or you can call Freephone 0800 220744 for information. Packets containing 21 sachets or bars, of one variety, cost £21 each. If you dislike a certain taste, you can exchange the packet you have started without charge.

How does it work?
Obesity is bad for you but 'home-made' diets are not nutritionally complete, Cambridge Health believe. The answer is to provide full nutritional needs with the minimum of energy.

The diet
A Cambridge counsellor checks that you don't have any medical problems, advises you on the most appropriate target weight, **61**

suggests the best plan for you and offers weight maintenance advice before supplying you with the diet.

For four weeks *all* your food is replaced with Cambridge Diet products. You take three sachets a day. Each of these is mixed with 8 fl oz (230 ml) of hot or cold water using a whisk or electric blender. You can have one Cambridge Diet Meal Bar per day as well, but this will slow down weight loss. You must cut down on caffeine, but you might suffer withdrawal symptoms if you stop drinking tea or coffee altogether. Alcohol is strictly forbidden. You are given suggestions for varying the drinks. You can, for example, make them into mousses by adding smaller amounts of water, or add different flavourings to drinks, or mix different flavours, to add variety. You must also drink at least a further 4 pt (2.3 l) of water a day to avoid dehydration.

A typical day's diet

Throughout the day	*No other food* *At least 4 pt (2.3 l) water*	*0*
Breakfast	*Cambridge drink*	*137*
Lunch	*Cambridge soup*	*132*
Evening meal	*Cambridge drink*	*137*
	Calories (approx)	400
	Cost	£4.00

You can, alternatively, follow the Meal-a-Day Plan which means that you can have one 400-calorie meal a day in addition to the drinks, but of course you lose less weight.

After four weeks – and no one can continue longer than this without a doctor's permission – if you are still above your target weight you move on to the Meal-a-Day Plan. Your counsellor will provide meal suggestions or you can use the 'Trimmer' range (see page 73). If, after a week, you still have weight to lose you go back on the Cambridge Diet and continue like this, with four weeks on and one week off until you reach your ideal weight.

Variations

- Men and tall women are advised to take one extra serving per day.
- There are new self-help 'Target Groups' for those wishing to lose 2 st (12.7 kg) or more, meeting at first twice weekly and then once a week. A Target Group consultant advises and motivates you to learn to change behaviour.
- Separate groups for men are available.
- Some people use the Cambridge Diet to replace one or all of their meals, others use 'Trimmer' products (see page 73).

Who shouldn't use it?

All potential dieters are encouraged to consult their doctor if they are on any medication (other than the contraceptive pill); adolescents and people over 70, gout-sufferers, heart and stroke patients *must* consult their doctor.

The following will not be allowed to use it: children under 14; pregnant or lactating women; people who have had strokes or heart problems in the previous three months or are insulin-dependent diabetics; those who have an eating disorder or severe kidney or liver problems, are severely depressed or are allergic to milk.

Additional information

You are given a booklet which explains how to use the diet and how it works, and which contains charts on which to record your weight. You are told to see your doctor at monthly intervals to check on your progress.

A full list is given of potential side-effects from a VLCD. Your counsellor can arrange to have your urine checked to make sure that you are drinking enough water.

BMI charts are given to help you work out a healthy weight. You are told that your ideal weight should be in the range BMI 20–25, exactly in line with current medical opinion.

Your counsellor encourages you to take sensible and appropriate exercise.

Expected weight loss

According to Cambridge Health, everyone loses weight at a different rate, but you might lose a stone (6.3 kg) in one month.

Keeping off the pounds

A paperback called *The Cambridge Weight Maintenance Programme* (£1.95) provides a structured eating plan for going back on to normal foods, hints and tips about how to maintain a healthy diet and low-calorie recipes; and you can of course continue to see your counsellor.

They say

'It's simple to follow, and you don't have to count calories. It's fast, safe and effective in achieving rapid weight loss.'

You say

'I like it and use it two or three times a year when I'm going to go on holiday or for a special occasion, usually for two weeks at a time.'

'I don't mind the taste – I add different herbs and spices to the drinks and I haven't felt any ill-effects.'

'It's very monotonous and boring. I lost 12 lb (5.4 kg) the first week, then I got ill because I didn't drink enough and got dehydrated.'

'I put on weight after I stopped smoking – I think I took up drinking instead. The first time I used it was great – I lost 2 st (12.7 kg). I enjoyed the diet – I really felt in control of my life. It took me two years to put it back on. It wasn't so easy the next time.'

We say

At least with this VLCD someone is looking after you and making sure you take the diet properly and don't take it for too long.

Calorie counting	×	Less than £10 to start	×
Weighing of food required	×	Personal support	√
Forbidden foods	√	Detailed 'who can't use'	√
Suit single person	√	Emphasizes fluid intake	√
Suitable for vegetarians	√		

Diet type
A very-low-calorie diet.

What is it?
Sachets of powder which you mix with liquid, to make drinks which replace all meals, and mineral/vitamin tablets.

Ingredients: Sachets: skimmed milk, vegetable oil and dextrose (sugar). Tablets: minerals and vitamins.

First marketed in Britain in 1983, Pranavite Slim can be bought from health food shops. A six-day pack costs £16.95.

How does it work?
The very restricted calorie regime makes the body find extra energy by burning up excess fat according to the manufacturers.

The diet
Three times a day, meals are replaced with one sachet of powder mixed in water, juice or coffee. You must also take two multimineral and multivitamin tablets twice a day, and an additional 4½ pt (2.5 l) of water. No alcohol is allowed. This regime is followed for six days, the seventh day reverting to a normal diet; the procedure can be repeated for three further weeks.

Who shouldn't use it?
Anyone in doubt about their health should consult their doctor before starting the diet.

Additional information
You are encouraged to take exercise and weigh yourself every day. No side-effects are detailed.

Keeping off the pounds
If, after a while, you put on weight you are advised to 'mix and match' sachets with sensible eating, by replacing up to two meals per day.

A typical day's diet

Breakfast	*drink mixed with water*	200
Lunch	*drink mixed with water*	200
Evening meal	*drink mixed with water*	200
Extras	*multimineral and multivitamin tablets*	0
	At least 4½ pt (2.5 l) of liquid	0
	Calories (approx)	600
	Cost	**£3.00**

They say

'Does what other diets promise . . . it has helped vast numbers of slimmers in Europe, and now in this country, to lose weight without loss of physical condition.'

You say

'I took it for a fortnight. It's less embarrassing buying a diet in a health food shop than going to a counsellor. It didn't taste too bad – a bit like milk shake without the ice-cream – but I put all the weight back on in a couple of weeks of curries and lager.'

'I lost weight very quickly but that was because the drink was so disgusting it made me sick. I lost 4 lb (1.8 kg) in a week.'

We say

This diet doesn't quite give enough information on the packet to make sure that you use it properly. The labelling reads: '[a] controlled dietary regime for six days, which may be repeated up to a maximum of four weeks', and clarification had to be sought from the company's head office as to exactly what this means: it means you eat normally on the seventh day.

There is no warning on the packaging about whom this diet would or would not suit. Further information in the packet, with more detailed instructions, would ensure that the diet is used by the appropriate people in the appropriate way.

Calorie counting	×	Less than £10 to start	×
Weighing of food required	×	Personal support	×
Forbidden foods	√	Detailed 'who can't use'.	×
Suit single person	√	Emphasizes fluid intake	√
Suitable for vegetarians	√		

Food Fact File

Hippocrates, the ancient Greek doctor whose treatises on medicine were the standard textbooks for over a thousand years, took a tough line on the treatment of fatness. He recommended that fat people should eat only once a day, sleep on a hard bed, never take baths and walk naked as much as possible. They should perform hard work before eating; ideally they should be panting with exertion. The only refreshment allowed was cold diluted wine.

A very-low-calorie diet can be a good idea if you are very seriously overweight but have no other medical complications and your doctor approves. Neither of the two diets reviewed here makes it clear that doctors do not recommend VLCDs for anyone less than 20 per cent overweight, though the Cambridge Diet does clearly specify that VLCDs are not appropriate for certain medical conditions.

If you eat a VLCD you will lose weight rapidly, but at first you are only losing water and stored carbohydrate. In a weekend of 'normal' eating, you could regain all the weight you have lost. You would have to be extremely careful to eat low-carbohydrate meals on the non-diet days of the Pranavite Slim diet if you did not want to regain all the lost weight. Because VLCDs have a diuretic effect and can make you dehydrated, it is very important not to take other diuretics while using them.

Key features of VLCDs

Name	Theory scientifically proven	Promotes long-term healthy eating	Suggests new habits	Exercise plan	Weight-loss maintenance programme
Cambridge Diet	√	✕	√*	✕	√
Pranavite Slim	√	✕	✕	✕	✕

* At the Target Weight groups.

Chapter 7

Meal Replacement Diets

What's the theory?

The manufacturers of meal replacement diets argue that because their products are already calorie-counted, it is easier to follow a reduced-calorie diet. For people who are out of the house at lunchtime it may be easier to use a meal replacement than to try to concoct a low-calorie meal. In addition you don't have to worry about getting the proper nutritional balance of minerals and vitamins while you cut down on the food you eat. Meal-replacement diets have been around since the 1930s, but really took off when there was a scare about the safety of very-low-calorie diets in the 1970s. They are sold through all sorts of outlets, and tend to appear and disappear very rapidly. Body Plan, which had been popular, disappeared in 1992. Limmits and Slender have recently ceased production. Crunch&Slim is, at time of going to press, being re-packaged (new design, revised wording), so I haven't included it here. In the meantime, supermarkets have developed own-brand products. In 1993 the market in Britain was estimated to be worth £69 million.

New varieties appear constantly and flavours change with the seasons. They come in the form of milk shakes, soups, biscuits, bars and drinks, and are marketed as snack-type foods which you use to replace one or two meals per day as part of a calorie-controlled diet. Most make it clear that they are not going to work any other way.

By law, all meal replacements must state their ingredients and give nutritional information on the amount of fat, fibre, etc., they contain, and for minerals and vitamins the proportion of the Recommended Daily Amount (see page 417) which they provide. They must state that meal-replacement diet products can work only as part of a calorie-controlled diet. EC legislation, now in draft form, if introduced, would set the minimum number of calories per meal replacement at 200; prevent diet manufacturers from saying how much weight the dieter would **69** lose, how rapid any weight loss would be, or that the products reduced hunger or made you feel full; and stipulate that it must be made clear that you should not use the product as your only source of nutrition. The details are still under discussion, but some form of this measure is expected to become law in 1995.

Do these diets work?

In theory you would lose weight if you stuck to any of the plans outlined by meal-replacement manufacturers, because all the plans contain fewer calories per day than the average person currently consumes. In one study 160 very overweight people were given Slim.Fast products for free (two meal replacements, one low-fat meal and two snacks per day) for 12 weeks. At the end of this period 149 people had lost an average of 17 lb (7.7 kg) each; presumably the rest had dropped out. There aren't any further scientific studies of meal replacements.

Drinks and soups for meal replacement are generally made up from sugar and milk, some kind of bulker or filler such as cellulose or gum, various amounts of fibre, and added vitamins and minerals.

The scientific work done to test whether or not cellulose affects appetite is mostly of poor quality. An experiment with overweight people reported in 1954 that methyl cellulose taken before meals resulted in an average weight loss of 12 oz (340 g) per week, and that was when it was taken in conjunction with a reduced-calorie diet. Another reported that very overweight women ate less at a meal if they were given 20 g (about ¾ oz) of cellulose beforehand. I couldn't find any recent studies, and anyway at that level of intake flatulence would be a serious problem. Cellulose in over-the-counter diet products is banned in the USA because the manufacturers couldn't provide any evidence that it worked.

Guar gum has been shown to make people feel less hungry and eat less. However, this was in quantities much greater than permitted under British law; after reports of the lethal possibilities of gums their level was restricted to 15 per cent of any tablet or supplement. Other gums and fruit pectin are also supposed to be filling and reduce appetite, but there's no scientific evidence that this is so.

70   The additional pills or tablets provided with some meal replacements contain ingredients supposed to aid weight loss. These come in three forms: those that have a diuretic effect, e.g., buchu or dandelion; those that act as laxatives, such as juniper, pectin or psyllium seed; and those that slow down stomach absorption, and might make you feel full, such as hydrangea and burdock. Others contain amino acids supposed to alter metabolism or hunger. One called phenylalanine has been found to alter food intake, but at much higher doses than are found in food supplements and vitamin and mineral supplements. Another, called chromium picolinate, is an insulin-sensitizing nutrient – it has not been found to affect weight loss in overweight people.

Some people claim to feel fuller after eating meal replacements. Because the diets contain quite a lot of fibre, it's possible that they do make you feel full. But does feeling full make you eat less, then or later? Scientists have carried out experiments on the role of fibre in stopping you feeling hungry while you are eating and reducing how much you eat at a later meal. Two groups were given meals of the same calorie content, but for one group they were high and for the other low in fibre. The people on the high-fibre meal (10 g or so) said that they *felt* fuller, but when offered food afterwards both groups in fact ate the same amount.

In another experiment overweight women were given tablets to take 30 minutes before a meal four times a day. Half of these tablets contained fibre and half did not, but no one knew which was which. All the women were also asked to follow a 1200-calorie-a-day diet. At the end of 12 weeks, all the women had lost weight, but the group taking the fibre pills had lost about 4 lb (1.8 kg) more than the women on the 'pretend' pills.

The ingredients in meal replacements are completely incomprehensible to the average dieter. If I gave the complete lists of ingredients for each one it would take up half this chapter and it wouldn't be much help, so I have missed out all but the main ingredients. The point is that these powders have to contain preservatives and anti-oxidants so that the contents don't go off; they need thickeners and emulsifiers to make them smooth, and anti-caking agents to keep the powder from clogging together. I've included all the commonly used ingredients in the food labelling section on page 419, so that next time you want **71** to know what tri-calcium orthophosphate is (an anti-caking agent, actually) you will know where to find out.

In theory meal-replacement diets should be easy to stick to, because they are easy to understand. You don't have to count calories if you stick to their meal plans, there's a lot of variety and you get the satisfaction of real meals as well as the replacements, which you don't with very-low-calorie diets. There aren't any figures on how easy people actually *do* find it to stick to meal replacements except for the Slim.Fast study described above; 12 weeks into the study 93 per cent were still on the diet, but this spectacularly low rate of drop-out may have been influenced by the fact that these people were not paying for any of their food while on the programme.

Keeping off the pounds

After eight months in the Slim.Fast study, 58 per cent of the original slimmers were still in the programme and able to be weighed; of these 84 per cent had maintained or increased their weight loss. A *Which?* survey found that 20 per cent of people who used them said they kept off all the weight they had lost.

Any problems?

Some doctors claim that the side-effects some people experience using very-low-calorie diets (see page 60) can also occur in people following a meal-replacement diet. It's essential that the diet gives very clear instructions about who shouldn't use it – *and that people read these*. I have come across people with high blood pressure using these products, which is potentially dangerous.

Many of the side-effects people experience are related to dehydration. The fibre and bulkers these diets contain may lead to dehydration if you don't keep up your fluid intake. You *must* drink more water than usual.

Any diet can have psychological effects, but there isn't any evidence to suggest that meal replacements are worse than any other dieting method. I haven't found evidence about effects on mood.

Diet type
Trimmer is a supervised, meal-replacement diet.

What is it?
Powdered drinks you mix with water, bars and muesli replace meals. Trimmer was first produced in 1992 by Cambridge Health, as part of their range of diet aids (see Cambridge Health Plan: Cambridge Diet, page 61), and since then has been used by approximately 100 000 people. It is available through the Cambridge Health Plan from their counsellors and through Trimmer distributors: call 01603 760777 or Freephone 0800 220744 for details.

Varieties: Drinks: raspberry delight, fruits of the forest, vanilla and chocolate orange (about 200 calories). Chocolate-coated bars: apricot and sesame, yoghurt dipped citrus (about 167 calories); and a muesli (about 195 calories).

Ingredients: Drinks: skimmed milk powder, sugar, flavourings, minerals and vitamins. Muesli: skimmed milk powder, wheat flakes, oats, nuts and fruit. Bars: oats, yoghurt, sugar, skimmed milk powder, with minerals and vitamins.

Drinks come in tubs of ten servings which cost £5.50, muesli is 85p a serving and the bars are 85p each.

How does it work?
It is difficult to eat a balanced diet while you are trying to count calories too, the makers suggest. With Trimmer all your nutritional needs are supplied by prepared products.

The diet
You replace two meals per day and have an evening meal from a special selection of recipes. You must drink ¾ pt (425 ml) of skimmed milk every day. You can use milk from this allowance to add to the muesli or in tea or coffee. You should drink plenty of water and try to avoid alcohol. Recipes are for one serving, and divided into starters, main courses and desserts. Some are vegetarian.

A typical day's diet

Throughout the day	¾ pt (425 ml) skimmed milk	145
Breakfast	Trimmer muesli, with milk from allowance	195
Lunch	Trimmer drink	200
Evening meal	Oven 'fried' fish and chips, made with 4–5 oz (110–150 g) white fish, 8 oz (225 g) potato Sautéed mushrooms Pears in berry sauce	480
	Calories (approx)	1000
	Cost	£2.81

Variations
You can use Trimmer either before you go on to the Cambridge Diet, or for the first week when you come off the Cambridge Diet.

Who shouldn't use it?
You are advised to speak to your doctor before beginning this or any other programme. Pregnant or breast-feeding women, children under 14, diabetics on insulin, people with coeliac disease, and people with eating disorders will not be supplied with the product. People over 70, adolescents, and those with any other medical problems, or who are taking medication of any kind, must see a doctor before beginning the programme. It is not suitable for anyone with a milk intolerance.

Additional information
The 'Slim Cuisine' method of cooking is described in a series of books which you can buy, priced £6.95 to £7.99. These are intended to help you learn to make healthy food choices. The height/weight charts show that the ideal weight for a medium-frame woman of 5 ft 4 in (1.63 m) is between 8 st 8 lb (54.4 kg)

and 9 st 9 lb (61.3 kg), equivalent to a BMI of between 20 and 23, which is in line with current medical opinion.

Although there is no advice on changing your habits, a counsellor will advise you on making healthy food choices.

There isn't an exercise plan, but you are encouraged to start to increase your level of activity, though taking it easy at first. The merits of various kinds of exercise – walking, dancing, rebounding and so on – are discussed.

Expected weight loss

How much weight you lose is up to you. If you reduce your intake to 790 calories per day of Trimmer products you would be expected to lose 4 lb (1.8 kg) the first week and 2 lb (900 g) in succeeding weeks.

Keeping off the pounds

There is a list of dos and don'ts concerned with weight-loss maintenance. You can ask your counsellor for a copy of *The Cambridge Weight Maintenance Programme*, a paperback book costing £1.95. This contains recipes, a calorie counter, nutritional information, charts on which to record your progress and a structured eating plan which over a month aims to find the correct calorie intake for weight maintenance for you.

They say

'Trimmer is simply healthy food made easy.'

You say

'It was good but the muesli didn't look very appetizing. The bars were better.'

'I liked the food. You didn't have to think at all about what you were eating, and it was tasty.'

'I liked my counsellor. I felt she did care and wasn't just pushing me the stuff. I did it for a couple of weeks and I lost another 5 lb (2.3 kg) – I'd been on the Cambridge before that.'

'It was a satisfying meal, but a little watery. You had to stick with it to lose weight.'

We say

You have the advantage of the counsellor with this meal-replacement system, and she would advise you to drink a minimum of 4 pt (2.31 l) of water per day. The packaging does not tell you how much you need to drink, but Cambridge Health tell me they are reviewing that policy. Doctors don't recommend diets of less than 1000 calories per day be followed without medical supervision, so I don't think the Trimmer booklet should discuss eating as few as 790 calories per day. Otherwise, they do seem to be encouraging healthy eating and exercise, and they do help with weight maintenance.

Calorie counting	×	Less than £10 to start	√
Weighing of food required	×	Personal support	√
Forbidden foods	√	Detailed 'who can't use'	√
Suit single person	√	Emphasizes fluid intake	√
Suitable for vegetarians	√		

Diet type
A meal-replacement diet combined with auto-hypnosis and supplemented with vitamin tablets.

What is it?
Cinergi is a 30-day meal-replacement programme. You get it through authorised independent Cinergi distributors, who advertise in the press.

The pack you buy contains breakfast shakes, an audiotape, an instruction and recipe leaflet, which includes a chart on which to record your weight loss, and LFL – 'Lean for Life' – capsules.

The 30-day system costs £49.95. There is also a Seven Day Trial Pack, which costs £14.95.

Varieties: Shakes: Hawaiian tropic pineapple, Dutch chocolate, wild strawberry and vanilla ice (164 calories).

Ingredients: Shakes: fructose (sugar), skimmed milk, more sugars, minerals and vitamins. LFL capsules: cellulose, gelatine, 1 and 25 mg each of the amino acids ornithine and arginine, boldo, and Bio-trim 52 (a blend of 52 minerals, vitamins and herbs, which is too long to enumerate, but includes citrus pectin, fennel, iron, guarana, rosehip, kelp and alfalfa).

How does it work?
Starvation diets, the manufacturers claim, lower your metabolic rate, and then when you eat again you get fat. Cinergi, they say, 'boosts your metabolism into life, to get you burning off fat by day and by night'.

The diet
Included in the diet pack is an instruction sheet; this explains how to use the diet, suggests a diet plan and gives instructions on cooking methods. The leaflet says that you replace one meal per day, but the tape says that you can replace two. There is a scoop in the packet. You whisk two scoops of the powder into 8 fl oz (230 ml) of skimmed milk or water for each serving. You

77

are to eat five or six meals a day, leaving out as much fat as possible, and drink plenty of liquid (at least six full glasses of water). You can drink as much fruit juice and eat as much fruit as you like.

Cinergi warn you not to eat protein after 8 p.m. at night and provide a list of 'after eight' snack ideas. If you aren't a 'shake person' you can sprinkle the mix on cereal, mix it with Angel Delight or fruit juice, or freeze a whipped shake and eat it like ice-cream.

At night you take three of the LFL capsules with water before bedtime.

A typical day's diet

Breakfast	*Shake with 8 fl oz (230 ml) skimmed milk*	*164*
Snack	*Piece of fruit, e.g., apple*	*60*
Lunch	*Baked potato with 4 oz (110 g) shelled prawns and 1 tbsp fat-free mayonnaise and green salad*	*250*
Snack	*Piece of fruit, e.g., banana*	*90*
Evening meal	*Bacon and tomato tagliatelle made with 3 strips of grilled bacon, boiled onion, 8 oz (225 g) tinned tomatoes, 2 oz (56 g) (dry weight) tagliatelle*	*450*
Snack	*Raw carrots, celery and pepper*	*40*
Extras	*6 glasses low-cal drink, two of which should be water 3 LFL capsules at bedtime*	*2*
	Calories (approx)	1050
	Cost	£4.03

Note: I have assumed that a single meal replacement is taken and included the suggested snack lunch, rather than a Hot Xero meal.

Variations

You can buy ready-prepared Hot Xero main meals from the
company. They come in seven-meal packs and each costs £2.50.
The guide menus suggest that you can have one of these for
lunch, or a baked potato and salad. The main meal suggestions
again include a Hot Xero meal, or one of seven meals, for which
recipes (for one) are given. Most of these contain meat or fish.

The 15-minute audiotape is designed to help you diet, with
separate sections for days 1, 7, 14, 21 and 28 of the programme.
You are to listen regularly to your tape, at home or in the car. A
man's voice encourages you to be positive, to change your eating
habits for life, drink water instead of eating snacks, boil food
instead of frying it, eat low-fat foods, and so on. You are given
a password that you have to think about for one week (e.g.,
'transforming'). The next week you go forward in the tape to
the next section and a new password. It's all designed to praise
you if you have lost weight, and encourage you to continue if
you haven't lost weight. The tape suggests that you try to
exercise three or four times a week for 20 minutes per session.

Who shouldn't use it?

You are advised to consult your doctor before starting any
weight-loss plan. Children and adolescents, pregnant and breast-
feeding women, diabetics and individuals with known medical
conditions should not follow a weight-reducing programme
unless under medical supervision.

Additional information

There is a progress chart on which to record your weight and
measurements, and for you to keep a note of your audiotape
passwords.

Expected weight loss

This isn't mentioned, but promotional material indicates that
one user lost 2 st (12.7 kg) in the first month on the diet, which
would be well in excess of recommended rates.

Keeping off the pounds

On reaching your target weight you should continue to take
your LFL capsules to help you maintain it.

They say

'Diets are Dead! Cinergi is a revolutionary new weight control programme which enables you to lose inches and burn off fat . . . no need to starve . . . no need to count calories!'

You say

'The shake is much better than others I've tried — it's not so sweet.'

'I didn't feel hungry because you had to eat five or six times a day. The milk shake fills you up and I lost the urge to nibble.'

'I lost 4 lb (1.8 kg) in a week, but it's very expensive.'

'I listened to the tape once. It didn't encourage me and the drink made me feel sick.'

We say

The information given with this diet is confusing. I can't recommend that anyone try it until the manufacturers alter the instructions.

- If you ate six meals a day and had a Cinergi shake as well, you couldn't possibly lose weight unless you reduced your total calorie intake.
- I think it is mistaken of Cinergi to suggest that 'the whole family' can eat the breakfast shake. The small print says that children shouldn't use the product without medical advice, but most people would understand 'the whole family' to include children. Children should not be given meal replacements, ever.
- You are told not to eat protein at night, but not why not. The list of snack ideas which you *can* eat at night includes items containing protein, such as bread and popcorn!
- It is extremely unlikely that the LFL capsules speed up metabolism. Tests have shown that the amino acids ornithine and arginine don't affect appetite in these quantities, nor does taking them lead to weight loss. The 'Bio-trim 52' blend doesn't contain any ingredients scientifically proven to produce permanent weight loss.
- The tape suggests that if you are overweight you will have a 'slow metabolism'; in fact overweight people tend to have a

higher metabolic rate. Nor is it the case that metabolic rate is elevated for hours after 'light' exercise.

The diet is not suitable for vegetarians, as the LFL capsules contain gelatine.

Calorie counting	✗	Less than £10 to start	✗
Weighing of food required	✓	Personal support	✓
Forbidden foods	✓	Detailed 'who can't use'	✓
Suit single person	✓	Emphasizes fluid intake	✓
Suitable for vegetarians	✗		

Food Fact File

Why aren't Eskimos (which means 'eaters of raw fish' – they prefer Inuit, 'human beings') ill, when they mostly eat only raw seals and raw fish, never eat vegetables and have the highest fat consumption in the world? As it happens the sea creatures they eat contain more polyunsaturated fat and far less saturated fat than land mammals, and if the offal is eaten as well this provides sufficient vitamins and minerals. Raw fish actually seems to protect against heart problems; on this diet Eskimos have very low rates of heart disease, and of arthritis, cancer and diabetes. When they start eating a typical North American diet they develop these diseases as frequently as do North Americans, so this is not a genetic difference.

Herbalife

Diet type
A meal-replacement diet with supplementary herbal, vitamin and mineral tablets.

What is it?
A meal-replacement system known as the Diet Disc Weight Loss Programme. It originates in the USA and is produced by the Herbalife Company. The diet is advertised in local newspapers and available from distributors, who may or may not come round to deliver the diet to your door. The programme consists of Formulas 1, 2, 3 and 4 (Formula 1 is essentially a tub of shake powder; Formulas 2, 3 and 4 are optional additional kinds of vitamin, mineral and herbal extract tablets), and a leaflet.

Varieties: Formula 1: Dutch chocolate, French vanilla and wild berry (166 calories when mixed with skimmed milk)

Ingredients: Formula 1: fructose (sugar), soy protein and 38 other ingredients including cellulose, citrus pectin, honey powder, guar gum, psyllium husks, papain, flavourings, minerals and vitamins. Formulas 2, 3 and 4: Various herbs, minerals and/ or vitamins; Formula 2 tablets, for example, contain more than 50 ingredients, including cellulose, fennel, chickweed, couch grass, echinacea, hawthorn and rosehip.

There seem to be different pricing systems for different combinations of shakes and tablets, but the whole course, which would last for 18–20 days, would come to about £85. If you're not delighted with the product, you can ask for your money back within 30 days.

How does it work?
Your Herbalife distributor will help you maintain motivation for this diet. No claims are made for the tablets or the powder in the literature you are given.

The diet
Recommended use consists in three meals and three snacks daily. Two of the meals are Formula 1 shakes and the third you

choose yourself; it should be low in fat and high in fibre. You mix two dessertspoons (25 g) of Formula 1 into 240 ml of skimmed milk for each meal replacement (about 1 oz of powder to 8 fl oz of milk). The two daily snacks can be either half a shake with 120 ml (about 4 fl oz) of skimmed milk, or a piece of fruit. There are details of more interesting ways to serve the drink, though as a result its calorie content will vary. For example, if you have the drink just with skimmed milk it would provide 166 calories, but if you have it as 'coffee shake' – vanilla flavour with skimmed milk, ½ a banana and 1 tsp coffee – the calorie content will be higher. There is brief guidance on the daily meal you are to take, of 350–500 calories; this doesn't make provision for vegetarians.

You must drink 4–6 glasses of liquid a day. This can be the

A typical day's diet

Breakfast	Herbalife drink with skimmed milk	166
Snack	½ Herbalife drink with skimmed milk	84
Lunch	Herbalife drink with skimmed milk	166
Snack	Piece of fruit, e.g., banana	90
Evening meal	90–120 g (3–4 oz) lean poultry 1 cup steamed vegetables 1 small baked potato 2 cups salad greens with low-cal dressing	350–500
Extras	six Formula 2, three Formula 3 tablets and three to six Formula 4 tablets Calorie free drinks	
	Calories (approx)	1000
	Cost (including milk and recommended vitamins but not special drinks)	£5.99

recommended Herbalife Watermill Purified Water or Herbalife Aloe, or other low-cal drinks.

You are also advised to take the Formula 2, Formula 3 and Formula 4 tablets. You take two Formula 2 three times per day; and one Formula 3 tablet and one to two Formula 4 tablets three times a day with meals.

Variations
People over 16 st (101.7 kg) may find it too hard to cut down to two shakes and a meal. They are recommended to have three shakes.

Who shouldn't use it?
You are advised that children, pregnant women, nursing mothers, people with chronic kidney problems and insulin-dependent diabetics should consult a doctor before considering weight control.

Additional information
You are encouraged to take mild daily exercise and to practise relaxation, but there isn't a specific exercise plan.

Keeping off the pounds
To maintain your weight, you are advised to replace one meal per day with a Herbalife drink and continue the tablets. If your weight goes up, you should replace two meals per day with a Herbalife drink. There isn't any more information.

They say
'Herbalife . . . helps you control and normalize your appetite and provides a full, satisfying feeling . . . you can lose inches as well as pounds, and it can also help reduce the appearance of excessive fat . . . assists the natural self-cleansing action of the body.'

You say
'The taste is nice, but I didn't notice any effect from the capsules.'

'I missed not being able to eat until the evening – by then I was ravenous. I lost 7 lb (3.2 kg) in two weeks, that's all I could take.'

'The recipes for mixing the powder with juices, essences, fruit, ginger ale, etc., were silly, and there weren't any recipes for the main meal. It said eat poultry, fish or meat with steamed vegetables and lots of salad, but don't they all?'

'It doesn't fill you up very much and the powder doesn't go very far. It's ridiculously expensive compared with other powders, and I think the pills must be water pills – I lost 5 lb (2.3 kg) in the first two days.'

We say

This is a very expensive meal-replacement system, but you do have the advice and help of the distributor. The tablets provide vitamins and minerals, which are always useful when slimming, but none of their ingredients have been shown scientifically to have any effect on weight when taken in these small amounts.

- The diet says that it can 'help reduce the appearance of excessive fat', a vague turn of phrase since you either lose weight on a diet or you don't. It is also said that the diet 'assists the natural self-cleansing action of the body' which could be taken to imply that it has a laxative effect. Certainly some of the ingredients in the tablets are traditionally thought to act this way.
- Because the product is low in fibre, you would need to make sure you ate a high-fibre meal every day, and the suggested fruit.
- The diet doesn't state, as it should, that the drinks should not be used as the sole source of nutrition.

Calorie counting	✗	Less than £10 to start	✗
Weighing of food required	✓	Personal support	✓
Forbidden foods	✗	Detailed 'who can't use'	✓
Suit single person	✓	Emphasizes fluid intake	✓
Suitable for vegetarians	✓		

Diet type
A meal-replacement diet.

What is it?
A powder you make into a drink, and meal-replacement lunch-bars with a recipe leaflet and advice about dieting, launched by Boots in 1993. NutraSlim can be bought in most branches of Boots. If you are dissatisfied, your money will be refunded on production of the receipt and the product.

Varieties: Drinks: summer strawberry, chocolate supreme, hot chocolate, banana, and butterscotch (each provides 193 calories). Lunchbars: milk-chocolate-coated tropical fruit, white-chocolate-coated lemon, orange, tangy apricot (193 calories each). The lunchbars used to be marketed in the Boots 'Shapers' line, but were reformulated, with added zinc and vitamin E.

Ingredients: Drink powder: skimmed milk, fructose and cellulose, with minerals and vitamins. Bars: chocolate, glucose syrup, and fruit, with vitamins, minerals, flavourings and preservatives.

Drinks cost £4.99 for 12 servings. The lunchbars are 59p each.

How does it work?
You should slim only if you are overweight, the makers say. To reduce weight you must eat fewer calories than your body needs each day. Reaching your target weight can help you look good and feel better, according to NutraSlim.

The diet
You mix the powder into hot water or cold skimmed milk, depending on the flavour, using the scoop provided.

The NutraSlim diet plan has two levels. You start off on the Rapid Weight Loss Plan, where you replace two normal meals per day with a NutraSlim drink or bar and eat two healthy snacks, one of which must be a piece of fruit. It is made clear that you must also have one proper meal per day, and it should be one of the under-400-calorie ideas from the recipe leaflet. This will provide about 1000 calories per day in total.

You should only follow the Rapid Weight Loss Plan for two weeks. If you still have weight to lose, you move on to the Steady Weight Loss Plan, which lets you have up to 1200 calories per day. You have the two snacks, a 500-calorie meal, and you still replace two meals a day with NutraSlim, but you should have an extra serving of NutraSlim as well. You are warned not to eat less than 900 calories per day in all.

You can have unlimited black tea or coffee, but no sugar. If you use skimmed milk in tea or coffee, you are allowed only five cups a day. You should drink as much water as possible.

The list of healthy snacks is designed to teach you about healthy eating; they are mostly fruit and raw vegetables, with some dairy and sweet products.

NutraSlim Rapid Weight Loss Plan: a typical day's diet

Breakfast	NutraSlim with skimmed milk	193
Lunch	Tropical fruit lunch bar	193
Snack	Piece of fruit, say apple	60
Evening meal	Cod in parsley sauce, made from 6 oz (170 g) cod, 2½ fl oz (70 ml) yoghurt, 1 tbsp parsley, mustard, lemon juice, seasonings 5 oz (140 g) carrots (boiled) 3 oz (85 g) French beans (boiled) Small wholemeal bread roll 3 oz (85 g) tomatoes	360
Snack	Piece of fruit, say banana	90
Extras	Black tea and black coffee with artificial sweeteners, if with skimmed milk no more than five cups per day	50
	Calories (approx)	1000
	Cost	£2.66

87

The recipe plan contains details of 13 meals, some under 400 and the rest under 500 calories, as single servings. To ensure a varied and balanced diet, you should select a different recipe each day. Some recipes are high in protein but low in carbohydrate, and you are advised to have a high-fibre snack that day. Others are high in carbohydrate but low in protein, so you are advised to have a high-protein snack on that day.

Who shouldn't use it?
You are advised not to use this diet plan if you are pregnant, have a medical condition or have a large amount of weight to lose, more than 20 lb (9.1 kg).

Additional information
A height/weight chart shows that a medium-frame, average-sized woman of 5 ft 4 in (1.63 m) is becoming overweight at above 9 st (57.2 kg). That is a BMI of about 22, but until you reached a BMI of about 27 there is no risk to health.

Exercise is encouraged, to increase energy output and to tone muscle. No specific instructions are given, but moderation is advised to start with. Pregnant women, those with a medical condition or a lot of weight to lose are advised to consult their doctor before taking up exercise.

Expected weight loss
The diet plan states that you should lose about 2 lb (900 g) per week after the first week.

Keeping off the pounds
As mentioned above, you start on the Rapid Weight Loss Plan and move on to the Steady Weight Loss Plan after two weeks. When you have finished dieting successfully you are to weigh yourself regularly, and if you put on a few pounds you are supposed to go back on the diet for a few days to help you control your weight.

They say
'Being the correct weight can help you feel and look good . . . our product is a comprehensive and balanced diet plan designed to help you achieve your desired weight.'

You say

'I like biscuits, so I liked the bars, but I didn't lose weight.'

'It [the drink] was too sickly sweet, it made me feel I was going to be sick, but I stuck at it and lost 4 lb (1.8 kg). I just didn't fancy having hot chocolate for lunch.'

'It wasn't as filling as others I've tried, but the taste was all right and it was cheaper than others. I did lose weight.

We say

NutraSlim is among the lowest in sugar and highest in fibre of all the meal-replacement diets, and the leaflet advocates a well-balanced diet, with lots of fruit and vegetables. You have the advantage of advice if required from a Boots pharmacist. However:

- The recipes are fine so long as you're not a vegetarian – there is only one recipe which doesn't include meat or fish.
- This is the only diet plan I've read that makes it clear you shouldn't diet if you are not overweight. Unfortunately the NutraSlim weight charts don't make it clear that there is a range of healthy weights – on their chart you're overweight or underweight, and there's nothing in between! These charts should be changed to show that weights corresponding to BMIs of 20–25 are the acceptable healthy range.
- A list of Boots Shapers snacks (see page 198) is also included, but the plan doesn't say when these are to be eaten. If it is in addition to the healthy snacks, this would obviously increase calorie intake. If it is instead of the healthy snacks, you might not get sufficient fibre or vitamins.
- The diet could be quite expensive, because you are encouraged to eat Boots Shapers items for your snack. I haven't included the cost of any Shapers products in working out the daily cost.

Calorie counting	×	Less than £10 to start	√
Weighing of food required	√	Personal support	√
Forbidden foods	√	Detailed 'who can't use'	√
Suit single person	√	Emphasizes fluid intake	√
Suitable for vegetarians	√		

Diet type
A meal-replacement diet.

What is it?
The Slim.Fast Plan has more variety than other meal-replacement systems. There are powders and soups which you mix with skimmed milk or water, cans of ready-to-drink shakes, and nutrition bars. A leaflet with instructions and recipes comes with the powders and soups. This tells you how to use the product, informs you about other flavours, encourages exercise and healthy eating, and has dieting tips and recipes.

Varieties: Shakes: French vanilla, coffee delight, chocolate royale, strawberry supreme, banana de luxe, hot chocolate, hot cappuccino (200 calories with skimmed milk). Ready-to-drink shakes: Chocolate royale, French vanilla, coffee delight (200 calories). Soups: creamy mushroom, rich tomato (200 calories mixed with water). Nutrition bars: Chocolate chip, tropical nut, fruit crunch, peanut butter crunch (110 calories).

Ingredients: Shakes: sugars, skimmed milk, minerals and vitamins. Soups: skimmed milk powder, maltodextrin, vegetables, minerals and vitamins. Ready-to-drink shakes: skimmed and whole milk, sugar, minerals and vitamins. Nutrition bars: sugar, oats, chocolate, and various fruits and nuts, with milk, rice, flavourings, vitamins and minerals and hydrogenated vegetable oil.

Slim.Fast is produced by Sun Nutritional Inc., the biggest retailer of meal replacements in Britain, taking 80 per cent of the market. After great success in its country of origin, the USA, Slim.Fast was introduced to Britain in 1990. It can be bought at all major chemists and most supermarkets. There is a Slim.Fast recipe book for £1.50 in some large chemists, or you can send away for it.

Meal-replacement shakes come in tubs of 12 servings for £6.49. Ready-to-drink shakes are 99p per can. Soups come in packs of four for £3.95. Nutrition bars are 54p each.

How does it work?
Women should lose weight on a diet of 1000 and men of 1500
calories per day. Three servings of Slim.Fast and a 400-calorie
meal will provide these calories together with all the nutrition
you need, but without the need for calorie counting, according
to the makers.

The diet
You eat meal-replacement servings for breakfast and lunch, have
another meal replacement as a snack and eat a low-calorie and
'sensible, low-fat, well-balanced dinner'. You mix one scoop of
powder or a sachet of soup with either hot or cold skimmed
milk or water, depending on variety, or have a ready-to-drink
shake. You can also have fruit or vegetables as snacks, and lists
are given of these. If you eat the nutrition bars as treats, you
should not have more than two per day. You should also drink
6–8 cups of water every day.

The recipes change as accompanying leaflets and recipe books
are revised. They are usually for one serving. Many but not all

A typical day's diet

Breakfast	*Slim.Fast meal replacement shake*	200
Lunch	*Slim.Fast meal replacement soup*	200
Snack	*Slim.Fast meal replacement shake*	200
Evening meal	*Fruity curried chicken salad, made with 2 oz (60 g) cooked chicken, 2 oz (60 g) cooked rice, 1 oz (30 g) red pepper, banana, 2 oz (60 g) grapes, lettuce, 3 oz (90 g) apple, with lemon juice, low-fat yoghurt, curry powder*	330
	Blackberry baked apple, made with a 5 oz (150 g) cooking apple, ½ oz (15 g) blackberries	70
	Calories (approx)	1000
	Cost	£3.41

contain fish or meat. Simple cooking instructions are given where required. The Slim.Fast recipe book has meat and vegetarian dishes, desserts and starters, all calorie-counted.

Variations
Men can take one extra shake and two pieces of fruit per day if they wish.

Who shouldn't use it?
Pregnant women, nursing mothers, anyone with a health problem, or anyone who wants to lose more than 40 lb (18.2 kg), or more than 20 per cent of initial body weight, should consult a doctor before using Slim.Fast.

Additional information
Height/weight charts indicate that a person of 5 ft 4 in (1.63 m) should not weigh more than about 10 st 4 lb (65.4 kg), corresponding to a BMI of 25. You are overweight at that height if you are between about 10 st 4 lb and 12 st 6 lb (79 kg), corresponding to BMIs of 25–30. If you are even heavier then you are fat or very fat. These tables are in line with current medical opinion.

There isn't any specific exercise plan, but you are told that taking exercise will help your diet work harder. You are advised not to undertake any strenuous exercise if you have a health problem without seeing your doctor first. There are also tips about avoiding temptation, such as not shopping on an empty stomach or keeping food in the house.

You can buy a Slim.Fast shaker (£1) if you find mixing up the drinks with milk in a blender too much of a chore.

Expected weight loss
You should be able to lose 2½ lb (1.1 kg) per week after a slightly higher loss in the first week, which is in line with current recommendations.

Keeping off the pounds
Once you reach your ideal weight, you can eat two ordinary meals with one meal replacement and one nutrition bar per day. You weigh yourself weekly, and if you find that you have put

92

on 2–3 lb (0.9–1.4 kg) then it's back to the Slim.Fast Plan and the higher number of meal replacements until you reach ideal weight again. There isn't a specific weight maintenance plan.

They say

'The diet which puts successful slimming within your reach . . . it's simple and it's effective. Just follow the plan and see the weight come off.'

You say

'I did tricks to make it work. I work at night, so I stayed in bed till lunchtime then went for a walk without any money, so that I couldn't buy sweets. Although I was always thinking about food, I stuck to it and lost 1 st 7 lb (9.5 kg).'

'I didn't like the recipes but it was more pleasant than others I've tried – less blobby.'

'Very boring and dissatisfying – made me fantasize about food and want to break the rules and have a Turkish Delight.'

We say

Slim.Fast give a great deal of information in their leaflets, all sensible, and they say that their nutrition bars have 45 per cent less fat than most similar products. Slim.Fast have more variety on offer than their competitors can manage, a point worth bearing in mind in view of the fact that many dieters become easily bored by meal-replacement diets.

Calorie counting	✗	Less than £10 to start	✓
Weighing of food required	✓	Personal support	✗
Forbidden foods	✗	Detailed 'who can't use'	✓
Suit single person	✓	Emphasizes fluid intake	✓
Suitable for vegetarians	✓		

Slimma-Shake

Diet type
A meal-replacement diet.

What is it?
A powdered drink, which you use to replace meals, and an instruction leaflet.

Varieties: Toffee, chocolate, fruit trifle and strawberry flavours (200 calories when mixed with skimmed milk).

Ingredients: Dried whey powder, dextrose, soya protein, fibre, minerals and vitamins, with flavourings.

This diet was first marketed in 1995. You can buy it from health food shops and chemists. A tub of 12 servings costs £5.49.

How does it work?
To lose weight, you should eat 1000 calories per day fewer than usual. According to the makers, Slimma-Shake can provide essential nutrients and help you feel full while dieting.

The diet
For each serving of Slimma-Shake you mix two rounded table-spoons of the powder with ½ pt (285 ml) of cold, skimmed milk. You can add ice-cubes if you wish. You replace breakfast, lunch and an afternoon snack with Slimma-Shake. You can eat a low-fat, nutritious meal for dinner. You decide how many calories you wish to have, then you subtract the 600 provided by the meal replacements, calculate how many calories are in your evening meal, and therefore how many are left over for snacks (which can include alcohol). You are advised that it is essential to have plenty of non-alcoholic drinks. A calorie counter and list of healthy treats is provided, but no recipes.

Total calories each day should not fall below 1250 for a woman or 1500 for a man.

Exercise
You are advised that brisk walking for 20–30 minutes every day will help to promote weight loss, but there isn't a detailed plan.

A typical day's diet

Breakfast	Slimma-Shake made with skimmed milk	200
Lunch	Slimma-Shake made with skimmed milk	200
Snack	Slimma-Shake made with skimmed milk	200
Main meal	Your choice	As many as you decide
	Calories (approx)	1250
	Cost	£2.56

Who shouldn't use it?
If you intend to lose more than 20 lb (9.1 kg), have a medical condition or are pregnant, you should take medical advice first.

Additional information
There is a chart on which to record your weight loss. Slimma-Shake's height/weight charts show that the average weight for a 5 ft 4 in (1.63 m) woman is about 8 st 7 lb (54 kg). You are told that if you weigh more than 10 per cent above the average for your height, you might gain medical benefits from losing weight, but this is misleading (see below).

Expected weight loss
You are told that 2 lb (900 g) per week is a safe and healthy speed at which to lose weight.

Keeping off the pounds
There is no detailed plan. It is suggested that you replace an occasional meal with a Slimma-Shake.

They say
'The best-tasting meal replacement ... slimming has never tasted so good.'

We say

It would be a good idea for Slimma-Shake to adjust their weight charts upwards as at the moment they are misleading. Ten per cent above 8 st 7 lbs (54 kg) is about 131 lb (59.4 kg), which represents a BMI of about 22. This is *not at all* overweight; there are no known benefits to health from weight loss if your BMI is under 27.

The product was too new for me to be able to find people who had used it.

Calorie counting	√	Less than £10 to start	√
Weighing of food required	√	Personal support	×
Forbidden foods	×	Detailed 'who can't use'.	√
Suit single person	√	Emphasizes fluid intake	√
Suitable for vegetarians	√		

Diet type
A meal-replacement diet.

What is it?
Supatrim is a tub of meal-replacement drink powder with which an instruction leaflet is enclosed – the Supatrim Weight Loss Plan.

Varieties: Vanilla, banana, strawberry and chocolate (200 calories when mixed with skimmed milk).

Ingredients: Mainly dried whey powder, soya protein and sugars, with added vitamins and minerals.

You can buy Supatrim in tubs of 12 servings at £4.99, or in individual sachets at 49p each. It is marketed by Superdrug Stores plc (it can be obtained only from their shops) and has been available since 1993.

How does it work?
Limiting your calorie intake is the only way to lose excess weight, Supatrim say. You have a natural desire to eat, but Supatrim gives you a long-term feeling of fullness, which stops you getting hunger pangs and, they believe, makes it easier to stick to a healthy eating plan.

The diet
You replace breakfast, lunch and a snack with a Supatrim drink. You mix two rounded tablespoons or 36 g of powder to 250 ml of skimmed milk (about 1¼ oz to 9 fl oz) – you don't get a scoop with the can. You are to have a nutritious meal of not less than 400 calories in the evening. You are advised to eat as much fruit as you want, and to eat not less than 1000 (women) or 1500 (men) calories in total, per day. You are warned that it is important not to miss a drink or a meal.

The recipes in the leaflet are all under 400 calories per portion; some are for four people and some are individual dishes. All of them contain meat or fish; only one has a vegetarian option. There are six suggested meal plans.

A typical day's diet

Breakfast	*Supatrim shake with skimmed milk*	202
Snack	*Supatrim shake with skimmed milk*	202
Lunch	*Supatrim shake with skimmed milk*	202
Evening meal	*Turkey Sicilian style, made with ¼ oz (6 g) butter, ¼ onion, ¾ oz (20 g) button mushrooms, ¼ oz (6 g) plain flour, ⅛ tsp ground ginger, ⅛ tsp grated nutmeg, 1½ fl oz (40 ml) chicken stock, 1½ fl oz (40 ml) skimmed milk, 3 oz (86 g) cooked turkey meat, salt and pepper, ⅛ oz (4 g) flaked toasted almonds*	275
	2 oz (56 g) (dry weight) rice	170
	Salad	20
Snack	*Piece of fruit, e.g., banana*	90
	Calories (approx)	1100
	Cost	£3.00

Variations
Men should have an extra Supatrim drink and a piece of fruit or a light snack every day.

Exercise
There isn't a specific plan, but you are advised to aim for 20–30 minutes of exercise at least three times a week. If your preferred exercise is walking, you should do some every day.

Who shouldn't use it?
Supatrim should not be used at all by pregnant women or nursing mothers, or by anyone with 40 lb (18.2 kg) or 20 per cent of body weight to lose, without consulting a doctor first.

98

Additional information

The calorie counter in the instruction leaflet shows the calories in 100-gram units of over 100 foods. Most of these are staple diet items, but some are unusual – calorific values for jellied eels and venison are given, but not those for jam or sugar.

There is also a chart on which to record your weight loss, but it isn't really clear that you are supposed to add each week's loss on to the one from the week before, and then the next week's loss, and so on. Supatrim's height/weight chart has only one weight given for each height, and that for an average-sized woman of 5 ft 4 in (1.63 m) is 8 st 11 lb (55.8 kg). This represents a BMI of 20, and doctors don't recommend a BMI much below this. The leaflet says that the weights shown are just a guide, but that you should fall within the averages shown. There aren't any averages shown, and there's no range to fall between. These weights are supposed to include 3 lb (1.36 kg) for light clothing.

There are dieting tips about not missing meals, and eating little and often. And you are told to 'Think positive!'

Expected weight loss

The plan claims that you will lose a significant amount of weight quickly; a reasonable target would be to lose 3 lb (1.36 kg) per week.

Keeping off the pounds

Supatrim suggest that you weigh yourself regularly once a week, and if your weight starts going up then you go back on to Supatrim. There isn't a specific plan.

They say

'. . . a safe and effective method of losing excess weight – the Supatrim Plan is flexible and easy to use.'

You say

'I've tried others like it and it's no better or worse, just cheaper and not so many different flavours.'

'The recipes are all right but they are boring after a while – you need more.'

'The taste is horrible but if you stick to it, it works; I lost 3 lb (1.4 kg) in a week.'

'I liked the taste and lost 6 lb (2.7 kg) over a fortnight, to go on holiday. I was happy with it.'

We say
Supatrim is good value, but there are a few niggles:

- Few dieters wear clothes when weighing themselves, and there is therefore a possibility that some people using the Supatrim weight charts might think they were overweight when in fact they were not. The height/weight chart should be changed to show healthy weights between BMIs of 20 and 25.
- Little advice is given on eating sensibly, and what there is is a bit confused. You are told to have three Supatrim drinks per day, which makes 600 calories, and to have a sensible, low-fat main meal of not less than 400 calories. But some of the recipes given in the leaflet provide less than 300 calories per serving, so if you followed the plan you could be eating fewer calories than you should, to stay healthy.
- The section on eating as much fruit as you like appears at first sight to be part of a section about men, and at least one of my dieters never noticed it.
- The diet doesn't emphasize, as it should, the importance of drinking plenty of water.

Calorie counting	✗	Less than £10 to start	✓
Weighing of food required	✓	Personal support	✗
Forbidden foods	✗	Detailed 'who can't use'	✓
Suit single person	✓	Emphasizes fluid intake	✗
Suitable for vegetarians	✓		

Diet type
A meal-replacement diet and tablets.

What is it?
Powdered shake and tablets with which you get an instruction leaflet, containing advice on healthy eating, healthy cooking, handy hints for successful slimming and so on, with the benefits of weight reduction on physical and psychological health outlined.

Varieties: Vanilla, chocolate mint, chocolate mocha (220 calories with skimmed milk).

Ingredients: Shake: mainly sugar, with cellulose, various gums, minerals and vitamins. Tablets: cellulose, chromium picolinate.

I believe this first appeared on the market in 1994. 10 Day Quicktrim is available from specialist shops, or by credit card order on 0181 503 1040. It costs £9.95 for a ten-day supply.

How does it work?
Quicktrim fills you up and takes the hunger out of losing weight, its makers claim.

The diet
For quick weight loss, the diet consists in taking a Quicktrim drink for breakfast, for lunch and as an afternoon snack, having a piece of fruit or other snack at mid-morning, and cooking a meal from the menu guide in the evening. A list of snacks is provided.

You measure out one scoop (provided in the box) of the powder and mix it with 8 fl oz (230 ml) of partially skimmed 2 per cent milk. If you shake the mixture in a container or blend for a few seconds only, your drink is in the form of a shake; if you blend it for longer, with ice, you get a mousse. You can freeze this, stirring occasionally, if you want frozen mousse. You get ten tablets, and you are to take one each night before bed with a glass of water. The tablets 'may help to regulate' your desire for sweet things.

Their leaflet contains ten recipes, all of which contain meat or fish, and most of which are measured in American cups. All are for one serving.

You are advised that you must drink 6–8 glasses of water per day.

A typical day's diet

Breakfast	Quicktrim shake with skimmed milk	220
Snack	Fruit	60
Lunch	Quicktrim shake with skimmed milk	220
Snack	Quicktrim shake with skimmed milk	220
Evening meal	4 oz (110 g) broiled flounder in orange sauce Steamed bean sprouts with low-salt soy sauce ½ cup steamed asparagus tips Salad with lemon juice dressing	450
	Calories (approx)	1100
	Cost	£4.74

Variations

Men should eat 180 calories more per day while on the diet, by taking two extra snacks or eating larger portions, and should eat 400 more calories per day while on the maintenance programme.

Exercise

You are advised to keep up your exercise, beginning with 20 minutes three to five times per week of an activity you find convenient and enjoyable, and moving up to a total of 200 minutes per week. Walking is recommended.

102

Who shouldn't use it?
Anyone who is pregnant or nursing, or who has a health problem (including cardiac problems), diabetes, kidney stones, gallstones, liver or kidney disease, anorexia, bulimia, or who is more than 50 lb (22.7 kg) overweight, should consult a doctor before starting any weight-loss programme. People with phenyl-ketonuria should note that the product contains phenylalanine.

Additional information
Quicktrim's BMI graph indicates that the highest ideal weight for a woman of 5 ft 4 in (1.63 m) is 10 st (63.6 kg) representing a top BMI of 24.

You are advised to keep a food diary for a week to help pin-point when and why you overeat. There are handy hints to help overcome temptation – chew gum, keep busy, reward yourself for success and so on. Above all, you must 'Stay positive!'

Expected weight loss
No mention is made of how much weight you will lose.

Keeping off the pounds
Quicktrim suggest that you continue with two shakes per day, increase the number of snacks to three, and have a low-calorie frozen meal for lunch. You are advised to have a frozen meal in which less than 30 per cent of calories come from fat, and which is low in salt. You choose an evening meal from the menu guide.

They say
'With Quicktrim, you'll feel great while you lose weight quickly and easily.'

We say
I couldn't find anyone who had used the product.

- It doesn't say on the packet, as it should, that the product can help slimming or weight control only as part of a calorie-controlled diet.
- The chromium picolinate in the tablets has not been shown to affect appetite in any systematic way.

- All the suggestions and tips are sensible, but there isn't really enough information in the menu plans. If you made the orange sauce (see the menu above) with flour and butter, for example, the calorie count could be much higher.
- The writing on the box detailing the variations that men should make to the diet could be much larger – I found it extremely hard to read.

Calorie counting	√	Less than £10 to start	√
Weighing of food required	√	Personal support	×
Forbidden foods	×	Detailed 'who can't use'.	√
Suit single person	√	Emphasizes fluid intake	√
Suitable for vegetarians	√		

As you can see from the dieters' comments above, the world is divided into those who enjoy meal-replacement drinks and those who feel sick when they try them.

The main reservation with meal-replacement diets is that with many there's no re-education for the rest of your life if you do lose weight. Usually, the only suggested way of keeping the pounds off in the long term is to continue with the diet. I don't think that drinking shakes for two meals a day is something anyone should do for the rest of their life.

You need to mix up the powders with skimmed milk or water, and it's *very important* to read the instructions on the packet properly and make the drink with the correct liquid, or you could be consuming too few calories. Some people mix the drinks with water even when they are supposed to use milk,

Key features of meal-replacement diets

Name	Scientifically credible	Promotes long-term healthy eating	Suggests new habits	Detailed exercise plan	Detailed weight-loss maintenance plan
Cambridge Health Plan: Trimmer	√	√	×	×	√
Cinergi	√*	×	√	×	×
Herbalife	√	×	×	×	×
NutraSlim	√	×	×	×	×
Slim.Fast	√	√	×	×	×
Slimma-Shake	√	×	×	×	×
Supatrim	√	×	×	×	×
10 Day Quicktrim	√*	√	√	×	×

* The meal replacement parts of the diets are scientifically credible; the extras are less so.

in hopes of a faster weight loss. This is not good for you, because the balance of vitamins and minerals supplied by the meal replacement is calculated on what you mix the powder with.

In addition, some meal replacements contain ingredients which swell up in the stomach, so it is also *very important* to make sure that you drink the recommended amounts of water, or you will become dehydrated.

Of the diets I have reviewed in this chapter, here are a few final points:

- All meal-replacement manufacturers should provide the correct height/weight scales approved by the Department of Health, which use BMI and not insurance company data. At present this is only done by Trimmer, 10 Day Quicktrim and Slim.Fast. The top and bottom of the chart should be clear, and in type large enough to read easily.

- Although in theory you should lose weight on a meal replacement diet, the only published evidence for this is the Slim.Fast study (see page 70).

- It should be made absolutely clear, as NutraSlim does, that you shouldn't diet if you're not overweight.

- Herbalife should provide more guidance on a healthy main meal to have with the meal replacements.

- You may be the sort of person who finds it relaxing to listen to tapes about dieting, but Cinergi's tapes are in places factually incorrect.

- Although manufacturers are legally required to state the ingredients of their diets, some don't specify the sugar content on all their products. New legislation in 1995 means that they should do so in future.

- The exact contents of meal replacements and snack bars vary considerably (see the table below). When planning your main meal of the day, it's important to remember how much fat, fibre, sugar and so on the replacement or snack provides, in order to be sure that you're getting a healthy, well-balanced diet. The sugar content appears to be high in most of the products (it's a fair assumption that much of the carbohydrate in the ones which don't state the sugar content on the packet *is* sugar).

Major ingredients of meal replacements (in grams)

Name	Protein	Carbo-hydrate	Of which sugar	Fat	Fibre	Calories
Cambridge Health Plan: Trimmer (drink made with skimmed milk)	14.6	32.2	30.6	1.7	0.9	194
Cambridge Health Plan: Trimmer bar	5	31.2	?	6.7	2.8	198
Cambridge Health Plan: Trimmer muesli (made with skimmed milk)	10.5	32.2	?	5.4	1.65	211
Cinergi (breakfast drink made with water)	9.9	30.1	?	1	2	163
Herbalife (drink made with skimmed milk)	16	23.4	?	1	2.5	166
NutraSlim (drink made with water)	12	31	18	2.3	5.8	193
NutraSlim lunchbar	4.3	26	23	8	4.6	193
Slim.Fast (drink made with skimmed milk)	14	31.3	?	3	6.3	200
Slim.Fast nutrition bar	1.5	17	11.5	3.7	1	108
Slim.Fast ready to drink	9.1	32.8	32.8	3.7	5.8	201
Slim.Fast soup (made with water)	14	31.2	?	3	6.3	200
Slimma-Shake drink (made with skimmed milk)	15	29.1	27.2	2.7	5.6	201
SupaTrim (drink made with skimmed milk)	14.59	29.58	24.6	3.01	6.11	202
10 Day Quicktrim (drink made with skimmed milk)	15.2	37	?	6.4	?	250

The advantage that meal replacements have over real food is in their fillers and bulkers, which may make you feel full. Some dieters told me that they felt so full after a morning drink that they skipped the lunch serving – and that's not how you are supposed to use these products. It is *very important* to eat all the servings or you won't get adequate nutrition.

Of course you could make yourself a low-calorie breakfast and lunch for much less money than a meal replacement, and in many cases it would be more nutritious too. But if you can't be bothered to count calories yourself, or it is inconvenient to cook, or you want something quickly, there is no harm in using these products as directed. Most people seem to tire of them fairly quickly.

Which meal-replacement diet suits you depends on your own taste buds and on your pocket!

Food Fact File

Surveys show that the majority of people in this country are familiar with current guidelines about reducing the amount of fat in our diet and believe this will lead to improved health. However, the majority of people feel that their existing diet is healthy and not high in fat; which is surprising, since many British people eat very high levels of fat indeed.

Chapter 8

Reduced-Calorie Diets

What's the theory?

The diets included in this chapter emphasize that if you restrict calorie intake to the level at which you have to burn up fat stores, then you wil lose weight – they don't include exercise programmes. Reducing calories as a method of weight control has been around since calorie tables were first drawn up, in 1906, by Irvine Fisher. Calorie, which should really be kilo-calorie, is a measure of energy; it's the amount of heat needed to raise the temperature of one gram of water by one degree Celsius.

Some diets in this chapter stress the effects of a high-fibre intake on both appetite and excretion of calories. Others include supplements and extras which they believe may speed weight loss. A supplement containing lecithin, cider vinegar and kelp was first promoted by Ann Crenshaw in 1974. The theory is that the cider vinegar acts as a diuretic, kelp boosts metabolism and the lecithin emulsifies fat. (Vinegar has been used as a diuretic since Roman times, and has been popular as an obesity cure for hundreds of years.) Fennel is also believed to act as a diuretic. Autohypnosis is used by some specialists to help promote weight loss.

Calorie counting is a way of life for some people; 24 per cent of women and 12 per cent of men apparently think about the calories in what they are eating most of the time.

Do these diets work?

Reduced-calorie diets do work. There is a mass of evidence from controlled studies to show that if calories are restricted to about 1000–1200 per day then almost anyone will lose weight.

Usually a calorie-restricted diet either lets you eat as much as you like of certain foods and bans others, or allows you specified portions of certain low-calorie foods. So, you may be allowed unlimited quantities of protein and fruit, but nothing else, or **109** small portions of a range of foods. So long as the amount of calories you eat is fewer than you ate before, on either diet you should lose weight.

High-fibre diets, which require you to eat very filling cereals, fruit and vegetables, may leave little room for high-fat food items, and so through calorie-reduction contribute to weight loss. As discussed in Chapter 7, there's not much evidence that fibre taken as part of a meal has any effect on appetite, and the amount of extra calories excreted on a high-fibre diet is very small.

As for extras with these diets, a mixture of lecithin, cider vinegar and kelp appears, in a 1976 study, to have been ineffective in speeding weight loss, and neither fennel nor autohypnosis has been scientifically proven to be helpful to dieters.

Keeping off the pounds

If you do not change your eating habits for good, and you revert to eating high-calorie foods after finishing your diet, you will put on weight.

There is no independent scientific evidence to prove that any of these diets work in the long-term.

Any problems?

There may be problems on any diet if you don't follow the instructions properly. If the diet says no alcohol, you shouldn't drink – there's always a possibility of dehydration on a low-calorie diet. Don't ever try to speed weight loss by eating less than the recommended amounts of food.

Diet type
A reduced-calorie diet.

What is it?
The Charleston Program is a 108–page, large-format book by Dr Robert M. Johnson and Shirley Linde. Dr Johnson, who developed the diet, specialized in the treatment of obesity. Apparently some 70 000 people have used it in the USA and Canada.

The book covers such topics as setting goals and getting motivated, tips to make the diet work, making the diet plan unique to you, the Charleston Program exercise plan, and learning the skill of will-power. The programme claims to bring health benefits apart from weight loss – a reduction in cholesterol and blood pressure.

The programme costs £12.95 plus £2.95 post and packing, by mail order from the Willow Tree Press, Dept Ch 131, Unit J1, Brooklands Farm Estate, Brooklands Lane, Weybridge, Surrey, KT13 8UY. It is advertised in the press.

You get your money back if you return the programme (for any reason) within 35 days. You can also get your money back if you don't begin to lose weight in five days. If you aren't losing weight on a regular basis after six months, you can still have your money back.

How does it work?
Overweight people are not doomed to be fat, the authors claim. The key element in successful weight control is for the dieter to assume responsibility for his or her eating choices. With 'pattern restructuring' you can pinpoint your problem areas with food and change your eating habits permanently, according to Dr Johnson.

The diet
The diet programme itself has 12 rules. These are based on good nutritional practice. You are encouraged to eat fresh, unprocessed foods and lots of fibre, minimize alcohol, fat and sugar, and drink plenty of water. You are to eat five times a day.

Foods are divided into groups. The first group contains items of which you can eat as much as you like (e.g., tomato juice, carrots). The second is foods of which you can have three portions a day (e.g., haddock, ham). You can have two portions from the carbohydrate group per day, and one portion each from the groups of higher-calorie vegetables, fruit and berries, and soups. 'X-rated' foods you are only to consume occasionally. This group includes alcohol, butter and doughnuts. No food is entirely forbidden.

You can choose what you want to eat yourself and should aim for between 800 and 1000 calories a day. Recipes are not included in the book. You are advised, however, on non-fattening cooking methods and to take vitamin/mineral supplements.

A typical day's diet

Breakfast	1 slice wholewheat bread	65
	1 boiled egg	75
	Black coffee	
Snack	1 apple	60
Lunch	Beef and noodle soup	85
	1 slice wholewheat bread	65
	Low-fat cottage cheese	100
Snack	1 low-fat yoghurt	110
Evening meal	1 baked potato	90
	Cod	180
	Sweet corn	100
	Carrots	50
	Black tea	
	Calories (approx)	980
	Cost	£3.57

Variations

Variations are listed but you are advised to see a doctor before trying any of them. You can use the programme to provide a low-carbohydrate or low-cholesterol diet. If you think that you have a food allergy, a rotation method is described. If you are a vegetarian, it is recommended that you see a doctor or nutritionist for advice before beginning the diet. Using a liquid diet formula (a very-low-calorie diet) is recommended as a way of starting the programme.

Exercise
Very brief advice is given on exercise, and on toning and strengthening. Unfortunately Dr Johnson states that exercising can raise basal metabolic rate for eight hours afterwards; this is no longer considered accurate (see page 29).

Learning new habits
To help you change your eating behaviour permanently, Dr Johnson includes practical tips to make the diet work. These include leaving a small amount of food on your plate after every meal, and wearing an elastic band round your wrist – you pop it every time you are tempted to eat something you shouldn't.

There is also advice on how to change your thinking habits so that you are less likely to break your diet. Basically you learn to replace negative thoughts ('I just can't handle it – I may as well eat and enjoy myself') with positive ones ('OK, I failed but I can try again tomorrow'). You learn to identify irrational thoughts and replace them with rational ones. You are to replace your fear of failure with a desire for success, and practise developing positive mental pictures of yourself.

You are shown how to be assertive without being aggressive towards people who try to sabotage your diet, how to cope at parties and on holiday, how to fat-proof your home, and what to do if you have problems. You are shown how to analyse the situations which may lead you into temptation. As one of the author's dieters comments: 'Food is the perfect lover; it's always available and it never says "no".'

Who shouldn't use it?
There are no warnings against anyone following this diet: the book poses nine questions, and if you answer 'yes' to any three of these then the suggestion is that you should go on a diet. The questions are to do with your clothes fitting more tightly, being

unhappy with your weight, people making remarks about you, and so on. You should go on a diet if you can 'pinch an inch' of flesh, or if anything that shouldn't jiggles when you jump up and down.

Additional information

Two weight charts are included: the 1959 and 1983 Metropolitan Life Insurance Company ones. For a 5 ft 4 in (1.63 m) woman the desirable weight range was 116–131 lb (52.7–59.5 kg) in 1959 (BMI 20–23) and 124–138 lb (56.3–62.7 kg) in 1983 (BMI 21–24). The Charleston Program thinks that you should aim for 10–15 per cent less than the 1983 chart, but this would mean going for a BMI of 18, which doctors would consider too low. One plus is that on starting the diet you are to stop weighing yourself.

Expected weight loss

This is not mentioned.

Keeping off the pounds

On reaching your target weight you follow US government guidelines and eat a diet of which 30 per cent is fat, 55 per cent carbohydrate and 15 per cent protein. If at any time your weight rises to 10 per cent above your ideal weight, you go straight back on the Charleston Program.

Dr Johnson says

'It's safe . . . the food is great . . . and it gets the weight off and keeps it off.'

You say

'At first I thought it would be easy – there are lots of things in the three portions a day bit. But there's only so much fish you can eat, and most of the things are fish.'

'This is the only exercise programme I've ever been able to follow – it recommends vigorous sex.'

'The food is good and it's very detailed.'

'I lost 6 lb (2.7 kg) in three weeks.'

We say

The techniques here for dealing with the problems faced by anyone who goes on a diet are excellent. This book encourages you to take control of your eating and shows you how to stay in control, no matter what temptations come along. The diet itself is based on sound nutritional advice. Even so:

- Doctors don't recommend anyone to diet on fewer than 1000 calories a day.
- It's a pity that the choice of foodstuffs hasn't been converted to suit the average Briton, to whom rutabaga, poi, weakfish and yellowtail are unknown, and pickled pigs' feet and tangerine juice rarities.
- The very-low-calorie diets listed in the Program are not available in Britain, and if you are going to try one of the ones which are available, you *must* read the section on who should use these diets in chapter 6 of this book.
- You don't have to count calories or weigh food, but you do have to remember what's on which list and what a portion is. I think you would have to photocopy the list and take it round with you.

Calorie counting	×	Less than £10 to start	×
Weighing of food required	×	Personal support	×
Forbidden foods	×	Detailed 'who can't use'	×
Suit single person	√	Emphasizes fluid intake	√
Suitable for vegetarians	×		

The Complete F-Plan Diet

Diet type
A reduced-calorie, high-fibre diet.

What is it?
The F-Plan Diet is low in fat and high in fibre. It is detailed in a 204-page book by Audrey Eyton who has been writing about weight problems in the popular and scientific press for many years. It explains the facts about fibre, illnesses related to lack of fibre and the usefulness of fibre in dieting. There are charts showing you the fibre content of common foods, six sample daily diet menus and recipes. Advice is given on keeping to your diet while eating in restaurants.

The Complete F-Plan Diet (592 pages) is exactly the same as *The F-Plan Diet*, but the type is bigger so it is easier to read. It also has a section called 'F-Plus' (see Variations below), which *The F-Plan Diet* does not. *The F-Plan Diet* was first published in 1982 and became Britain's best-selling dieting book of all time. It has been translated into 16 languages. Both *The F-Plan Diet* (£4.99) and *The Complete F-Plan Diet* (£6.99) are published by Penguin.

How does it work?
Fibre is good for dieting in several ways, says Audrey Eyton. Fibrous foods take longer to eat than non-fibrous foods. Because it takes at least five minutes before any food has a satisfying effect on hunger, with fast foods you could eat 2000 calories in less than five minutes, well before you have even begun to feel the effects. With fibrous foods, you are still chewing away when the 'filling up' signs start and you can adjust your intake to stop eating when you feel full. When people eat meals quickly they feel hungry again sooner than if they ate the same meal slowly, and as you have to eat fibrous foods slowly because you have to chew them, you won't feel hungry again so soon.

An additional benefit is that because they need more chewing, fibrous foods also need more swallowing. Ms Eyton believes that chewing and swallowing probably affect brain control mechanisms which cause us to feel full.

116 A higher intake of fibre means that a satisfyingly greater volume of food can be eaten than on a normal diet, even while reducing calorie intake. Weight is also lost more quickly, because, Audrey Eyton claims, a high-fibre diet causes calorie loss through undigested food particles being excreted.

The diet

You choose the calorie content of your own diet, of between 1000 and 1500 calories per day, depending on your sex and the amount of weight you have to lose. You do have to count calories and weigh food.

You must have ½ pt (285 ml) of skimmed milk and an apple and an orange every day. You must also make up a kind of muesli to Audrey Eyton's recipe. This is called 'fibre-filler' and it alone will provide ½ oz (15 g) of dietary fibre per day. It's made from various bran cereals and dried fruits, and you have it with milk from the daily allowance. You are allowed low-cal drinks, but fruit juices are forbidden, and you are advised to cut out alcohol. If you can't and are allowing yourself a daily ration of alcohol, you are shown how to recalculate your calorie intake to allow for it.

All the recipes are given for a single serving, except for some of the more complex ones which can also be frozen, where quantities are given for four. Ms Eyton does not believe that most dieters want to cook one thing for the whole family.

Variations

The F-Plus section of *The Complete F-Plan Diet* contains additional meal plans to the ones given in *The F-Plan Diet*. These are shown by calorie count (1000, 1250 or 1500) in each of eight sections, catering for working women, snackers, keen cooks, convenience food, men, children, freezer-owners and a section just on popular menus. The strict F-Plan rules are relaxed a little; you don't have to have fibre-filler on the convenience food diet or the men's; men don't have to have skimmed milk and can drink alcohol.

Who shouldn't use it?

You are advised that anyone who suffers from a health problem of any kind should consult a doctor before embarking on a diet programme.

A typical day's diet

Throughout the day	½ pt (285 ml) skimmed milk	100
	Fibre-filler	250
	1 apple	60
	1 orange	60
Breakfast	½ fibre-filler with milk allowance	125
Lunch	Sandwich, made with 2 slices wholemeal bread, 1 oz (28 g) cottage cheese, 1 tsp French mustard, 1 oz (28 g) sweet corn, 1 oz (28 g) lean ham	250
Snack	½ fibre-filler	125
Evening meal	Frankfurter bean bake, made with 8 oz (225 g) baked beans, 1 tsp ketchup, ½ tsp mustard, 1 tsp dried onion flakes, 2 oz (56 g) frankfurters	300
	Calories (approx)	1200
	Cost	£3.57

Side-effects

You are warned that flatulence may be a problem in the first weeks of the diet. If it persists, you are to concentrate on foods other than peas and beans.

Additional information

Advice is given about the range of illnesses that doctors think are connected to a low intake of fibre, and on the benefits to children's teeth and men's haemorrhoids of a high-fibre diet.

118   There is no exercise plan. Although you are advised that exercise will speed weight loss, you are told that you don't need to exercise to lose weight on this diet.

You are encouraged to slow down your eating style.

Expected weight loss
You are expected to lose 3 lb (1.4 kg) per week – this is higher than the recommended rate.

Keeping off the pounds
Audrey Eyton suggests that the parts of the diet which are easy to follow can become a lifelong habit, because by the end of the diet you will have come to prefer such foods – wholemeal bread instead of white bread, bran flakes instead of corn flakes. On reaching your target weight you can increase calorie intake, but still aim for the sake of your long-term health to keep up the fibre content of your diet.

Audrey Eyton says
'The ultimate diet for weight loss and fitness.'

You say
'I couldn't stick to it for long – it made me feel so fat and bloated.'

'I liked the recipes, but I like beany things anyway.'

'I actually quite enjoyed the diet, and lost 3 lb (1.4 kg) in two weeks – but I stopped because I couldn't stand the wind.'

We say
Although the benefits of fibre for dieters haven't turned out to be as great as it seemed they might be when Audrey Eyton wrote this book, the importance of a high-fibre diet in promoting health remains a fact. However:

- There is no real evidence that your tastes will automatically change to prefer high-fibre foods, so there is a danger of relapsing when the diet is over.
- Levels of fibre don't have to be as high as this diet advocates for beneficial results.
- The original book was criticized in some quarters because the **119**

diet was considered boring. The new version has more recipes and allows more variation on the diet.

- I am sorry that Audrey Eyton has included a children's diet, because children shouldn't diet.
- The effects of chewing on appetite, claimed by Audrey Eyton, haven't been scientifically validated.
- The number of calories excreted on a high-fibre diet is very small.

Calorie counting	√	Less than £10 to start	√
Weighing of food required	√	Personal support	×
Forbidden foods	√	Detailed 'who can't use'	×
Suit single person	√	Emphasizes fluid intake	×
Suitable for vegetarians	√		

Diet type
A reduced-calorie, high-protein diet.

What is it?
The diet, compiled by Dr Herman Tarnower, is a high-protein, low-fat and low carbohydrate one. A 240-page book by Dr Tarnower and Samm Sinclair Baker describes the development of the diet. It includes testimonials from grateful users, recipes, two question-and-answer sections, nutritional advice, a calorie/protein/fat/carbohydrate counter, and advice on long-term weight-loss maintenance.

Dr Herman Tarnower was a physician specializing in heart disease who developed his diet for his own patients. His book is said to be the world's best-selling diet book ever. Dr Tarnower's Scarsdale Diet was famous before his death, but when one of his long-term lovers, a respected and successful headmistress, killed him in a fit of jealous rage his diet became mega-famous. (He actually thanks his murderer-to-be Jean Harris, in the foreword of the book, for her assistance in writing and researching it.)

The British edition has been revised by Dr David Delvin to make it more understandable and to substitute British equivalents for unobtainable US ingredients. It is published by Bantam at £4.99.

How does it work?
Other diets, the book says, don't work because they are too complicated or too slow. On this diet you are told exactly what to eat each day, so the decisions are taken away from you. There's no need to worry about what you're going to eat, and the simplicity of the diet makes it easy to stick to, according to Dr Tarnower.

The diet
You don't count calories or weigh portions. The rules are simple. You are permitted no alcoholic drinks; black tea or coffee and low-cal drinks are all you are allowed. Snacks are strictly forbidden between meals; you may, however, have as much carrots and

celery as you want. You are not allowed oils or fats; meat must be lean, and you should stop eating when you are full. You mustn't substitute or add food to your daily menu plan. Meat, fish, fruit and vegetables are permitted in unlimited quantities.

You follow the diet for 14 days only, and then you go on to the diet's Keep-Trim programme for weight-loss maintenance. After 14 days on that, if you still have weight to lose, you can go back on the Scarsdale Diet. You keep on alternating between the two – called 'Two On, Two Off' – until you have reached your desired weight.

A typical day's diet

Breakfast	½ grapefruit	20
	1 slice wholemeal bread	60
	Black coffee	
Snack	Carrots and celery	45
Lunch	6 oz (170 g) assorted cold lean cuts of meat	350
	Sliced tomatoes	50
	Black coffee	
Snack	Carrots and celery	45
Evening meal	4 oz (110 g) Fish	200
	Salad and vegetables	100
	1 slice wholemeal bread	60
	Grapefruit	40
	Black coffee	
	Calories (approx)	1000
	Cost	£3.57

Variations

Dr Tarnower adapted the original diet when people complained that they couldn't afford to eat so much meat, and came up with the Money-Saver version (cheaper cuts of meat and cheap fish). There are also Gourmet, Vegetarian and International variations. On the International diet you cook different dishes on different days, e.g., Pineapple Surprise Aloha on Hawaiian Day, Tuna Shimi on Japanese Day. Fairly elaborate recipes are included for all the main dishes, and serve either one or two.

Who shouldn't use it?

You shouldn't go on this or any other quick reducing diet without first consulting your doctor. Alcoholics and diabetics in particular should not use this diet without medical supervision.

Additional information

Dr Tarnower wasn't keen on anyone over 40 taking up strenuous exercise, and exercise is not mentioned much in the book. You are told that sex is a fine exercise, but eating a small apple will put back all the calories expended; it takes half an hour of energetic cycling to use up 300 calories, which you can put back with a chocolate cupcake.

You keep a progress chart of your weight loss.

The Metropolitan Life Insurance Company's height/weight charts are included. These give the range of desirable weights for a 5 ft 4 in (1.63 m) woman as 7 st 12 lb (50 kg) to 8 st 11 lb (55.8 kg), representing a BMI of 19–21. This is too low. A note under the tables points out that these scales have been revised, and says that it is OK to be 'a few pounds higher' than is shown on the scales – but the note doesn't say how many 'a few' is.

Dr Tarnower quotes the ancient Chinese philosopher Confucius: 'What is past, one cannot amend . . . for the future one can always provide.' He emphasizes that you should think about future success, not past failures.

Expected weight loss

You are expected to lose 1 lb (450 g) in weight per day; weight losses of 20 lb (9.1 kg) in two weeks are said not to be unusual. This is a far higher rate of weight loss than current recommendations.

Keeping off the pounds

You are not allowed to follow the Scarsdale Diet for longer than two weeks, even if you still have weight to lose. You go on to the Keep-Trim programme.

This is still a low-fat, low-carbohydrate diet, without calorie counting or weighing. Just about everything fattening is forbidden. Sugar, cakes, sausage, mayonnaise, cream, potatoes, pasta, desserts, butter, oil or any kind of fat are not allowed, and you can have only two slices of wholemeal bread per day. You alternate the Keep-Trim programme with the Scarsdale Diet every two weeks until you reach target weight. Dr Tarnower says that 90 per cent of successful dieters on the Scarsdale Diet maintain weight loss, but provides no evidence for this.

Once you have reached target weight, you are advised to weigh yourself every day, nude. If you are more than 4 lb (1.8 kg) over your desired weight (this is the 'Four Pound Stop Signal') you are to go straight back on to the Scarsdale Diet until you have lost the excess weight.

Dr Tarnower says
'It works.'

You say
'It's a crash diet, very strict, and you couldn't deviate. If it said fruit, you had fruit. I lost 5 lb (2.3 kg), but I couldn't stick to it. I had to substitute for things I didn't like, so it fell through after a couple of weeks.'

'I just couldn't stick to it.'

We say
This diet has been much criticized by nutritionists for providing too little carbohydrate and too much protein, in complete contrast to today's views of a healthy balance of nutrients. Others question whether any diet which allows free consumption of such high-calorie foods as meat and fish can work for very overweight people, who could easily pack away big quantities of grilled chicken before they felt full, with no consequent reduction in daily calorie consumption. With the addition of ½ pint (285 ml) of skimmed milk the diet would be nutritionally sound as it stands, to offset a low level of calcium.

The diet could only appeal to someone who didn't want to think about what to eat at all, because it really is very restrictive

124 indeed. Dr Tarnower didn't approve of any substitution or change to the diet in any way. What a pity (as I learned recently) that Dr Tarnower was always a stone overweight himself, according to his own charts. You can tell by reading the book that he was a man who liked fine food – but one of the questions in the 'Question and Answer' sections directly asked if he'd ever had a weight problem, and I'm afraid he lied.

Calorie counting	×	Less than £10 to start	√
Weighing of food required	×	Personal support	×
Forbidden foods	√	Detailed 'who can't use'.	√
Suit single person	√	Emphasizes fluid intake	×
Suitable for vegetarians	×		

Food Fact File

Sesame prawn toast, a spring roll, beef and black bean sauce, a vegetable chop suey and a toffee apple is about 1890 calories.

Diet type
A reduced-calorie diet and food supplement.

What is it?
A tub of 60 capsules and a five-page leaflet outlining a high-protein, low-carbohydrate diet. The 'KCVL' (Kelp, Cider Vinegar and Lecithin) capsules are made from soya bean oil, lecithin, cider vinegar, kelp and vitamin B6. No calorie content is stated, but the amounts of these ingredients are very small and so the calorie content is probably negligible.

The Newlook Weight Loss Course started in 1992, since when more than 3000 have been sold. About 95 per cent of users are women. You can get it by mail order from Newlook Health, PO Box 363, Kilmacolm, Renfrewshire, PA13 4TN, or call the credit card line on 0150587 4460. Advertisements for the product appear in women's magazines.

The diet plan and enough capsules for 30 days costs £20. You can then re-order capsules using a Freepost envelope or by calling the credit card line. These cost £12.95 for 30 days' supply. If, after two weeks, you are dissatisfied, you can get your money back by returning the remainder of the course.

How does it work?
Taking certain supplements in conjunction with a calorie controlled diet, the makers say, will prevent calories being laid down as fat and burn up existing body fat.

The diet
You take one capsule twice a day (no special time is specified) and follow the leaflet's diet plan, which is to eat 1000 calories per day. There are eating plans for six days, each of three meals per day, two of which call for a pre-packed diet meal of less than 400 calories for dinner.

You make up your own diets using the eating plans as examples. This will help you to feel in control, and a diet is more enjoyable if you eat foods which suit you, the makers suggest. You are invited to complete and return a questionnaire detailing your success.

No recipes are given, nor would be required as the diet is very basic.

A typical day's diet

Breakfast	1 KCVL *capsule* 1 *boiled egg* 2 *slices toast*	 75 120
Lunch	7 oz (200 g) *cottage cheese* 1 *banana*	200 90
Evening meal	7 oz (200 g) *chicken (no skin)* 7 oz (200 g) *parsnips* 4 oz (110 g) *peas* 1 KCVL *capsule*	300 84 108
	Calories (approx)	1000
	Cost	£4.23

Variations
Men can eat 1500 calories per day.

Who shouldn't use it?
If you are in any doubt about your health, consult your GP before starting the diet.

Additional information
A list of the calorific content per 100 g of some popular foods is enclosed. You also get a list of do's and don'ts, which contains brief advice about not starving yourself, drinking plenty of water and taking exercise.

Expected weight loss
In the advertisement a user says that she lost 5 st (31.8 kg) in six months, an average of 2–3 lb (0.9–1.4 kg) a week. This is a slightly higher rate of weight loss than is considered to be healthy in current medical opinion.

Keeping off the pounds

Two methods are described. In the first, you cut out all junk food. You won't have to count calories if you stick to foods which are not manufactured or refined, described as fruit, pasta, and wholemeal bread, and totally avoid sugar, white flour and fat.

If you find that this method doesn't work, you will have to count calories. You start by eating 2000 calories per day and watch for weight changes. If your weight remains constant, you increase calorie intake gradually until you start to put on weight, and when you do you know what your daily calorie limit is. If you put on weight at 2000 calories per day, you are to decrease calories until your weight is constant.

They say

'By reducing calories (and this can be done painlessly by following this course) we are sure you will gain very rewarding results.'

You say

'The advert is very convincing, so I was disappointed it was a few sheets of photocopied paper and some anonymous pills.'

'I thought the recipes were boring and very hard to stick to.'

'It was pathetic and I felt really cross.'

We say

Although it is true that eating fewer calories will make you lose weight, there isn't any scientific evidence that the ingredients in Newlook capsules will help burn up fat or prevent it being laid down.

- The diet sheet is very basic – no real descriptions are given. I assume that the 'cottage cheese' should be low-fat and the 'bread' wholemeal, and that the chicken should be roasted or grilled, not fried, but if you didn't realize this the calorie content of the diet would be much higher. The calcium content of the diet is too low.
- There isn't any guide as to what is and is not a healthy diet. Once you have reached your target weight you are told to avoid all white flour, sugar and fat, but fat is an *essential* part

128

of a healthy diet and to cut it out completely could lead to vitamin deficiencies.

- You are told not to eat junk food, which is defined as foods that are 'manufactured' and 'refined'. Then you are told to stick to natural sources such as pasta and bread. Both of these are manufactured and refined. Newlook tell me they intended to mean 'heavily refined'.

- The calorie counter of popular foods is too brief and sketchy to be very useful. It doesn't list sugar, butter or alcohol, which I would describe as popular foods.

Calorie counting	√	Less than £10 to start	×
Weighing of food required	√	Personal support	×
Forbidden foods	√	Detailed 'who can't use'	×
Suit single person	√	Emphasizes fluid intake	√
Suitable for vegetarians	√		

The Revolutionary 3 in One Diet

Diet type
A reduced-calorie, high-protein diet combined with aromatherapy and autohypnosis.

What is it?
It is a two-page leaflet explaining the high-protein, high-fat, low-carbohydrate diet, an audiotape, a bottle of aromatherapy oil and 28 patches. The aromatherapy oil contains *Foeniculum vulgare* (the Latin name for fennel) and natural spring water.

You can obtain it by mail order from Robell Research (UK) Ltd, PO Box 142, Horsham, West Sussex, RH13 5FJ, or call 01403 242727 for credit card orders. It costs £39.95 including post and packing.

How does it work?
The aromatherapy oils, the manufacturers say, decrease appetite and act as a diuretic. The audiotape offers positive suggestions for beneficial eating patterns and the diet plan presumably helps weight loss. No claims are made.

The diet
On this diet you follow a specified set of menus for three days per week, and then on the other four you eat sensibly and healthily, avoiding chips, pies, chocolate, butter and the like.

Suggested menus are given from which you choose what items to eat on the three key days. You must eat meat or fish at breakfast, lunch and dinner and before going to bed. You must completely avoid vegetables, salads, all fruit except citrus fruit, cereals, dairy products and any food containing flour, such as pasta or bread. You should eat sufficient food to appease your hunger and are not to miss any meals. You are advised not to diversify from the diet and are told that if you cheat you will get fat.

Only five average-sized cupfuls of fluid are allowed per day. If you consider it essential you may take a little wine.

No recipes are given as the diet is very simple. You can cook the food any way you like, but only vegetable fat should be used for frying and fish may not be battered. Sauces must be used sparingly.

The diet is not at all suitable for vegetarians.

A typical day's diet

Breakfast	Bacon (say, 3 rashers)	170
	Citrus fruit (e.g.,	20
	½ grapefruit)	
	Black tea	
Lunch	Fish (say, 2 oz (56 g) cod)	100
	Chicken (say, 4 oz (110 g)	200
	fried breast)	
	Citrus fruit (e.g.,	50
	2 nectarines)	
Tea	Boiled egg	75
	1 Ryvita	25
	Black coffee	
Evening meal	Meat (say, 4 oz (110 g)	300
	steak)	
	Citrus fruit (e.g., orange)	60
Before going to bed	Meat (say, 2 oz (56 g) ham)	300
	Calories (approx)	1200
	Cost	£5.00

Treatment
The aromatherapy patches are applied singly and must be attached within half an hour of getting up in the morning. You are to apply 2–3 drops of oil to a patch and stick it to a different part of your body every day.

Variations
It is claimed that aromatherapy will also help cellulite, reduce the symptoms of PMT and the menopause, and stimulate the production of oestrogen, thereby postponing some of the degenerative effects of ageing.

Learning new habits

The audiotape runs for about 15 minutes on each side. You are to find somewhere comfortable where you will be undisturbed, and after listening to side 1 several times move on to side 2. You are to listen to the tape as frequently as possible, but never listen to it while driving a motor vehicle.

A woman's voice, to a background of New Age type music, tells you about the diet in a repetitive manner. She stresses that you will be able to take control of your life and of your eating; you will be able to put less food in your mouth each day. On the second side you are invited to enter a light hypnotic state, and she then tries to instil a feeling of confidence in your ability to control your eating, through visualizing all the benefits that being slim will bring you; you have chosen to be slim, and no one can stop you. Again this is accompanied by music, and at the end she counts you up out of your trance state.

Who shouldn't use it?

The aromatherapy patches are not to be used by epileptics, pregnant women or children. You should consult your doctor before starting the diet.

Side-effects

A dry mouth may be a problem.

They say

'Be positive – you will reach your target weight.'

You say

'I didn't notice any effects from the patch.'

'I hated the tape at first – this silly voice droning on and on – but it did make me think about eating less and I fell asleep every time I listened to the relaxation side.'

'The diet made me feel physically ill – I got light-headed and I got diarrhoea. You weren't allowed to drink enough.'

132 'I lost 4 lb (1.8 kg) in a week but it's an effort just eating meat and citrus fruit.'

We say

The diet itself is very like the Scarsdale Diet (see page 121), which is also based on protein and citrus fruit. Like the Scarsdale Diet, you must follow the menu plans but you aren't told how much to eat.

- You could easily find yourself eating far more calories than you should, and the low quantities of dairy produce mean that you could be short of calcium, folic acid and vitamin A.
- Autohypnosis methods remain unproven.
- There is no scientific evidence that aromatherapy can help you to slim or that it will affect specific ailments such as PMT or symptoms of the menopause. If the aromatherapy oil did have a diuretic effect (as fennel is supposed to), and you stuck to the small amount of fluid you are allowed, and the citrus fruit had its usual effects (increased peeing and diarrhoea when eaten to excess), then you could easily become dehydrated. This could cause an apparent loss of weight, which would return just as soon as you started eating normally again.

Calorie counting	✕	Less than £10 to start	✕
Weighing of food required	✕	Personal support	✕
Forbidden foods	✓	Detailed 'who can't use'	✓
Suit single person	✓	Emphasizes fluid intake	✕
Suitable for vegetarians	✕		

Vegetarian Slimming

Diet type
A reduced-calorie diet.

What is it?
A holistic approach to slimming that aims to get your body, senses, mind and emotions working together to make you slim and healthy. This 320-page book by Rose Elliot contains three vegetarian slimming plans. First you are shown how a vegetarian diet is healthier for humans, kinder to the environment and reduces the suffering of animals. There are height/weight charts, recipes, tips for success, methods of increasing motivation, and discussions of the benefits of alternative therapies.

The book is published by Chapmans/Orion and costs £4.99 in bookshops. First published in 1991, it has sold 40 000 copies. The author has been a vegetarian since the age of three.

How does it work?
First you are encouraged to look at yourself naked, weigh yourself and compare the weight with the tables given, and then decide if *you* want to slim for yourself. Rose Elliot doesn't think that you can succeed unless you want to. If you decide to go ahead, you first identify with the aid of food diaries why your calorie intake is exceeding your output, and work out why, how and when you overeat. There is information about nutrition from vegetarian and vegan viewpoints, with the health benefits outlined of a diet high in carbohydrate and fibre but low in fat and sugar.

The diet
There are three diets, the Vegetarian Slimming Plan for Calorie-Counters, the Vegetarian Slimming Plan for Food-Combiners, and the Vegetarian Hip and Thigh Diet. In general the diets are high in fibre and carbohydrate but low in fat. On the first you have to count calories and weigh ingredients, on the others simply weigh ingredients.

Overall, the Calorie-Counters plan provides 1000 calories per day, but if you have 1 st (6.3 kg) or more to lose you should start on 1200 calories, and if over 3 st (19.1 kg) on 1500 calories per day. Men with more than 1 st (6.3 kg) to lose should start on 1500 calories per day, but if they need to lose less than this, 1200 will allow them to lose weight quickly.

On the Calorie-Counters plan there is a daily allowance of ½ pt (285 ml) of skimmed milk, two pieces of fruit and as much as you like from the 'free' list, which consists of low-calorie vegetables. Black tea and coffee and low-cal drinks are also unlimited. There are three meals per day. You are allowed to 'swap' meals for vegetarian convenience foods, or to 'swap' calories for alcoholic drinks. You can divide the meals up as you like, and save any items for later to be eaten as snacks.

Recipes and menus have symbols to mark suitability for vegans, hip and thigh dieters, and so on. Advice is given about take-aways and eating out. Melon is the recommended starter, followed by plain boiled vegetables, or chips and a plain salad, with fruit to follow.

The Vegetarian Slimming Plan for Calorie-Counters: A typical day's diet

Throughout the day	½ pt (285 ml) skimmed milk 2 pieces of fruit Unlimited black tea, black coffee or low-cal drinks	200
Breakfast	5 fl oz (140 ml) plain low-fat yoghurt with 1 tsp honey 1 slice wholewheat toast with scraping of butter	200
Lunch	Baked potato with 1 oz (28 g) cottage cheese Unlimited salad	250
Evening meal	6 oz (170 g) baked beans with unbuttered wholewheat toast Unlimited salad	350
	Calories (approx)	1000
	Cost	£3.57

Recipes are for one, but you are shown how to adapt them to meet the needs of a family. There are recipes for entertaining at home.

Variations

The other diets described in the book include the Rice and Fruit Diet, which consists of only five pieces of fruit and 8 oz (225 g) of boiled rice per day, plus home-made lemonade. Rose Elliot says that you can follow this for up to 14 days, and will lose 1–2 lb (450–900 g) per day during the first week. There are two crash diets, each to be followed for one day only: the Pineapple and Bananas Diet consists of unlimited fresh pineapple and two bananas per day; the Strawberries and Buttermilk Diet has 1 ½ pt (850 ml) buttermilk and 2 lb (900 g) of strawberries.

The Food-Combiners Diet doesn't involve any calorie counting and follows the general principles of the Hay System (see page 245). Rose Elliot seems to think that it works because of the simple limitations it places on eating; for example, you can't combine carbohydrate and protein in the same meal, and fruit can't be eaten with anything else. But she points out that it's not possible to separate carbohydrate and protein completely. Dr Hay classed potatoes and grains as carbohydrates but both contain some protein.

On the Vegetarian Hip and Thigh Diet you follow either of the crash diets detailed above or the Rice and Fruit Diet for up to 14 days for 'excellent weight loss and general cleansing'. You then follow the Food-Combiners diet, choosing the recipes marked as suitable for Hip and Thigh dieters (these are low-fat menus).

There is a list of herbal remedies and foods believed to aid slimming (as appetite suppressants, diuretics, metabolism boosters or aids to digestion). Aromatherapy, sitz baths, skin-brushing, Bach Flower remedies and wearing particular colours of clothes are recommended as ways of keeping yourself calm and stress-free while slimming. To combat 'cellulite', aromatherapy oils and anti-cellulite creams are suggested. Rose Elliot also discusses the importance of getting in touch with your emotions and feelings as a way of releasing pent-up energy which can be used in more productive ways.

Exercise
A simple exercise routine involving stretching, bending and toning is illustrated, to help improve flexibility. The benefits of bioenergetics and T'ai Chi are discussed and there is also a yoga routine.

Learning new habits
You are encouraged to weigh yourself every day, and to record your weight, your thoughts, feelings and anything that you find interesting in a slimming book, which you use every day. You are encouraged to give yourself treats for reaching certain weight-loss goals.

Who shouldn't use it?
You are told that as with any diet it is wise to ask your doctor's advice before starting the Vegetarian Slimming Plan if you are in any doubt about your health.

Additional information
The height/weight charts show the minimum, average and maximum recommended weight of a 5 ft 4 in (1.63 m) woman as 7 st 10 lb (49 kg), 8 st 8 lb (54.5 kg) and 9 st 12 lb (62.6 kg). These correspond to BMIs of 18, 21 and 24.

Expected weight loss
You are expected to lose 2 lb (900 g) per week on the Vegetarian Slimming Plan, which is considered by doctors to be a safe rate.

Keeping off the pounds
To maintain weight loss having reached your target weight on the Calorie-Counters Plan, you must continue to count the calories. You increase your intake by 200 calories per day for a week and if you haven't put on any weight you can increase it by the same amount for another week, until you find that you are putting on weight, at which point you go back to the calorie intake of the previous week. If you exceed your target weight by more than 7 lb (3.2 kg) you are to start dieting again.

Rose Elliot says

'Make slimming a joy and create for yourself a new way of eating that you will love . . . you will be healthier and slimmer – and stay that way.'

You say

'The recipes were quite difficult to follow. On the Rice and Fruit Diet, how do you feel when you've only had rice and two pieces of fruit? Who could stick to that? Not me, for sure. It's only when you feel you're eating normal food that diets work. It would make you binge.'

'The recipes are varied and quite good, because it's hard to find calorie-counted vegetarian food books. They generally rely on pulses, nuts, sour cream and cheese – but these are high-fat foods, and you can be a fat vegetarian.'

We say

Although a vegetarian diet is an exceptionally healthy one to follow if a wide variety of food is chosen, the plans detailed above are low in zinc, iron, niacin, folic acid and vitamin B6. Rose Elliot advises you to take vitamin and mineral supplements if you are worried about your intake of nutrients. In the first edition she recommended kelp tablets as good supplements. However, it is now known that excessive use of these can interfere with the body's thyroid gland (because kelp, being a seaweed, is rich in iodine), and she intends to change the text at the next printing.

The other herbs mentioned in the book may have diuretic or laxative effects, but taking diuretics and laxatives doesn't make you thin. Throughout the rest of the book Rose Elliot emphasizes that you can lose weight only by eating a reduced-calorie diet.

Calorie counting	✓	Less than £10 to start	✓
Weighing of food required	✓	Personal support	✗
Forbidden foods	✓	Detailed 'who can't use'.	✗
Suit single person	✓	Emphasizes fluid intake	✗
Suitable for vegetarians	✓		

Any diet which reduces calorie intake significantly below previous intake should cause weight loss.

Nutritionists are concerned whether diets that allow you
unlimited quantities of such high-calorie foods as meat and fish
can really work for very overweight people. They may be used
to eating far higher volumes of food than you should consume
on such a diet, and could easily manage to eat large quantities
before they felt full, with no consequent reduction in daily
calorie consumption.

Doctors believe that the best sort of diet is one you can
continue for the rest of your life. For the sake of your health,
this means eating a varied diet, which is why high-protein diets

Key features of reduced calorie diets

Name	Theory scientifically proven	Promotes long-term healthy eating	Suggests new habits	Exercise plan	Weight-loss maintenance plan
The Charleston Diet	√	√	√	×	√
The Complete F-Plan Diet	√*	√	×	×	√
The Complete Scarsdale Medical Diet	×	×	×	×	×
The Newlook Weight Loss Course	√*	×	×	×	√
The Revolutionary 3 in One Diet	×	×	×	×	×
Vegetarian Slimming	√*	√	×	×	√

* Most of it.

139

are not now recommended. In the table I have not ticked a diet for promoting long-term healthy eating if it doesn't stress the importance of a mixture of carbohydrates, proteins, fats and fibre for long-term well-being.

Crash diets are never advised; nor are weight losses in excess of 1–2 lb (450–900 g) per day. Although it is true that you don't need to exercise to lose weight on a reduced-calorie diet, it's still recommended as a way of toning up flabby flesh at the same time, and a maintenance programme has been proved to be useful in keeping off the pounds in the long term.

All reduced-calorie diets should emphasize the importance of drinking plenty of water.

Food Fact File

Favourite foods outside the home, judging from how much is spent on them – about £8 billion per year:
Sandwiches
Hamburger and chips
Fish and chips
Pasta or pizza.

Chapter 9

Reduced-Calorie Diets
with an Exercise Plan

What's the theory?

The diets included in this chapter emphasize that if you restrict calorie intake you will lose weight, and if you exercise as well you will lose weight faster and be fitter and healthier. Some diets in this chapter also stress the benefits of eating different amounts and different kinds of food at different times of the day, which the authors believe leads to a speedier weight loss. Others advocate reduced-fat diets or high-fibre diets as the easiest ways to reduce weight.

Do these diets work?

Reduced-calorie diets have been scientifically proven to work. However, there's no scientific evidence that eating larger or smaller meals of differing composition at different mealtimes actually influences weight-loss (see page 22) and the effects of fibre on appetite are not clear-cut (see page 71).

Recently it's been suggested that the most important change you can make to your diet is to reduce the fat content, on the grounds that you get far more calories per gram of fat (9) than you do from a gram of carbohydrate (4). Research has shown that it is in fact possible to reduce your weight simply by cutting down on fat, but it's a slow business unless you reduce calorie intake and increase output as well, and it does depend on how much fat you ordinarily eat.

It had been suggested that if you cut down on fat you could eat as much carbohydrate as you liked, but a comparison of weight loss in men and women on a low-fat, controlled-calorie diet with those on a low-fat, eat-as-much-carbohydrate-as-you like diet found that the groups on the controlled-calorie diet actually lost more weight; women lost twice as much weight when calories were controlled. Another study found that women

141

on a low-fat, eat-as-much-carbohydrate-as-you-like diet lost 1 lb (450 g) or so more after six months than those on a low-fat, reduced-calorie diet – not a very significant difference, but they did enjoy their diet more.

It is also scientifically proven that appropriate aerobic exercise will use up extra calories and help speed weight loss on a calorie-reduced diet.

Keeping off the pounds

If you do not change your eating habits for good, and you start eating high-calorie foods in the same quantities as before after finishing your diet, you will put on weight, which is why a diet which incorporates a sensible weight-loss maintenance programme is important. There's no independent scientific evidence to prove that any of these diets work in the long term.

Any problems?

Don't ever try to speed weight loss by eating less than the recommended amounts of food. Most of the diets in this chapter have been assessed by experts for nutritional quality, and if you don't follow them properly you could be putting your health at risk, as with any diet.

Diet type
A reduced-calorie diet combined with an exercise plan.

What is it?
This high-carbohydrate, low-fat diet is the result of a collaboration between the author, Eve Cameron, and Channel 4, makers of the Big Breakfast television programme. It is presented in an amusingly written 192-page book describing the diet, with quotes from famous stars about their diets. Chapters include 'Rise and Dine', 'Let's Do Lunch' and 'Guess What's for Dinner'. There are tips on healthy eating and an A–Z crash course in nutritional know-how. *The Big Breakfast Diet* was first published in 1994 by Pan Books at £4.99.

How does it work?
Low-calorie diets cause your metabolism to slow down to conserve energy, the book claims. When you eat normally again you get fatter than before. If you have a big breakfast, a medium lunch and a small dinner you will lose weight steadily and safely. Regular aerobic exercise will help you burn calories as well.

The diet
You are encouraged to eat lots of fresh fruit and vegetables, and cut down on fat and sugar. You should eat less red meat and more white meat and fish.

The first principle of the diet is that you must have a really Big Breakfast. It is claimed that this will make you feel less hungry and so less likely to nibble, with the result that you will be happier throughout the day. Lunch should be healthy and filling. Your evening meal should be light and taken about three hours before you go to sleep to allow you to burn off more of the calories.

No calorie counting is needed, but portion sizes must be weighed properly. How much you eat is up to you. Recipes are for one, two or four people, or 'nutters', 'Zoggians' or 'codtented citizens' in Big Breakfast-speak. They are in three sections: breakfast, lunch and dinners.

A typical day's diet

Breakfast	2 oz (56 g) porridge oats, mixed with water, plus skimmed milk, and a banana chopped in	400
Lunch	1 small baked potato, with filling made of ½ chopped onion, ½ red pepper, ½ clove garlic, 2 oz (56 g) sweet corn and 1 tbsp crème fraiche	200
Evening meal	Orange soup, made with ¼ tbsp olive oil, ¼ onion, ¼ carrot, ¼ potato, juice of ¼ orange, ¾ pt (213 ml) vegetable stock	100
	Pasta and chicken salad, made with 4 oz (110 g) pasta, 4 oz (110 g) chicken breast, small amounts tomato, pepper, onion, with lemon dressing	400
	Calories (approx)	1100
	Cost	£3.57

Variations

Big Lads can eat more than the recommended amounts of some dishes.

Exercise

The exercise sections are full of good ideas to get you exercising, or 'movin' and 'a-shakin' as the book prefers to call it, illustrated with photographs of The Big Breakfast crew. A workout using weights, tone-up exercises and a tums, bums and thighs programme are included. Equipment ranging from good training shoes to the use of hula hoops (not the edible ones) or spacehoppers is discussed, as are skipping, running and so on.

Who shouldn't use it?

If you have a medical condition or are pregnant, the diet and

144 exercises should only be carried out after consultation with your

doctor. Children should not go on a weight-loss diet unless recommended by a doctor.

Additional information

There are jokes, beauty tips, food facts, cooking quizzes, a list of aphrodisiacs, atrocious puns and so on, just as you would expect if you have seen the television programme. You're also told that being thin doesn't mean that people will like you more, that you'll fall in love and live happily ever after or land a fantastic new job.

The height/weight charts give the acceptable weight range for a woman of 5 ft 4 in (1.63 m) as 108–138 lb (49–62.6 kg), which corresponds to a BMI of 18–24. The men's range is from 20 to 25. Both are in accord with current medical opinion.

Expected weight loss

It is claimed that you will lose around 2 lb (900 g) a week if you follow the diet exactly, which is in line with what doctors would recommend.

The Big Breakfast say

'WARNING! This book may seriously affect your figure.'

You say

'Aargh! No puddings!'

'The recipes are good and it's funny to read.'

'I didn't do the exercises. I couldn't make the lunches as I was at work, and I couldn't make myself stop eating carry-outs at night, so I didn't lose weight.'

We say

This is a terrific and amusing way to present good nutritional values to people who don't know anything about them, though the diet could be rather low in calcium.

- You are advised to cut down on alcohol if you can't cut it out entirely. Given that most people's socializing takes place where alcoholic refreshment is taken, more advice about the low-cal alternatives might have been useful.

145

- It is claimed that working out regularly can speed up your metabolism. This isn't strictly true.
- Dieting does not make you fat; after losing weight once you will put on and take off weight at the same rates as someone who has never dieted.
- It is assumed that you are interested in cooking and that you will be able to cook the meals for yourself. No hints are given about how to make your parents do it for you, or on how to keep the rest of the family or your flatmates happy while you hog the kitchen rustling up your personal choices.
- Experienced dieters are likely to be well aware of most of the information here, though perhaps not about the aphrodisiacs.
- There is no evidence that eating larger or smaller meals at different times of the day makes any difference to weight loss or mood.
- There is no specific weight loss maintenance plan.

All in all, one for the younger dieter. Recommended exercise includes roller-skating and trampolining.

Calorie counting	✗	Suitable for vegetarians	✓
Weighing of food required	✓	Less than £10 to start	✓
Forbidden foods	✓	Detailed 'who can't use'.	✓
Suit single person	✓	Emphasizes fluid intake	✓

Diet type
A reduced-calorie and exercise diet.

What is it?
There are three components in this programme: dieting, exercise and changing the way you think. The diet is a low-fat, high-carbohydrate one, moderately high in fibre and protein.

The programme is described in a large-format, 88-page book by Janet McBarron-Liberatore who became a doctor after starting as an auxiliary nurse at the age of 16 and who now specializes in bariatrics (an American term for the branch of medicine concerned with the problems of overweight people). She herself suffered from excess weight all through her adolescent years. She went on innumerable diets, had aversion therapy and her ears stapled, and put on weight. All the time she pretended to herself that she was dieting, while compulsively eating in cupboards and in her car. At one time she weighed 15 st (95.3 kg), but has since lost over 60 lb (27.2 kg).

Topics include 'Eat and Be Thin', 'A Diet You Can Live With', 'Walk to Keep the Weight Off' and 'Stay Thin and Win'. Included are recipes and advice on cooking methods, healthy nutrition and exercise.

The book is available by mail order (£12.95 plus £2.95 for post and packing) from the Willow Tree Press, Dept Ch 131, Unit J1, Brooklands Farm Estate, Brooklands Lane, Weybridge, Surrey, KT13 8UY. Alternatively, look out for advertisements in the press.

How does it work?
To lose weight and keep it off, the diet gives you a few basic rules which are both practical and mental. They include setting yourself a realistic target and a realistic time in which to complete it, rewarding yourself when you reach your target, and learning how to stop blaming other people (it is you and you only who is responsible for how much you weigh). You are to weigh yourself only once a week, at the same time on the same day – preferably a Monday.

No diet works if you eat differently for a while and then go

147

back to your old ways when you become thin, the author suggests. On Day One, you are to start thinking thin and eating differently for ever.

The diet

The plan is one which you can follow with a family, when entertaining or going out, *so long as* you stick to the rules for yourself. You can eat up to six times a day, providing you take as a snack one of the items included in a daily plan, or choose one from a list of 150-calorie snacks. You should never eat less than four hours before bedtime, and you must drink eight 8 fl oz (220 ml) glasses of water per day.

There are three eating plans; you don't have to stay on the same one throughout, but you shouldn't change to another until you have been on one for at least a week. The first plan is for those who have a high level of activity throughout the day, and allows you a big breakfast, moderate lunch and light dinner. The second, for business executives, allows a light breakfast, heavy lunch and moderate dinner. The third, which Dr McBarron-Liberatore says is the most popular, is for a light breakfast, moderate lunch and big dinner.

You don't have to count calories, but you do have to weigh portions, and lists are provided for these in the different categories of food item. Every plan allows for ten 70-calorie portions of carbohydrate (e.g., 1 cup skimmed milk, ½ cup cereal, ⅓ cup noodles, ½ cup peas). Every day you are to have four portions of bread or pasta and two each of dairy products, vegetables and fruit. You should also have four 100-calorie portions of protein (e.g., 2 oz (56 g) chicken, 1 egg, 1 oz (28 g) cheddar cheese), two 50-calorie portions of fat (e.g., 1 tbsp cream, 1 tsp butter) and one 150-calorie snack, the list of which includes 4 fl oz (110 ml) wine, 2 oz (56 g) cake, 1 oz (28 g) butterscotch. There are also 'bonus veggies' which are optional, some of which can be eaten in unlimited quantities, like bean sprouts or celery. You aren't allowed to eat foods not on the lists, red meat should be limited to four times per week, and coffee and tea are restricted – Dr McBarron-Liberatore believes that caffeine interferes with the release of fat from fat cells. Different amounts of fat, carbohydrate and protein are allowed for the different meals on the three plans.

There are 14 pages of recipes, mainly for four people, and all are in American cup measures. There aren't any main meals for vegetarians who don't eat fish.

A typical day's diet

Breakfast		
2 carbohydrate portions	1 cup skimmed milk	85
	1 slice wholewheat bread	60
1 protein	2 oz (56 g) slice baked ham	100
Lunch		
3 carbohydrate	¼ honeydew melon	80
	2 slices wholewheat breats	120
Bonus vegetables	Lettuce, onions, sprouts	10
2 protein	2 oz (56 g) chicken	100
	½ cup low-fat cottage cheese	100
1 fat	1 tsp mayonnaise	50
Evening meal		
5 carbohydrate	1 cup skimmed milk	85
	½ cup brown rice	100
	1 small roll	50
	1 pear	60
	⅓ cup corn	40
Bonus vegetable	½ cup broccoli	25
2 protein	3 oz (85 g) crab meat	80
	1 oz (28 g) Gruyère cheese	100
1 fat	2 tbsp light cream, for coffee	50
	Calories (approx)	1300
	Cost	£3.57

Exercise

Dr McBarron-Liberatore believes that getting some exercise is more important than dieting. She advocates vigorous walking for at least 30–45 minutes per day, at least six days per week. She gives lists of excuses that she commonly hears from people who say they can't take exercise, and debunks them, while stressing the emotional and physical benefits. She claims that **149** exercise speeds the metabolism by up to 30 per cent for 24 hours after vigorous walking, which unfortunately isn't so.

Learning new habits

There are quizzes to help you analyse the way you think. You are advised how to analyse your eating patterns, discover times when you are likely to overeat, and overcome temptation by 'acting thin', such as taking smaller bites at meals, using a smaller plate, planning meals and not eating before bedtime.

Dr McBarron-Liberatore judges from her experiences in running a clinic for people who want to lose weight that lack of self-confidence is one of the main problems. There is advice to help you feel more confident in your ability to shed the pounds, such as frequently reminding yourself that you are a good person who will lose weight and get thin. You must keep a food diary, because this makes you take responsibility for what you eat, helps you stay on track and gives you insight into your eating habits.

Who shouldn't use it?

Quizzes help you to decide whether you are ready to try the diet. If you think that you want to starve yourself, want an instant fix for your problems, or want to lose weight quickly without adjusting your attitude to food, you should *not* begin the programme. You are advised that, before starting this or any other weight-loss programme, you should see your doctor. The approach overall is about patience: it took you some time to reach the weight you are and it will take some time to become thin again.

Additional information

There are appendices of nutritional information on healthy eating and information on shopping. There is also a section on cooking methods – put your frying-pan to the back of the cupboard and steam, microwave or boil food instead.

Dr McBarron-Liberatore is adamant that you shouldn't aim for an unrealistic goal. It's unrealistic to expect to weigh as much as you did as a teenager, or less than you did ten years ago, for example. It's unrealistic to aim for a weight you can't possibly maintain. It's better to aim for one that you were previously able to maintain for at least six months.

There are no height/weight charts, but she suggests that for a 5 ft 4 in (1.63 m) woman it would be reasonable to weigh between 7 st 10 lb (49 kg) and 9 st 6 lb (59.9 kg), representing a BMI of 18–23.

Expected weight loss
You should expect to lose between 1½ and 2 lb (700–900 g) per week

Keeping off the pounds
The whole book is about keeping the pounds off, as this is one of the cornerstones of the diet. You are to consider yourself a food addict who has overcome addiction, and be constantly on your guard both against people who try to sabotage your plans and against yourself if you find that you are slipping back into your bad old ways rather than thinking thin, exercising and eating correctly.

After reaching your target weight, you are to weigh yourself daily for a month and then follow detailed instructions about how to maintain your weight loss, depending on how much you gain or lose over the next six months.

Dr McBarron-Liberatore says
'The successful new weight-loss programme that helps you lose weight by "eating healthy" . . . it's easy and it works!'

You say
'I lost weight on this diet – it was easy to follow and I liked the recipes.'

'I don't have time to walk vigorously for 45 minutes a day, but I still lost 6 lb (2.7 kg) on the diet.'

'Because it's all about counting it's a bit hard at first, but as you're allowed so much carbohydrate I didn't feel hungry and stuck to it for two weeks.'

We say
This is an excellent diet plan, completely in line with nutritionists' advice. Dr McBarron-Liberatore identifies one of the most frequent causes of failure to maintain weight loss as the situation

in which dieters set up IOUs for when they have finished dieting, as in 'I've given up cakes/ice-cream/butter on this diet and when I finish the diet I'll be able to have as much as I like of them.' This certainly seems to be true for some people, so the idea of starting as you mean to continue for ever is a sensible one. Although there are forbidden foods at first, these can be introduced again later. There are just a few small reservations:

- The recipes don't give values for carbohydrate, fat and protein, which is a pity as it is quite complicated to work out from the programme exactly what you can eat each day, even with the lists.
- Some of the items aren't readily available in Britain, such as collards (a type of kale) and triscuits.
- Unfortunately exercise doesn't speed up metabolism to any significant extent, as the book claims.
- I can't find any evidence that caffeine interferes with fat release from fat cells.

Calorie counting	×	Suitable for vegetarians	×
Weighing of food required	√	Less than £10 to start	×
Forbidden foods	√	Detailed 'who can't use'	×
Suit single person	√	Emphasizes fluid intake	√

Diet type
A reduced-calorie diet combined with an exercise programme.

What is it?
The diet is a low-fat, high-fibre one, with no calorie counting, and is given in a 416-page book by Barry Lynch. This is an expanded and updated version of two previous books, *The BBC Diet* (1988) and *The New BBC Diet* (1990), with combined sales of 2–3 million copies. Topics include 'How Fat is Fat and Does it Matter?', 'A Dozen Dieting Myths', 'Getting Yourself on Your Side'. There are case-histories from people who followed the original diet detailing their successes, recipes (with an index) and personal record charts (e.g., food diaries, activity levels). The health risks of being overweight and why people get fat in the first place are discussed. Dieting myths – different combinations of food help you burn up fat, alcohol doesn't affect your weight, 'I don't eat enough to keep a sparrow alive' – are dismissed.

The Complete BBC Diet was first published in 1994 by Penguin and costs £4.99.

How does it work?
There is no such thing as a miracle diet, the book maintains. The only way to lose weight is to take in fewer calories than you expend and increase your level of physical activity.

The diet
The first step is to choose the diet that will suit your food preferences, your lifestyle and you. Decide whether you want to follow one of the book's nine two-week set plans or choose one of the five flexible plans. On all plans it's important to drink as much water as possible, and all allow some skimmed milk and low-fat spread. In some of the plans there is a weekly allowance of alcohol, if you wish. You should avoid sweetened drinks, cream, high-fat meat products, full-cream milk, biscuits, cakes, pastries and salted snacks. You do have to weigh high-calorie foods, but you can eat as much as you like of some other items – usually low-calorie vegetables.

You can swap the meals about on the two-week diet plans, **153** and swap the plans about by having two weeks on one and then two weeks on another. The principle of the diets is to cut down on fat and sugar and increase the amount of fibre in your diet.

There are two set plans of 1,000 calories, five of 1250 and two of 1500 calories. You choose the one that will suit you depending on your height, your sex and how much exercise you normally take. The 'typical day' illustrated here is an example of the Middle Way set plan; it is suitable for most women and, at 1250 calories per day, weight loss will be steady. This features slightly plainer, more traditional food than most other diets. The five flexible eating plans are the Quickfire, Vegetarian,

A typical day from the Middle Way Diet

Daily allowance	½ pt (285 ml) skimmed milk	85
	½ oz (14 g) low-fat spread	50
	7 fl oz (200 ml) fruit juice	70
	Unlimited water and low-cal drinks	
Breakfast	5 fl oz (140 ml) orange juice	50
	2 Weetabix with skimmed milk from allowance	130
Snack meal	2 slices wholemeal bread	120
	2 oz (56 g) mashed sardines	100
	Cucumber and cress	10
	1 diet yoghurt	50
Evening meal	6 oz (170 g) grilled gammon	300
	Pineapple ring	20
	2 oz (56 g) sweet corn	70
	4 oz (110 g) baked tomato	20
	Baked banana and orange, made with 1 banana, 5 tbsp orange juice, nutmeg	120
Optional	Alcoholic drink	100
	Calories (approx)	1250
	Cost	£3.57

154

Gourmet, Hearty-Eating and No-Bother (convenience foods) Plans, providing from 1000 to 1500 calories per day. On these you choose a breakfast, a snack meal and a main meal from lists of options. Recipes are mostly for one or two people, but some are for four servings. There are recipes for starters and snacks, pasta and rice dishes, fish, poultry, meat, salads, side dishes, soups and puddings.

Exercise

The health benefits of exercise are explained, and you are advised how to increase your activity level gradually, either outside – walking, swimming – or at home by skipping or using the stairs. A chart shows how many minutes of exercise you should aim to take on at least five days a week. Warm-up, stretching and body-shaping exercises are illustrated.

Learning new habits

The book suggests ways to motivate and keep on motivating yourself. These include analysing why you want to be thin, keeping a food diary, enlisting the help of friends or your partner, coping with temptation and making a contract with yourself along the lines of, 'I promise I shall lose a certain amount of weight, and after I have lost the first set number of pounds I shall buy myself a reward.'

Who shouldn't use it?

If you are worried about your health, you are advised to check with your doctor before starting the diet.

Additional information

The height/weight charts show the desirable weight for a 5 ft 4 in (1.63 m) woman to be between about 8 st 4 lb (52.7 kg) and 10 st 2 lb (64.5 kg), which is a BMI of 20–24, exactly in accordance with medical opinion. You are told that no food can make you fat if you only eat it once a week.

Expected weight loss

In the first two to three weeks you can expect to lose 7–12 lb (3.2–5.4 kg) overall, in the next two weeks 1–2 lb (450–900 g) **155** per week, and in the following month 1–2 lb (450–900 g) per week, with the same loss thereafter until you reach your target weight.

Keeping off the pounds

A chapter suggests ways to cut down the fat in your diet, by eating leaner meat, avoiding butter and margarine as much as possible, reducing sugar and alcohol, using low-fat cooking options and incorporating the principles of the diet into your lifestyle permanently. You should continue to weigh yourself once a week. If you find that you just can't live without chocolate, chips and the like, you can eat sensibly for six or better still six and a half days a week and then eat what you like for the other meals.

They say

'Medically approved, easy to follow and tremendously success-ful, *The Complete BBC Diet* . . . is your key to a slimmer, healthier you and is the only diet book you'll ever need!'

You say

'I've changed my way of eating. I don't diet now, I've lost 7 lb (3.2 kg), but I still follow the book. There are good recipes and it's a well-balanced diet – I do cheat a bit and I have a glass of wine every night.'

'It's quite a good book – the most sensible I've read – but some of the food was very expensive, some of it was silly and some I didn't like. There was more cooking than I could do.'

We say

This is an excellent set of diets, with something for every taste, age and circumstance, lots of information about healthy eating and good advice on changing your eating habits. You are advised that the guidelines of the diet are perfectly suitable for women who are breast-feeding or pregnant and for overweight children. While this is true, as the guidelines are perfectly in line with modern nutritional thinking, no such person should go on a reducing diet without seeing a doctor first, as Dr Lynch suggests.

Calorie counting	×	Suitable for vegetarians	√
Weighing of food required	√	Less than £10 to start	√
Forbidden foods	√	Detailed 'who can't use'	×
Suit single person	√	Emphasizes fluid intake	√

Food Fact File

The ACE vitamins (the anti-oxidants) are creating a lot of interest at the moment, because they are thought to help prevent the development of cancer and heart disease. Vitamin A is made in the body from carotenoids, the chemicals which give some fruit and vegetables, such as carrots, their yellow or red colour. Vitamin C comes from fruit, especially citrus, and vegetables. Vitamin E is found in eggs, nuts, vegetable oils, butter and cereals. Not surprisingly, many dieters' daily intake of vitamin E tends to be low; it is not a good idea to go on very-low-fat diets for this reason. Another reason to keep up vitamin E intake is that, although there is no hard evidence, it is supposed to enhance sexual performance and combat ageing!

Diet type
A low-fat, reduced-calorie diet, combined with exercise.

What is it?
A 30-day eating and exercise plan by Judith Wills, in a large-format, 160-page book. She describes the benefits of reducing the amount of fat in our diet, explains how much and what kinds of fat we need, and shows how to modify our eating and cooking habits to improve the health of the whole family. She also shows how to convert high-fat meals into low-fat versions, although both meals weigh the same. Fat addictions – to cheese or chocolate – are discussed, and strategies to combat them outlined.

There is an exercise plan, a chapter on keeping the pounds off permanently, and before-and-after photographs and stories of people who lost weight (and inches) on this diet. *Fat Attack* was first published by Vermilion Arrow in 1995 at £4.99.

How does it work?
Judith Wills believes that a diet that lets you eat all the foods you like while still keeping fat intake within recommendations, combined with a simple exercise plan to increase output, is the best way to go about achieving weight loss.

The diet
The diet is a low-fat, high-fibre, moderately salty one. You can eat things you like, by swapping high-fat items for low-fat ones, altering cooking methods, and altering the balance of food towards more carbohydrates and less fat-rich meals. There are no forbidden foods. You don't have to count calories or weigh carbohydrate portions accurately.

There's an allowance of $4\frac{1}{4}$ fl oz (125 ml) of skimmed milk every day, and you can have one treat per day from a list that includes alcoholic drinks, ice-cream, cheese, sweets, chips and butter. All kinds of low-calorie drinks, very low-calorie vegetables and condiments are permitted freely.

Every day you choose a breakfast from a range of seven, all of which include a fruit choice, and then have the lunch and

A typical day's diet

Daily allowance	4 ¼ fl oz (125 ml) skimmed milk	40
Breakfast	1 oz (25 g) plain cereal with 4 oz (100 ml) skimmed milk	130
	1 slice white or brown bread, low-fat spread and low-sugar jam	75
	1 piece of fruit	50
Lunch	Pasta and tuna salad, made with 1 oz (25 g) pasta shapes, 1 tbsp low-fat natural yoghurt, 1 tbsp Kraft free choice, 4 oz (100 g) tuna, 4 oz (100 g) cannellini beans, with green beans, parsley, celery, cucumber, lettuce, skimmed milk, sugar, apple, mustard	305
Evening meal	Greek-style spicy lamb kebabs, made with 4 oz (100 g) lamb fillet, 1 tbsp low-fat Greek yoghurt, ½ tsp paprika, cumin, coriander, ¼ red pepper, onion, 1 tsp mint, olive oil, and garlic and bay	226
	1 piece of fruit	50
	Tomato rice, made with 2 ½ oz (70 g) long-grain rice, 4 oz (100 g) chopped tomatoes, and onion stock, orange, cumin and carrot	280
	Cucumber, pepper and lettuce salad	40
Treat	1 oz (25 g) bar of chocolate	150
	Calories (approx)	1300
	Cost	£3.57

evening meals laid out for the individual days. There are two options for each meal, and at lunch one of these could be made up as a packed meal.

You are allowed to eat the dessert part of the lunch or evening meal as a separate snack at some other time. The evening meal options include one dish which is quick and easy to prepare, or a convenience ready-made dish, and another for which the recipe is given. The diet is not suitable for vegetarians; most evening meal options contain meat.

Recipes for the lunch and evening meals, all for four servings, are given in a separate section. These give the calorie and fat content. There are soups and starters, and the main meals include all sorts of ethnic foods – chilli, fajitas, beef rendang, chicken tikka masala – and low-fat versions of popular dishes. There's a section on baked potato fillings and toast toppings, and others on sauces and puddings.

Variations

If men have just a little weight to lose, or are shorter than average, they follow the basic plan. Otherwise, they are to increase the amounts of all carbohydrates and skimmed milk, and have one extra treat per day.

Exercise

The 'Take Thirty' exercise plan asks you to spend 30 minutes per day on each of five days a week, and is based on walking. First, the advantages of this kind of exercise to health and weight loss are described. Then advice is given to fit the 'Take Thirty' plan into your week; for example, you can take a packed lunch to work, walk for 15 minutes to a park to eat it and afterwards walk back for 15 minutes. You are advised to warm up gradually, and then walk briskly enough still to be able to talk. Pulse tests help you decide whether you are going at the right pace. Gradually you increase the pace until after six weeks you should be able to walk at 5 mph (8 kph) for 30 minutes.

If you aren't able to find the time to walk in daylight, or the weather is bad, there are alternatives. Warm-up stretches, toning exercises and cool-down stretches are illustrated.

Learning new habits

There are specific recommendations for dealing with problems caused by bingeing on high-fat foods. If you're a sweet-eater or a cheesaholic you have to decide whether you're overeating because of low blood sugar, because it's a habit, because it's a comfort or because it's a reward. Ways to prevent bingeing in these circumstances are outlined, and cheesaholics are given lower-fat alternatives. There is advice on overcoming bad habits, with alternative strategies to eating for comfort.

Who shouldn't use it?

If you are pregnant or have a medical condition, you shouldn't follow the diet and exercises without first consulting your doctor.

Additional information

BMI charts are shown and the acceptable level is stated as 20–25, exactly in line with current recommendations. You are also shown how to calculate your waist-to-hip ratio, in order to see whether you have the classic 'apple' shape known to be more prone to heart disease. If your BMI is between 25 and 30, you can tell whether you need to lose weight by comparing your waist-to-hip ratio with the average values given.

Expected weight loss

Men will lose 10–14 lb (4.5–6.3 kg) over 30 days, and women between 8 and 12 lb (3.6–5.4 kg), which is in accord with current medical opinion.

Keeping off the pounds

To maintain weight loss you are advised to stick to the diet's guidelines, which allow for 20–25 per cent of all calories from fat, and to keep saturated fats to a minimum. You are to fill up on carbohydrate, fruit and vegetables. Low-fat protein foods are listed, as are foods with high levels of saturated fat. Nothing is forbidden, but you shouldn't let more than 10 per cent of your total intake of calories come from saturated fat.

Judith Wills says

'The no-hunger way to a fitter, leaner body and a healthy heart.' **161**

We say

This is a well-balanced diet, nutritionally. It incorporates all the latest ideas about trans-fatty acids, saturated fats and vitamins and their role in preventing heart disease and promoting good health.

It is certainly true that a low-fat, high-carbohydrate diet is one that doctors recommend for weight loss, and in addition this diet is high in fruit and vegetables. By allowing alcohol, chocolate, convenience foods and chips, and by introducing modified recipes for ethnic foods and old family favourites, this diet could fit your lifestyle quite easily. The book is too new for me to have had reports on it as yet.

Calorie counting	✕	Suitable for vegetarians	✕
Weighing of food required	✓	Less than £10 to start	✓
Forbidden foods	✕	Detailed 'who can't use'	✓
Suit single person	✓	Emphasizes fluid intake	✕

Diet type
A reduced-calorie diet combined with exercise.

What is it?
There are eleven diet plans, recipes, a convenience-food calorie-counter, exercises, food diaries, nutritional advice and case-histories (some with before-and-after photographs), in a 176-page book by Sally Ann Voak. There is also a quiz to complete; this finds out how much you *really* eat, and so what your current calorie intake *really* is, as opposed to what you pretend it is. The book is the result of a BBC TV project in the village of Fatfield in Tyne and Wear. In two years on the diet, the villagers lost 2 tons in weight. *The Fatfield Diet* is published by Michael O'Mara at £3.99 and is available in bookshops.

How does it work?
Dieters fail to lose weight long-term because diet meals are boring or too small, in this book's view, and when you come off them you have to eat normally again, and you tend to put on weight. With this diet you eat large meals of normal food and, combined with exercise, this will help you to lose weight.

You are advised to read the whole book from cover to cover before you begin the diet. You must be honest about your true eating habits and stop feeling guilty – guilt is time-wasting, destructive and fattening. You are encouraged to think positively about why you want to diet, and develop 'body image awareness'.

The diet
The diet plans are high in fibre and carbohydrate but low in fat. There are no forbidden foods – you can even have chips, so long as they're oven chips – but you are advised to cut back on sugar and alcohol, though there is no need to cut them out. You are not allowed anything in unlimited quantities except water and salad vegetables like cucumber and celery. The book includes low-fat cooking methods and food preparation. You *must* eat all you are supposed to eat each day.

There is a basic plan of 1350 calories per day for women and 1600 for men. Some recipes are given, but most of the meal plans are very simple and don't need elaborate preparation. Servings are for one, four and sometimes eight.

A typical day's diet

Throughout the day	½ pt (285 ml) skimmed milk	100
Breakfast	½ grapefruit	20
	1 oz (28 g) bran cereal with milk	150
	1 slice wholemeal bread with 1 tbsp honey	120
Treat	1 wholewheat crispbread with 1 oz (28 g) cottage cheese and scraping of Marmite	60
Lunch	Sandwich, made with 2 slices wholemeal bread, salad, ½ oz (15 g) Edam cheese	200
	1 diet Ski yoghurt	45
	1 orange	60
Treat	10 grapes	30
Evening meal	5 oz (140 g) lean pork chop	375
	Bubble and squeak, made with 2 oz (56 g) cooked cabbage, 8 oz (225 g) mashed potato, ½ carrot, onion, nutmeg, ½ tbsp crumbs, ¼ oz (7 g) cheddar	125
	Salad	20
	½ glass wine	50
	Calories (approx)	1350
	Cost	£3.57

Variations

There are ten variations on the basic plan, including Vegetarian, Boozer's, Shift Worker's and Lazy Cook's Plans. You can use different plans at different times to suit your lifestyle, so, for example, women can move to the Anti-Bloating Plan before a period.

Exercise

You do 20 minutes' exercise three times per week, and if you are unfit or very overweight it is recommended that you start off with swimming before moving on to anything more vigorous. If you can't stand the idea of revealing your body in public, there are some exercises that you can do in the bath. There are also 'couch potato' exercises which you can do while watching TV, and stretch exercises.

Learning new habits

Before you start the diet, you complete the 'Fatfield Charter', which is given at the end of the book. You promise to follow the diet faithfully and diligently until you have reached a certain weight, to try to take more exercise, and to give yourself a present or a treat when you have lost the first 7 lb (3.2 kg). Then you cut out the charter and put it up in the house where you will see it regularly, or you can send it to Sally Ann Voak with a photograph of yourself. When you have reached your target weight you send her another photograph. She will return it to you, endorsed with the Fatfield Seal of Excellence.

You are strongly encouraged to keep a food diary.

Who shouldn't use it?

If you are overweight, on medication or diabetic you must consult your doctor before starting the diet.

Additional information

To increase your motivation you can join the Fatfield Slim Pals. This is a nationwide network of slimmers who keep in touch with each other by letter and phone. *The Fatfield Way* is a video costing £10.99 in the shops: it tells you about the diet and shows you the exercises. You can buy *The Fatfield Recipe Book* for £3.99 from the same publisher.

No height/weight charts are shown. It is up to you to set your target weight.

You are advised to be extra-loving to your partner while you

165

are slimming; it can be upsetting for him or her to watch you changing.

Expected weight loss
No expected weight loss is given.

Keeping off the pounds
The maintenance plan allows 1500 calories per day, and you can add treats to this if you find that you are still losing weight (the allowance is 1800 calories per day for men). Meal plans are given.

Sally Ann Voak says
'Eat more and weigh less!'

You say
'This is the easiest diet I've tried for fitting in with a family, and I've lost 7 lb (3.2 kg) so far.'

'You can eat just about everything you ate before but you have to be careful not to go back to your old ways of cooking afterwards.'

We say
This is ordinary family food; gourmet dining it's not. You can have roast dinners, fish fingers, beef burgers, chips, convenience foods and keep drinking alcohol and eating sweets; it should fit into British family eating easily. The point is that you can't have so much of them, you have to cook them in different ways and you have to eat lots of vegetables with them. It's a very well-balanced diet nutritionally.

- It wouldn't be a good idea to stay on the Lazy Cook's Plan for very long. Convenience foods tend to be high in calories and fat, and although you are encouraged to eat vegetables and fruit as well, two convenience meals a day isn't a recipe for long-term health.
- Many overweight people would rather die than exercise. I like the idea of 'couch potato' and 'bath' exercises – at least they will get you going, and then maybe you can do a bit more.

- Keeping a food diary and making a commitment to lose weight are good ways to keep up motivation.

Calorie counting	×	Suitable for vegetarians	√
Weighing of food required	√	Less than £10 to start	√
Forbidden foods	×	Detailed 'who can't use'	√
Suit single person	√	Emphasizes fluid intake	√

Food Fact File

The Edwardian country-house guest was awakened with tea, toast and biscuits in bed. At breakfast, he or she helped themselves to porridge, cream, tea (Indian and China), coffee and lemonade; hot dishes included haddock, bacon, eggs (boiled, fried, poached or scrambled), kedgeree, kidneys and mushrooms; among cold dishes were ham, ptarmigan, grouse and pheasant; followed by more toast, scones, butter, jam, honey and marmalade. This was only the first of several gargantuan meals throughout the day.

High Speed Slimming

Diet type
A reduced-calorie diet combined with an exercise plan.

What is it?
A low-fat, high-carbohydrate diet formulated by Judith Wills, with eating plans, recipes, an exercise programme and advice on keeping off the pounds permanently, in a 192-page book. First published in 1992 by Sphere, *High Speed Slimming* has sold 70 000 copies to date and is available in bookshops at £3.99.

How does it work?
Judith Wills' theory is that a good, fast weight loss at the beginning of a diet motivates you to reach your target weight.

First, you work out your correct calorie level – the lowest number of calories you should eat to lose weight quickly and safely. Judith Wills has a theory that metabolism is boosted by means of various stratagems, such as eating six times a day, eating lots of complex carbohydrates or eating cold, raw food. She claims that you can 'save' up to a maximum of 425 calories per day by using these tricks. You can save another 250 by, for example, fidgeting, having less sleep and keeping cool. Another 520 are saved by increasing exercise, to a maximum of 1195 calories above normal expenditure. This means that by following her recommendations and eating a reduced-calorie diet, even of 1000 calories a day, weight will be shed very quickly because output is so much higher than input.

The diet
There are three diet plans. Plan One provides 1400 calories per day, Plan Two 1200 and Plan Three 1000. Which one you start with depends on your age, body build, sex, level of activity and how much weight you need to lose. There is also a list of 50, 100 and 150-calorie extras, of which you can have a set number each day. If your weight loss slows down you may move to a lower-calorie plan, but otherwise you keep to the plan you are on until you reach your target weight. Lunch is the biggest meal of the day, but you can swap lunch and evening meal menus

occasionally if you need to. On this diet 60 per cent of total calories come from carbohydrate and 20 per cent each from protein and fat.

A moderately active woman of 5 ft 4 in (1.63 m) between the ages of 31 and 40 with less than 2 st (12.7 kg) to lose, whose activities are sedentary, who walks an additional 30 minutes or so per day and whose body shape is rounded rather than muscular or tall and skinny, would be on Plan Three.

A typical day's diet

Daily allowance	5 fl oz (140 ml) skimmed milk	45
	1 additional 50-calorie item, e.g., fruit	50
Breakfast	1 oz (28 g) 'no added sugar' muesli with 4 fl oz (110 ml) skimmed milk	140
	1 orange	60
Snack	1 banana	90
Lunch	1 boiled egg	80
	Large green salad, with dressing, made from 1 tbsp reduced-calorie mayonnaise and natural yoghurt, ¼ tsp curry powder	80
	1 slice wholemeal bread and a little low fat-spread	70
Snack	1 diet yoghurt	50
	1 apple	60
Tea	5 oz (140 g) baked beans	100
	1 slice wholemeal bread	60
Snack	1 apple	60
	Calories (approx)	1000
	Cost	£3.57

All recipes serve four and have been chosen because they don't need elaborate preparation or lengthy cooking. There are vegetarian dishes and suggestions for altering non-vegetarian dishes.

Exercise

There are two exercise routines. The first, called the AM plan, you do preferably after breakfast. It is designed to strengthen, tone and exercise you in about 20 minutes. Both this plan, and the one you do in the evening after tea, the PM plan, are fully illustrated. The PM plan also takes 20 minutes to go through, and is a programme of aerobic activity which you choose yourself. Activities include walking, swimming, cycling and rowing on a machine. Both AM and PM should be done six times per week. Warm-up and cool-down routines are given.

Additional information

The height/weight chart gives the acceptable weight range for a 5 ft 4 in (1.63 m) woman as between 108 and 138 lb (49–62.6 kg), corresponding to a BMI of 18–24. This matches current medical opinion. The overall message is: Use food – don't let it use you.

Expected weight loss

You can lose up to half a stone a week (3.2 kg), a stone (6.3 kg) in a fortnight or in the longer term 3–4 lb (1.4–1.8 kg) every week that you are on the diet. This is well above the medically recommended rate of weight loss.

Keeping off the pounds

You can follow the principles of the diet for the rest of your life. A chapter explains the maintenance plan, the basics of which are that slim people need fewer calories than overweight people. In the long term you should follow the high-carbohydrate, low-fat diet plan, although you may gradually increase your intake, and up your fat intake to nearer 25 than 20 per cent of total calories. You must also keep up the exercise programme. Lists of foods are given: Green ones, which you can eat plenty of; Amber ones, which must be eaten with caution; and Red ones, which should be eaten sparingly.

Judith Wills says
'The breakthrough diet for fast, safe and permanent weight loss.'

You say
'I went on it for nearly the whole two weeks and I lost 7 lb (3.2 kg).'

'I enjoyed reading the book. It was full of interesting things and I liked the recipes.'

We say
What Judith Wills suggests is generally correct. She is an expert and knows the subject extremely well. There are a few points:

- I can't find any evidence that losing weight quickly is bad for you, if you follow a nutritious diet, which this is. As stated earlier, it can help motivate people at the beginning of a diet. However, medical professionals prefer people to lose weight at a steady 1–2 lb (450–900 g) per week. Doctors don't recommend that people diet on less than 1000 calories a day without medical supervision.
- There is no advice on who shouldn't use the diet.
- It is not correct that exercise increases metabolic rate by any significant amount, though if you follow the exercise plan you will improve your health and expend more calories. Learning how to fidget could be quite hard.
- Eating spicy or cold food and eating lots of small meals does use up more calories, but the gain is really very small.
- Alcohol is not mentioned, so this diet is not for those of us who like a tipple.

Calorie counting	√	Suitable for vegetarians	√
Weighing of food required	√	Less than £10 to start	√
Forbidden foods	×	Detailed 'who can't use'	×
Suit single person	√	Emphasizes fluid intake	×

The Ryvita Diet

Diet type
A reduced-calorie diet combined with an exercise plan.

What is it?
Ryvita is a high-fibre crispbread, which has been used as a
reduced-calorie slimming aid for over 60 years. The company
producing it have also published a 96-page book by Jennie
Shapter, outlining their Zip into Shape eating plans. It contains
healthy-eating advice, photographs of exercise routines to help
you tone your body as you lose weight, and lots of recipes. It is
available in bookshops and main supermarkets at £4.99, and
has sold nearly 50 000 copies to date.

How does it work
To lose weight you must reduce the amount of calories you eat,
the author says. It is better to lose weight slowly. Recent
evidence shows that high-fibre foods take longer to chew, and
are more satisfying, reducing hunger while you reduce calories.
Crispbreads like Ryvita are useful sources of dietary fibre, she
maintains, and with an exercise routine to burn extra calories,
can help you to lose weight.

The diet
There are two diet plans, one for those who don't want to count
calories, the Day by Day Diet, and one for those who are too
busy for a detailed plan or who don't mind counting calories –
the Mix and Match diet. Both of these plans provide 1200
calories per day for women and 1500 (with extra allowances)
for men.

You are supposed to use the Day by Day Diet for 14 days. If
you haven't lost enough weight you can repeat the diet or go on
to the Mix and Match Diet. On the Day by Day Diet you are
given exact details of what to eat for three meals and two snacks
per day, which will provide 1100 calories. On the Mix and
Match days you use the same recipes to make up your calorie
allowance of 1100. You are to have a breakfast, a light meal, a
snack and a dessert each day, from the different parts of the
recipe section. On both diets you are allowed ½ pt (285 ml) of

A typical day's diet

Daily allowance	*½ pt (285 ml) skimmed milk*	*100*
Breakfast	*1 Ryvita Original crispbread with 1 tsp low fat spread 1 boiled egg 1 Ryvita sesame crispbread with reduced-fat spread and 2 tsp reduced-sugar marmalade*	*200*
Snack	*Carrot soup, made with 4 oz (110 g) carrots, 1 onion, 1 stick celery, ½ pt (285 ml) vegetable stock, spices and herbs 2 Ryvita Dark Rye crispbreads*	*100*
Lunch	*Crab snackers, made wtih 2 oz (56 g) crab meat, 2 tbsp red pepper, mushrooms, 1 tbsp reduced-calorie mayonnaise, spices 2 Ryvita Oat Bran crispbreads, 2 stuffed olives, chicory leaves*	*200*
Main meal	*Warm Chinese salad, made with 1 chicken breast, 1 tsp honey, ½ tbsp sherry, ½ tbsp sesame oil, 1 tbsp soy sauce, ½ stick celery, small amounts red and green pepper and Chinese leaves, 3 oz (85 g) boiled new potatoes*	*400*
Dessert	*Banana special, made with ¼ oz (7 g) butter, juice and rind of ¼ orange, 1 banana, ½ oz (14 g) muscovado sugar, 1 tbsp rum, 1 tsp flaked hazelnuts*	*200*
	Calories (approx)	1200
	Cost	£3.57

skimmed milk for use in tea or coffee, which will bring your total daily intake to 1200 calories. Some of the recipes are suitable for making up and taking with you to work. You are advised to drink lots of mineral water.

If you feel the need to snack, there is a section on small treats you can give yourself, providing you adjust your calorie intake accordingly at your other meals. Most of these are, not surprisingly, things you can do with Ryvita (Ryvita with Marmite, Ryvita with strawberries, Ryvita with cheese, etc.), but fruit, alcohol and chocolate are included.

Some recipes are for one and others for four servings, and all give the calorie content. There are no vegetarian options on the Day by Day Diet, but there are lots of vegetarian dishes in the Mix and Match section. Essentially, this is a high-fibre, low-fat and low-salt diet.

Variations
Men can eat 1500 calories per day.

Exercise
The exercise plan is from *Slimmer* magazine. It warns you to start gently and build up to more vigorous activity. It includes warm-up and cool-down exercise, and advice on how often you should do the routines. This is one of only two diet books I've seen with photos of *men* doing exercises!

Who shouldn't use it?
If you are not in good health you should consult your doctor before dieting, and you must not diet while pregnant unless medically advised to.

Additional information
The height/weight charts indicate that a healthy weight for a 5 ft 4 in (1.63 m) woman is between about 7 st 12 lb (49.9 kg) and 9 st 7 lb (60.4 kg). These represent BMIs of between 19 and 23, in accord with recommended weights.

Expected weight loss
If you follow the plan for four weeks you are expected to lose at least 6 lb (2.7 kg) and perhaps 10 lb (4.5 kg) or more. If you

lost no more than 10 lb, this would be in accord with current medical opinion.

Keeping off the pounds

There is a calorie, fat and fibre guide to common foods which you can use to design your own healthy eating plan once you have reached your target weight, with recipes for snacks and salads, family food, entertaining and desserts. You are advised to keep up your healthy lifestyle with a diet that includes plenty of fruit and vegetables, and to continue your exercise routine.

Jennie Shapter says

'Zip into shape . . . no fussy, faddy "magic" food or systems . . . a nutritious, sensible and pleasant diet.'

You say

'It's a really good diet and I lost 7 lb (3.2 kg) on it. If I feel I'm gaining weight I go back on it. I love Ryvita and I stick to this diet now several days a week since I lost weight on it.'

We say

I found this diet most appealing: the food is presented in beautiful colour photographs which had me drooling, and you have to have a dessert every day! A slice of wholemeal bread is about the same calorie content as two Ryvita crispbreads, but not as high in fibre; however the effects of fibre on appetite are not scientifically proven (see page 71). It all depends how much you like Ryvita. . . .

Calorie counting	√	Suitable for vegetarians	√
Weighing of food required	√	Less than £10 to start	√
Forbidden foods	×	Detailed 'who can't use'	√
Suit single person	√	Emphasizes fluid intake	√

Seven Days to a Slimmer You

Diet type
A reduced-calorie diet combined with an exercise plan.

What is it?
A book of advice and seven-day eating diet plans written by Michele Simmons. It is 144 pages long, with chapters on 'How Diets Work', 'A Strategy for Successful Slimming' and 'Exercise', and a number of eating plans. The book, published in 1994 by Headway, costs £4.99 and is available in bookshops.

How does it work?
Diets, Michele Simmons writes, bear little resemblance to the way we actually live. Food should be one of the joys of life, and people usually give up diets because they are so boring. We all want to eat food that suits our mood.

Motivation is a key to successful slimming, and ways to help keep you motivated are recommended. One of these is to be honest with yourself. There is no point in lying about what you eat, for you cheat only yourself. You should also be realistic about how quickly you can lose weight, and you should try to keep a food diary. Exercise will speed weight loss, the author believes.

The diet
There are some basic rules about what and how you are to eat on this diet. You should drink water before meals if you are worried that you might eat too much, and in any case you should have at least eight glasses of water per day. You can have as many low-cal drinks and as much undressed salad and vegetables as you want. Sweets, chocolate, sugar and the like are to be avoided. You are allowed two 'treats' per day, from a choice including biscuits, bread and fruit.

Michele Simmons says there are plenty of other low-fat, low-calorie diet and recipe books, but hers is better because it takes account of the fact that not everyone wants to cook every night; many people don't have the time or the patience, and for some fast food is the only option at lunchtime. To work, a diet must keep you full and satisfied. A mixture of foods will provide maximum nourishment. All the meals described are low-fat, low-sugar and high-fibre.

On the Seven Days to a Slimmer You Diet, each week's food plan is looked at as a group of seven days. You can follow as many of these seven-day plans as you wish or as you need to. They allow you to plan for the circumstances of your life – whether or not you have time to make a lunch for yourself, if you have to cook for others, if you eat out a lot. The menu plans

A typical day's diet from 'On the Home Front'

Daily allowance	½ pt (285 ml) skimmed milk	85
Breakfast	2 oz (56 g) high-fibre cereal with a little chopped banana Tea or coffee with milk from allowance	200
Treat	1 mini-box raisins	40
Lunch	Egg sandwich, made with 1 egg, 2 slices of wholemeal bread, scraping of low-cal mayonnaise, salad low-cal drink piece of fruit, say banana	200
		90
Treat	4 oz (110 g) grapes	65
Main meal	½ grapefruit	20
	Hot tuna topping pasta, made with ¼ onion, ¼ garlic clove, 2½ oz (70 g) tuna, ¼ tin tomatoes, ¼ pepper, seasoning	200
	4 oz (110 g) pasta	120
	Salad	20
	Baked apple	180
	Calories (approx)	1200
	Cost	£3.57

are around 1000 to 1200 calories each. You are advised to take a daily multivitamin tablet to ensure sufficient minerals and vitamins. There is no calorie counting, but you must weigh portions accurately.

Some recipes call for preparation; others need hardly any. You can mix and match the seven-day sets. There is a section of breakfast recipes and one of lunches. Seven further chapters give rules and recipes for seven days of eating-at-home, vegetarian meals, eating out, using ready-meals, fast foods and diets for Fat Days when you are feeling particularly hungry and Thin Days when you want to eat light meals. Recipes given are for different numbers of people – the 'Eating Out' chapter has recipes for one, the 'Veggie Way' for four, 'On the Home Front' for four or six. You are shown how to convert high-calorie dishes, such as spaghetti carbonara, into low-calorie ones.

Exercise

Michele Simmons admits she was a late convert to the idea of exercise, but medical evidence has persuaded her that exercise is beneficial to slimmers. She claims that it increases metabolic rate, decreases hunger, increases the amount of lean tissue by toning up the muscles, and makes you less prone to depression and insomnia. She recommends three sessions of vigorous exercise, for 20–30 minutes, per week. Having explained the difference between aerobic and anaerobic exercise, she discusses how to choose the best sort of exercise for you and emphasizes that you should choose an activity you really do enjoy.

Learning new habits

Slimming strategies to beat the urge to eat mean changing the way you eat. You are to eat slowly, putting down your knife and fork between mouthfuls, and chew thoroughly. You should stop eating when you are full, even if you haven't finished all the food, you are not to have seconds, and you should learn to recognize moments of weakness at particular times of the day. If you feel tempted towards a bakery or sweet shop, Michele Simmons suggests that you brush your teeth for five minutes. 'If in doubt have nowt' is the overall message.

Who shouldn't use it?
There are no warnings against anyone following this diet.

Additional information
You are shown how to calculate your own BMI, and Michele Simmons suggests that a BMI of between 20 and 25 is what you should aim for, exactly in accord with medical opinion. However, your ideal weight is left to you to decide. The book includes a chart on which to record your weight loss, and a metric converter.

Expected weight loss
Michele Simmons calculates that you should lose about 10 lb (4.5 kg) per month, which at 2 lb (900 g) or so per week is the recommended rate.

Keeping off the pounds
Having lost weight, you should be able to maintain that weight loss if you stick to the guidelines for shopping and cooking that Michele Simmons outlines. These include not buying meat products, checking the levels of sugar stated on the labels of food items before you buy them, removing fat from meat before cooking, and looking out for low-fat recipes in magazines.

If you ever do overindulge, at least you will know that you have done so, and you can compensate by being extra careful about what you eat the next day. If you find that your weight is rising, even slowly, you should go back to one of the seven-day eating plans.

Michele Simmons says
'The aim of this diet . . . is to help you reduce your weight with the least possible change to your lifestyle and your taste buds.'

You say
'I thought it was easy to understand; it was all kept simple.'

'It takes into account problems with living with a family — joining in the afternoon tea with just one little crumpet. . . .'   **179**

'Some of the advice about keeping to the diet is a bit impractical. How could you brush your teeth if you were walking along the street and felt an urge come over you to go and buy sweets?'

We say
This book is full of sensible advice, particularly about changing to healthy eating habits, and the diet is in general the low-fat, high-carbohydrate sort which nutritionists recommend. It's a little low in calcium and zinc, and very low in fat, but otherwise well-thought-out – Michele Simmons suggests that a multi-vitamin pill be taken daily, again in line with nutritionists' recommendations for dieters. There are one or two niggles:

- It really wouldn't be a good idea to stay on the ready-meals plan for very long. A week already seems too long to me, because this particular diet is higher than the others in fat and sugar.
- There isn't any scientific evidence that exercise raises metabolic rate to any significant degree, even for a couple of hours after the exercise period, unless you are an athlete. Nor is it true that exercise suppresses hunger: exercise seems both to depress and to increase appetite in different individuals at different times, depending on how vigorous the exercise is, the person's weight and their sex. Exercise may improve depressed people's mood and help insomniacs, but exercise doesn't make people without these problems cheerier or prone to sleep longer.
- All calorie-reduced diets should state explicitly who should not use them.

Calorie counting	×	Suitable for vegetarians	√
Weighing of food required	√	Less than £10 to start	√
Forbidden foods	×	Detailed 'who can't use'	×
Suit single person	√	Emphasizes fluid intake	√

Diet type
A reduced-calorie diet combined with an exercise plan.

What is it?
A six-step self-help programme for weight loss and weight maintenance in a 320-page book by Judith Wills. A new style of eating is proposed, where you can still eat the foods you like, but with far less fat and protein and much more carbohydrate, by *gradually* making swaps in the way you shop and cook. You proceed through the book step by step, and you are asked to check your progress by doing things all the way through (keeping diaries, checking lists, making lists for actions).

The book was first published by Arrow in 1994. It costs £4.99 and has sold 60 000 copies to date.

How does it work?
Telling people to eat less doesn't help them to understand *why* they have been eating too much. If they understand *why* they overeat they can learn *how* to control intake, Judith Wills believes. An exercise routine will help to shed the pounds.

The diet
A chart shows you how to work out which of four types of body profile you have, and you use this to choose your diet plan. You are urged to consider the plan and work out your choices on a monthly rather than a weekly basis, and weigh yourself monthly rather than weekly. Judith Wills uses a triangle system, with each triangle representing 50 calories of food. A 'food pyramid' shows how many of each type of food triangle you should have each day. Different body types are allowed different numbers of triangles, on different kinds of dieting days – days when you want to try very hard (22 triangles), for example, or days when you want to relax and eat a bit more (up to 40 triangles). Lists of snacks, fruits, extras, breakfasts, hot meals, desserts and takeaways are given, with their triangle value. There is a Red Extras list of foods on which you are only to use 10 per cent of your triangles per day – biscuits, sweets, alcohol, sugar and the like. No foods are forbidden, and you are urged to eat at least three times per day.

An Optimum diet day

Throughout the day	5 fl oz (140 ml) skimmed milk	△
Breakfast	1 diet fromage frais 1 apple Glass of orange juice	△ △ △
Snack	1 crispbread, scraping of low-fat spread and reduced-calorie jam Coffee (with milk from allowance)	△
Lunch	3 oz (85 g) prawns, chopped apple and stick of celery, with 1 tbsp low-cal mayonnaise Green salad 1 slice bread Tea (with milk from allowance)	△ △ △ △
Snack	2 fig-roll biscuits Tea (with milk from allowance)	△ △
Main meal	1 small ready-made pizza base topped with tomato sauce, 2 tbsp mozzarella, choice of topping, (mushrooms/peppers/onions) Salad 5 apricots Coffee (with milk from allowance)	△ △ △ △ △ △ △ △ △ △ △
	Calories (△ = 50 calories)	1100
	Cost	£3.57

The diet plans are flexible, depending on your lifestyle and how much weight you need to lose. I have worked out here a typical day's diet for a woman over 26 years of age, 5 ft 3 in (1.6 m) to 5 ft 6 m (1.68 m) tall, who wants to lose 1–2 st (6.3–12.7 kg) in weight. I've chosen an Optimum diet day, which allows the fewest triangles.

Recipes for two people are included. There are cold and hot main dishes, and desserts. There isn't a specific vegetarian section, but you can always choose a vegetarian option.

Exercise

A section on exercise emphasizes the benefits in terms of improved health and weight loss. There are tests of muscular strength and tone, and of flexibility, to help you choose a suitable programme, as well as a photographic guide to the Slim for Life Flexi-Programme – a ten-minute, 3-times-a-week routine to improve basic body strength, tone and suppleness.

Learning new habits

Judith Wills includes lists of statements about being fat which you use to assess why you want to be slimmer (for health, sexual or personal reasons, for example), and she shows you how to focus on your motivations and take control of your eating through the use of diaries and check lists. You are shown ways of combating people who for their own reasons will try to sabotage your diet, and how to build up your confidence.

Who shouldn't use it?

Anyone with a medical condition, or who is pregnant, must consult a doctor before using the diets or exercises in the book.

Additional information

There is a section for parents which describes the different nutritional needs of children and suggests how to help them stay slim and healthy. Judith Wills gives advice on all sorts of topics. She stresses that keeping cheerful is good for you and those around you, and that although losing weight will improve your life in many ways, it won't solve all your problems.

The height/weight charts give the minimum acceptable weight for a 5 ft 4 in (1.63 m) woman as 8 st 2 lb (51.7 kg), corresponding to a BMI of 19, and the highest acceptable weight as **183**

9 st 12 lb (62.6 kg), which is a BMI of 24, in line with current medical opinion.

Expected weight loss
No expected weight losses are given.

Keeping off the pounds
The book concludes with food charts detailing the triangle value of all common foods, which you can use to devise healthy eating plans for the rest of your life. Once you reach your target weight, you use the charts to plan meals, using the triangle system as before but with various added allowances of triangles per day.

Judith Wills says
'If diets work for you then this book will!'

You say
'It's quite complicated to understand the system, but I did get the hang of it and I lost 10 lb (4.5 kg).'

'I enjoyed reading the book because it's full of interesting facts and she gives you good ideas about how to stop overeating.'

'You can do this with a family, because she tells you how to keep them fed and happy while you're dieting.'

We say
Nutritionally, this diet is fine – although it would be important to keep up your intake of niacin and vitamin B6. *Slim for Life* is based on the latest scientific thinking about nutrition, and is full of tips to help you stay motivated. It suggests sensible ways to acquire new eating habits, with its emphasis on keeping track of your actions and emotions, and thus maintaining control of your life. I think that you would have to begin by carrying this book around with you, though, as I found it far from easy to remember the triangle values.

Calorie counting	✗	Suitable for vegetarians	✓
Weighing of food required	✓	Less than £10 to start	✓
Forbidden foods	✗	Detailed 'who can't use'	✓
Suit single person	✓	Emphasizes fluid intake	✓

The Weight Watchers Complete Diet Book

Diet type
A reduced-calorie diet combined with an exercise plan.

What is it?
This is a full-colour, large-format, 160-page book, drawing on the experiences of Weight Watchers slimming clubs which have been around since 1971. It covers such topics as 'I can do it!', 'How do I start?', 'What can I cook?' and 'How do I stay slim?'. There is a chapter on exercise, and information on Weight Watchers meetings near you, with telephone numbers for further information. There are fashion tips on how to look good (with a section for men), and the whole book has full-colour before-and-after photographs of Weight Watchers slimming successes, men and women, with their case-histories. Advice is given on healthy eating while pregnant or breast feeding, on food for children and on healthy cooking methods.

Published in 1994 by Simon & Schuster at £9.99, *The Weight Watchers Complete Diet Book* has sold 65 000 copies to date. You can buy it in bookshops or from Weight Watchers at a reduced rate.

How does it work?
The best diet is one which you can follow for the rest of your life, according to Weight Watchers. By changing your eating habits and stepping up your level of exercise, you will lose weight permanently.

The diet
The diet programme itself is a 14-day set of menus and exercise plans. To make choosing healthy foods easier, foods are divided up into Selections. Women should eat 4 carbohydrate, 3 fat, 3 fruit, 2 milk, 5 protein and 3 vegetable Selections per day, which would average 1200 calories. There are at-a-glance colour photographs to show you what a Selection of any food is. Combination foods are also shown; for example, a beefburger with bun is 2 carbohydrate Selections and 1½ protein Selections. Convenience, high-calorie and treat foods are described in terms of Selections.

You don't have to count calories, but you do have to weigh **185** portions exactly. There are no forbidden foods. Each day's menu is set out on a separate page, and includes a Food for Thought section (tips on food choices for healthy eating) and an exercise or stretch routine.

There is an Optional Daily Allowance of 100 calories, which you can eat in any form you choose (e.g., alcohol, sugar, jam), or you can save these up for a more substantial treat. The menu plans for each day include vegetarian options. You should drink 6–8 glasses of water every day, about half of which can be tea

A typical day's diet

Daily allowance	*Optional daily allowance*	*100*
	½ pt (285 ml) skimmed milk	*85*
	Unlimited vegetables	*50*
Breakfast	*4 fl oz (110 ml) fruit juice*	*40*
	1 oz (28 g) cereal (not sugar-coated)	*100*
	¼ pt (140 ml) skimmed milk	*45*
Lunch	*Egg in tomato mayonnaise, made with ⅓ tsp ketchup, 1 boiled egg, 1 tsp mayonnaise, low-fat natural yoghurt, ½ tsp cream, basil, lettuce*	*120*
	2 oz (56 g) French bread	*160*
	4 tsp low-fat spread	*70*
	2½ oz (70 g) low-fat natural yoghurt	*35*
Evening meal	*4 oz (110 g) grilled salmon steak*	*200*
	8 oz (225 g) potato	*160*
	Green salad and tomatoes	*40*
	1 medium apple	*60*
	Calories (depending on unlimited vegetables)	1250
	Cost	£3.57

or coffee. There is a list of low-calorie vegetables of which you can have as much as you want, raw, steamed or boiled, at any time.

Recipes are given where necessary for each day of the diet. These are for one serving, and there is always a vegetarian option. Another section details low-calorie dishes, some provided by successful Weight Watchers dieters. There are light lunches and snacks, meat, fish and vegetarian main meals, and desserts. Servings are for 1, 2, 4 or 8 people. There's an index, and all the dishes are marked with the number of Selections involved.

Variations
Men and young people add extra selections of carbohydrate, fat, protein and fruit to the diet plan, and 100 extra calories of any food they like. Young people should have an additional skimmed milk allowance as well.

Exercise
The exercise section stresses the benefits of exercise and outlines ways to increase your activity levels (with a warning for those who drink or smoke heavily or have medical problems to consult a doctor first). You begin with a warm-up, take your pulse and calculate your optimum training pulse rate. Full-colour photographs and a very clear text show you what to do. You should exercise at least three times per week.

Learning new habits
Having explained the physical and psychological reasons why losing weight can be good for you, the book suggests that you keep a personal weight chart on which to record both your changes in weight, and your body measurements. Having a photo of yourself taken every month will keep you motivated. There is a short section on what happens at Weight Watchers meetings, if you feel that you would like some company while you are dieting, and a question-and-answer section.

Who shouldn't use it?
You are advised that you should not embark on a weight-loss programme without your doctor's supervision.

Additional information

The height/weight charts indicate that the healthy weight range for a woman who is 5 ft 4 in (1.63 m) and between 26 and 45 years of age is 8 st 2 lb (51.7 kg) to 9 st 8 lb (60.8 kg), which is a BMI of between 19–23, in line with current medical opinion. You are to calculate your healthy weight range and aim for that, but are not to weigh yourself more than once a week, at the same place, at the same time and in the same clothes.

Expected weight loss

After an initially higher weight loss, on this diet you are expected to lose 1–2 lb (450–900 g) per week, but your personal weight loss will depend on how closely you stick to the guidelines given. This is the rate of weight loss recommended by current medical opinion.

Keeping off the pounds

On reaching your target weight, you start to add Selections or Optional Calories gradually. You may choose to eat a little more each day or to save up and eat more at weekends. The point is to discover how much you can eat before you start to put on weight, or lose weight. If you lose weight you add a Selection or two; if you gain weight you cut out a Selection or two. By recording your weight weekly you will learn to adjust your intake accordingly. You should keep up your healthy eating and continue to exercise. There are guidelines for ways to keep off the pounds permanently.

They say

'If you follow the Programme to the letter you will succeed.'

You say

'It's an easy-to-follow diet, and you can drink if you want. I lost 3 lb (1.4 kg) in a week, but eight glasses of water a day is pushing it, it's hard.'

'It's healthy eating. You get to recognize the portions so you don't have to use the scales, and I've lost 9 lb (4.1 kg) in four weeks.'

188

We say

This book is full of sensible ideas, practical advice and heart-warming success stories, all entirely in accord with the general principles of the Weight Watchers organization and the best nutritional advice. However, all calorie-reduced diets should state explicitly who shouldn't use them.

Because no foods are forbidden, you can easily fit this diet into most lifestyles. The point is that you are allowed a *little* of everything, as Weight Watchers believe it is important to start training yourself to eat moderately for the rest of your life.

Calorie counting	×	Suitable for vegetarians	√
Weighing of food required	√	Less than £10 to start	√
Forbidden foods	×	Detailed 'who can't use'	×
Suit single person	√	Emphasizes fluid intake	√

Overview

The reduced-calorie diets described in this chapter nearly all offer you a choice of a set plan to stick to or more flexible eating plans where you choose between food options. Which suits you depends on your personal circumstances, but it's been shown many times that a diet that fits in with your lifestyle is most likely to be successful in the long term.

Nutritionists recommend that you should aim for approxi-

Key features of reduced-calorie diets with an exercise plan

Name	Theory scientifically proven	Promotes long-term healthy eating	Suggests new habits	Exercise plan	Weight-loss maintenance plan
The Big Breakfast Diet	√*	√	×	√	√
The Columbus Nutrition Plan	√	√	√	√	√
The Complete BBC Diet	√	√	√	√	√
Fat Attack	√	√	√	√	√
The Fatfield Diet	√	√	×	√	√
High Speed Slimming	√*	√	×	√	√
The Ryvita Diet	√	√	×	√	√
Seven Days to a Slimmer You	√	√	√	√	√
Slim for Life	√	√	√	√	√
The Weight Watchers Complete Diet Book	√	√	√	√	√

* Most of it.

mately 30 per cent of your total calorie intake from fat. If your diet is too low in fat, vitamin deficiencies can result.

The benefits of exercise can't be overemphasized, but remember what all these diet programmes stress — don't try to do too much too soon.

Food Fact File

The Blobbendales are just like the Chippendales – except that they are enormously fat. The heaviest weighs 49 st (311 kg). They jiggle and gyrate their gigantic bellies and bums to music and drive fans wild all over the world. Even this amount of exercise was sufficient to cause one of the Blobbendales to lose weight; he was warned that if he lost much more he'd be out of a job.

Chapter 10

Slimming Foods

What's the theory?

These are foods with reduced calories or reduced fat, and so, in theory, by substituting ordinary food with products from this range, you will be eating a calorie-reduced diet. The first type of 'slimming foods' were artificially sweetened canned foods in the 1950s. Since then the market for slimming foods has expanded into every type of food product. From low-calorie beers, ice-cream, yoghurt, sauces and salad dressings to complete meals, you can buy a reduced-calorie version of almost anything. You can even buy sugar-free sweets. The whole range of 'healthy eating' products is worth some £650 million per year in Britain.

Many people who aren't trying to lose weight use slimming foods when they want a convenience food, or when they are being careful about what they eat. These foods aren't always marketed as slimming aids, and are sold as healthy, low-calorie options. For example, Bird's Eye Healthy Options is not included here as the company do not promote the food as an aid to weight loss.

Does it work?

It is believed that many people actually gain weight when they first start to use low-fat products, because they think they can eat as much as they like without getting fat. Although foods may promote themselves as 'low-fat' they won't always contain many fewer calories than the real food item they replace. Often the difference is made up with sugar and if you substitute sugar for fat you may still put on weight.

It seems that when people change to low-sugar products they tend to increase sugar consumption from other foods, as if rewarding themselves for being good in one area by having treats in another. The same is true for low-fat foods: it's the 'I've been good by using low-fat spread so I'll have an ice-cream' scenario common to all us dieters.

While low-sugar and low-fat foods may have changed some individual eating habits, they haven't changed the overall picture of sugar and fat consumption. Although people think they are eating less fat, in general they are not. Dieticians are concerned that eating low-fat and low-calorie foods does nothing to help people change to a healthier lifestyle.

Keeping off the pounds
There isn't any evidence that weight loss lasts with these products.

Any problems?
You shouldn't experience any physical problems if you follow the diet plans given with ready-to-eat meals, because they are all devised by expert nutritionists. It is important as with any diet not to eat less than the recommended amounts, and to vary your diet. There are no known psychological problems.

Food Fact File

Fish and chips with mushy peas is 900 calories.

Diet type
Slimming foods.

What is it?
A range of frozen slimming food dishes, all calorie-counted. These weigh from 250 to 400 g (9–14 oz) and provide 300–400 calories. Light Meals can be heated and then eaten straight from the dish, and each provides 200–250 calories. Ingredients vary with the different dishes, but are all listed on the packs.

Varieties: There are 14 products available, including, eg, chicken tikka masala, prawn curry, beef lasagne, fisherman's pie and glazed chicken. There are four Light meals, one of which is vegetarian; two are based on rice and two on pasta.

Lean Cuisine was launched in the USA in 1981 and came to Britain in 1985. Products can be bought in grocers and supermarkets nationwide and prices range from £1.49 to £2.29. You can obtain the Lean Cuisine *Healthy Eating* and *The Lean Plan* guides free, by calling 0800 200 222. Currently over 4000 tonnes of Lean Cuisine dishes are sold in Britain every year.

How does it work?
Simply — too many calories result in excess body fat, according to the manufacturers.

The diet
The Lean Plan diet is based on three meals a day and a daily milk allowance. There are breakfasts, light meals based on sandwiches, soups, baked potatoes or salads, and main meals. Nearly all the main meals and some of the light meals are Lean Cuisine products.

To make up your correct calorie allowance you have to do some calorie counting, but *The Lean Plan* guide has lists of foods of different calorie contents from which you can choose the foods you prefer. You do have to weigh and measure ingredients.

There is a list of 'free' foods, which you may have in unlimited quantities; these are low-calorie vegetables. You are advised to drink as much water as possible, and to try to change to low-cal drinks. The menu plan as a whole is designed to be low in fat and sugar but high in fibre and carbohydrate.

A typical day's diet

Daily allowance	1 pt (570 ml) of skimmed milk 1 low-cal drink	190
Breakfast	1 slice wholemeal toast, with 1 tsp reduced-fat spread and 1 tsp yeast extract ½ grapefruit	150 20
Light meal	Instant low-cal soup Sandwich, made with 2 slices wholemeal bread, 2 oz (56 g) lean ham and sliced cucumber	40 255
Main meal	Lean Cuisine Beef Julienne 1 apple 1 glass wine	451 60 100
	Calories (approx)	1200
	Cost	£4.37

Variations
Men are allowed 1600 calories a day.

Exercise
The Lean Plan guide includes recommendations for exercise in your normal daily schedule. There is an illustrated set of simple exercises and suggested times and numbers of required repetitions.

Additional information
The height/weight charts show the acceptable healthy weight for a woman of 5 ft 4 in (1.63 in) as about 7 st 10 lb (49 kg) to

10 st 4 lb (65.3 kg), representing BMIs of 18–25. This is within the range approved by doctors. Lean Cuisine advise the reader that these are only guidelines; if you have more muscle or bone than the average person then the charts will not apply to you.

Lean Cuisine have produced two guides, as described above, perforated for clipping into a personal organizer. *Healthy Eating* covers government guidelines on healthy eating, discusses food groups, their importance in the diet and how to balance intake from each of them, assesses your health rating and advises on sensible limits to alcohol consumption. The second guide, *The Lean Plan*, describes the 14-day reducing diet and includes height/weight charts, advice on eating out, exercises and healthy eating tips.

Who shouldn't use it?
You are advised to consult your family doctor before starting any programme of exercise or weight loss.

Expected weight loss
You are expected to lose 1–2 lb (450–900 g) per week on the plan.

Keeping off the pounds
There aren't any specific guidelines on this.

They say
'Healthy eating can be easy, convenient and enjoyable with Lean Cuisine.'

You say
'I would use them when I came home from work and couldn't be bothered to cook, and on a diet. I don't think about the price – my time is worth more.'

'I'm a mundane cook and some of them I like, but some are a bit exotic.'

'If you've got a target they're easy to use – you don't feel so deprived, because they're tasty – but the portions tend to be small. They're OK with lots of vegetables.'

'It's dear to do it all the time.'

We say
The leaflets are informative and accurate, and easy to follow.

Calorie counting	√	Suitable for vegetarians	√
Weighing of food required	√	Less than £10 to start	√
Forbidden foods	×	Personal support	×
Suit single person	√	Emphasizes fluid intake	√

Food Fact File

Traditionally, rich Englishmen ate meat, meat and more meat; on being asked about vegetables the noted nineteenth-century dandy Beau Brummell confessed, 'Once, I ate a pea.'

Diet type
Slimming foods.

What is it?
Ready-prepared meals, part of a range of calorie-counted foods and drinks; most are ready to eat but some you have to heat. They range from snack-type foods – chocolate bars, crackers with paté or cheese, sandwiches – to more substantial pot meals and chilled salads. There are soups, lunch packs, dips, salads, cheeses, desserts, ice-creams, yoghurts, ice-lollies, marmalade, pickles and mayonnaise, all reduced-calorie, low-calorie or calorie-counted.

Ingredients vary depending on the particular product, but nutritional information is clearly displayed. There are at present over 140 varieties, with new ones being added and old ones discontinued, which vary with the seasons.

Prices range from 21p to £1.99. Shapers are produced by Boots and are available in most of their stores. They have been around since 1970. The range of foods available has increased greatly since then. Boots is believed to have sold £24 million of Shapers products in 1992.

How does it work?
To reduce weight you must reduce the number of calories you consume, but calorie-counting can be inconvenient and time-consuming. With Shapers foods the work of calorie-counting has been done for you, and the manufacturers believe that you can be certain of getting all the nutrients you need.

The diet
Each food is clearly marked with the calorie content, and you make up your own diet plans.

Who shouldn't use it?
There are no restrictions on who can use the meals.

Additional information

If you are prepared to record your food intake (including size of portions), for three or seven days, and send the record with some personal details to Boots' Health and Nutrition Centre, Freepost, The Boots Company plc, Nottingham NG2 3AA, you can have your diet analysed by the Computer Diet Analysis Service. This costs £5.95 for the three-day and £9.95 for the seven-day analysis. You get a full report on the nutritional quality of your diet, with suggestions on how you can improve it if necessary. You can also obtain free advice on any aspect of diet or health from the Centre, and leaflets and fact sheets can be supplied.

They say

'The freedom to eat flexibly and lose weight, whilst knowing you are receiving the right balance of nutrients.'

You say

'I found it really boring, the flavours were just OK.'

'The soups are a bit watery but the sandwiches and meals are very nice. I have them for lunch and sometimes for supper as well. I've lost 3 lb (1.4 kg) in a month. They need more information on the packets.'

'I like the sandwiches and they change the flavours all the time. It's easier at lunchtime than trying to think of something slimming when you really want something to eat.'

We say

There is no specific advice on the packets, but Boots assure me that in every store the pharmacist will be pleased to advise anyone with a query about diet or health.

Calorie counting	√	Suitable for vegetarians	√
Weighing of food required	×	Less than £10 to start	√
Forbidden foods	×	Personal support	√
Suit single person	√	Emphasizes fluid intake	×

Diet type
Slimming foods.

What is it?
It is a diet programme where meals are delivered to your home, or any other specified location, by courier. The meal plans are high in cabohydrate, minerals, vitamins and fibre, but low in salt and fat. The company began supplying meals in 1994, since when more than 700 people have joined the programme. Call the Target Weight Hotline Freephone on 0800 15 30 30 for information. It costs £10 to register with Target Weight and then £42 per week thereafter, if you have the whole range of meals on offer.

How does it work?
The Target Weight concept means that everything to ensure you lose weight is done for you – you don't have to do anything. Target Weight believe this will make it easier to diet.

The diet
After completing a medical history and being accepted for the programme, you are assigned an individual counsellor. He or she will advise you on your target weight and help you choose a suitable diet plan, depending on your present weight and medical history. He or she will call you every week (or more frequently if necessary) to discuss any problems, review your progress and weight loss and help you decide on your eating plans for the following week. You can call your counsellor any time you have a problem.

Food ordering is done on a weekly or fortnightly basis. The programme allows you to choose and then order up to three main meals, a snack and a dessert for each day. To these you add vegetables, fruit and milk as detailed in your individual diet programme. There are several plans, including ones of 1100–1200 or 1400 calories per day, and a vegetarian plan providing 1100–1200 calories. You also receive the Target Weight Multi Mineral Supplement. You are given leaflets explaining the importance of correct nutrition and exercise.

The food is 'shelf-stable' and so doesn't need to be refrigerated. It comes in cartons or packets and most items require

A typical day's diet

Daily Allowance	¾ pt (425 ml) skimmed milk 1 piece of fruit	150 50
Breakfast	Pancakes* low-fat natural yoghurt ½ tsp cinnamon Tea with skimmed milk from allowance Multivitamin supplement*	140 15
Morning snack	Serving of strawberries Coffee with skimmed milk from allowance	30
Lunch	Chow mein noodles* Mixed salad, including tomatoes, celery and mushrooms Tea with lemon	195 40
Afternoon snack	Popcorn* Diet drink	179
Evening meal	Lancashire hot-pot* Wholemeal roll* 1 tsp margarine Carrots Cauliflower Chocolate dessert*	231 97 35 20 20 84
Evening snack	Fresh fruit salad 4 fl oz (110 ml) skimmed milk	100 50
	Calories (approx)	1400
	Cost (delivered food + milk, fruit, vegetables)	£7.00

* Foods supplied to you.

minimal preparation. All main meals can be microwaved (the popcorn is already popped) but some dishes have to be cooked; for example, the pancake mixture has to be mixed and fried. It's up to you what kind of dishes you choose.

You are encouraged not to drink alcohol while on the programme, but you should drink eight glasses of water per day. You should have only two low-cal drinks, but you must have ¾ pt (425 ml) of semi-skimmed or skimmed milk, depending on your sex, and two or three servings of fresh fruit each day.

Exercise
A very detailed Activity Plan shows you how to decide which level of exercise to start with, how to put together a programme and how to set long-term activity goals. You are advised to choose activities which you enjoy, and when you reach your goals you record your achievement and then set yourself a new goal.

Who shouldn't use it?
Children under 14 are not allowed to take part in the programme, nor are pregnant women or nursing mothers whose baby is under four months of age. If you answer 'yes' to any query on a questionnaire about medical conditions, Target Weight will consult your doctor on your behalf before starting you on the programme.

Additional information
Target Weight counsellors advise women to aim for a BMI of between 20 and 24, and men for a BMI of 22–25, both in line with current medical opinion.

You are given advice about eating habits and other habits you should change which may have hindered weight loss in the past.

Expected weight loss
How much weight you lose each week is up to you, but your counsellor will advise you. Promotional literature suggests that you could lose 2 st (12.7 kg) in three months, which is in line with recommended rates.

Keeping off the pounds

For the first eight weeks of the maintenance plan you continue to follow the Target Weight Meal Plan as described above, but for only four days of each week. On the other three days you design your own menus, using sample meal plans and charts which detail how many 'serves' of particular foods you should have. Your counsellor will help you with this.

After eight weeks of this you move on to designing your own meal plans for five days of the week, and finally you stop using the product when you feel able to design all your own plans.

You are permitted alcohol on the maintenance plan, but on a limited basis and are advised to keep on increasing the amount of exercise you take.

They say

'No dreary powders, no liquid diets or meal replacements, Target Weight provides delicious portion-controlled and nutritionally balanced meals . . . to make your diet enjoyable.'

You say

'It's good because you don't have to think. I lost 10 lbs (4.5 kg) over three months – it's not so easy to lose weight at my age, I'm 72. It is expensive but it's easy to prepare – just pop it in the microwave.'

'I was on it for two months, then I lost my job and I had to stop, but I'd lost a stone. You had to drink a lot of water on it, and I tried to keep up, and I did stick to what they gave me, and they told you how much vegetables to have.'

'I just couldn't stand the food. I didn't like it at all.'

We say

Similar food-delivery services have been criticized in the past for not providing any guidance about changing to healthy eating habits permanently, and for serving up rich sauces and providing heavily refined products. Target Weight does provide wholemeal rolls, crackers, muesli and bran, and does encourage healthy eating. The main dishes are served with sauces, but these are low-fat and low-sugar.

Of course you couldn't have *all* your food delivered to you, **203** because then you wouldn't be eating anything fresh. So you have to do some shopping on this diet, and you would have to be careful you didn't end up buying 'extras' while you were doing so.

Calorie counting	×	Suitable for vegetarians	√
Weighing of food required	×	Less than £10 to start	×
Forbidden foods	√	Personal support	√
Suit single person	√	Emphasizes fluid intake	√

Food Fact File

Eating an average of 150 ants a day, the !Kung people of the Kalahari Desert provide themselves with about 2 oz (60 g) of protein, as well as calcium, iron, phosphorus and vitamins B1 and B2.

Weight Watchers from Heinz

Diet type
Slimming foods.

What is it?
There are two main kinds of frozen meals: Plus, weighing about
300 g (12 oz) and under 300 calories, and a Big Deal range
where portions are about 400 g (14 oz) and under 400 calories.
Depending on the product, you boil in the bag, microwave or
oven-cook the dish conventionally.

There are over a hundred other items in the Weight Watchers
from Heinz range. Apart from ready-prepared meals, there are
soups, desserts, jams, sauces, spreads, breads, cereals, puddings,
cakes, ice-cream and (of course) baked beans. A variety of
ingredients is used, depending on the particular product, but
nutritional information is clearly displayed.

Varieties: Plus meals come in Heinz vegetable, pasta, menu,
Oriental and seafood varieties; Big Deal are larger-sized portions
of chicken or beef dishes; varieties change frequently.

Weight Watchers from Heinz products have been for sale since
1985; apparently more than 40 per cent of households in Britain
bought one of these products in 1993. They're available in most
supermarkets and grocery stores. Meals vary from £1.09 to
£2.09.

How does it work?
Eating well and keeping to a healthy weight doesn't necessarily
mean small portions, but it does mean reducing your fat and
sugar consumption, according to Weight Watchers from Heinz.

The diet
There isn't a specific diet plan available, but you are given
general advice about healthy eating and healthy cooking meth-
ods in the leaflet *Eating Today*, which can be obtained from
Weight Watchers from Heinz, 15–17 Huntsworth Mews,
London NW1 6DD.

Exercise

The benefits of exercise to physical health and weight loss are emphasized, but there is no specific exercise plan. There are guidelines on gradually increasing your activity level and on appropriate kinds of exercise.

Who shouldn't use it?

There are no restrictions on use.

Additional information

You are given details of how to contact a Weight Watchers meeting near you, and vouchers entitling you to attend a meeting free, or you can choose a free cookbook if you decide to join Weight Watchers By Mail.

Included in the *Eating Today* booklet is a chart showing that a person of 5 ft 4 in (1.63 m) should weigh between about 7 st 4 lb (46.3 kg) and 10 st 2 lb (64.5 kg), corresponding to a BMI of between 18 and 24, which is in line with what doctors would recommend.

Expected weight loss

No expected weight loss is stated, but you are advised not to try to lose weight too quickly – 1–2 lb (450–900 g) a week is recommended.

Keeping off the pounds

There is no specific advice on weight maintenance.

They say

'Eating well is about getting the balance right.'

You say

'It is well-balanced and good nutrition, so you don't have to think about it yourself.'

'I go to the classes as well and they give you money-off coupons for it. I do eat the foods and I have lost weight.'

'Some of the portions are too mingy.'

'I have them on nights I'm in a hurry or if I'm really hungry – it stops me grazing.'

'It's really convenient. I mix them up with vegetables to make it seem more and I have them several times a week.'

We say
The popularity of these foods speaks for them.

Calorie counting	√	Suitable for vegetarians	√
Weighing of food required	×	Less than £10 to start	√
Forbidden foods	×	Personal support	×
Suit single person	√	Emphasizes fluid intake	×

Which?, the magazine of the Consumer's Association, looked at a variety of healthy or calorie-reduced slimming foods some time ago, and concluded that they were generally lower in fat than standard similar convenience foods, but at a price. Fewer calories cost more money. It is certainly true in general that the proportions of calories which come from fat and sugar are reduced in these foods.

Although eating calorie-controlled, ready-prepared dishes seems like an easy option when slimming, if you can afford it, it's important to remember that the different dishes do vary considerably in what they provide. To get a proper balance of nutrients it would be best to follow any plans the manufacturers give, rather than devise your own, because they use the advice of expert nutritionists. Some rely more on calorie-counting and weighing than you would imagine.

The following table gives the nutritional breakdown of the dishes included in the menu plans above. Values are given for the *whole* product, not per 100 g. For Weight Watchers from

Major ingredients of slimming foods (in grams)

Name	Portion size	Protein	Carbo-hydrate	Of which sugar	Fat	Of which saturated	Fibre	Calories
Lean Cuisine Beef Julienne with rice	400	25.2	59.2	11.3	8	1.7	6.7	410
Shapers Pasta Bolognese	300	14	30	6.9	6	2.7	5.4	230
Target Weight Lancashire Hot-Pot	300	8.1	7.1	1.4	1.8	0.9	1.4	231
Weight Watchers from Heinz Beef Lasagne	400	24.4	42.4	12	12.8	6	2.4	380

Heinz I've chosen one of the company's most popular dishes. The Shapers dish was the closest in ingredients to the others.

As it is self-evident that you will lose weight if you eat fewer calories, all these products are 'correct' in dietary terms. However, Target Weight has a slight edge as exercise and weight-maintenance plans are already included (with the others, you have to apply for the relevant leaflets), and they give more information than the other manufacturers in this chapter about who shouldn't use their products.

Food Fact File

Prunes were so highly regarded as aphrodisiacs that they were given away in brothels in Elizabethan times. Hyena eyes, slugs, haggis, oysters, goose tongues, asparagus and scores of other delicacies have at one time or another been considered to have the same effect.

Chapter 11

Appetite Suppressants,
Pills and Supplements

Pills to help you slim have been sold for hundreds of years, with the most appalling ingredients, including strychnine, camphor, digitalis and arsenic. Some were laxatives or made you sick; others were said to have 'magic' anti-fat properties (which they didn't) or to suppress appetite (which they couldn't).

The Ancient Cretans were reputed to have a wonder-drug that allowed them to eat as much as they liked without getting fat; tragically, the secret was lost. Two thousand years ago the mathematician Philon of Byzantium provided a recipe for a 'Hunger and Thirst Checking Pill', but not as a slimming aid. He was interested in maintaining food stocks for besieged cities and armies on the march. The pill was made from lily bulbs, sesame, honey and opium (which would certainly have had an effect). Eating soap was an early medical treatment, and an Edinburgh doctor reported some success with it in the eighteenth century (frothing at the mouth an optional extra).

However, in the nineteenth century, ephedrine was discovered to be effective in increasing metabolic rate, and would-be slimmers drank copious quantities of it in tea. The study of how ephedrine worked led to the development of amphetamines in the 1930s and eventually to the new drugs (available on prescription only) used today. An estimated 400 000 people a year are prescribed slimming pills, at a cost to the National Health Service of over £1 million; thousands more are given prescribed drugs at private clinics.

There is a huge variety of over-the-counter tablets and supplements available by mail order and from specialized shops and chemists. Nearly 9 per cent of the population use them, though in most cases not very often. They are heavily advertised in the press and the market is worth millions of pounds – £5 million worth of Ayd Slim and Bran Slim alone were sold in 1993.

What's the theory?

Many products come and go very quickly, but their basic principle nearly always relies on suppressing the appetite.

Over-the-counter tablets and supplements contain a variety of ingredients intended to help you slim. High-fibre tablets and supplements taken some time *before* a meal are supposed to fill you up so much that you won't feel so hungry and will eat less; these generally contain bran, pectin, fibre and/or vegetable extracts. Other substances called bulkers swell up in the stomach, as bran does, and this is supposed to reduce appetite. One bulking agent is guar gum (variously described as *Cyamopsis tetragonoloba* or *Cyamopsis psoraloides*). Gum Arabic is also used in some tablets. Sterculia, from the china-chestnut tree, is another gum, also referred to as karaya. Other bulkers include methyl cellulose, which with water bulks up in the stomach to a hundred times its original volume.

Fifty years ago it was thought that wheat and kidney beans could reduce the absorption of starch through inhibition of a certain enzyme. The purified ingredient was extracted from the kidney bean, and named Phaseolamin in 1975. Billions of starch-blocker pills were consumed by people in the USA in the 1980s, in the belief that these would allow undigested starch to pass through the bowel, thus reducing its calorific effect. Another theory suggested that if blood sugar were raised in such a way that venous and arterial values were different (too complicated to go into; take my word for it), loss of appetite would occur.

In the body, amino acids, such as arginine, lysine, ornithine and phenylalanine are essential to the process of breaking down food, including fat. These are included in some diet products in the belief that taken by mouth they can suppress appetite or affect metabolism.

The first use of iodine as a treatment for obesity took place more than a century ago. Seaweed tablets made from kelp or brown seaweed (*Fucus vesiculosus*), contain iodine. Iodine is used to make thyroxine, the thyroid hormone which regulates metabolism.

Some tablets contain diuretics, from natural sources, which will make you pee more and *apparently* lose weight. These include all sorts of natural herbs, extracts and oils, including dandelion, buchu (oil from the leaves of a Cape Province shrub) and fennel (which is effective). Hydrangea, orange peel, meadowsweet, bearberry, pokeberry, horsetail and juniper are also believed by herbalists either to irritate the bowel, with a laxative effect, or to act as diuretics. This is when they are properly prepared – please don't start munching things direct from the garden. Boldo (bark from the South American *Peumus boldus* tree) has been widely used traditionally for healing and gastrointestinal problems.

Many tablets contain lecithin from soya oil, which is used as an emulsifier to make the tablets smooth. It is sometimes suggested that lecithin has fat-burning qualities as well, but it has no known effect on metabolism or on body fat when taken in this form.

Prescribed drugs fall into two rough classes. Both stimulate the parts of the brain that control appetite, but in different ways. The first group are more like the old amphetamines, but are not so addictive. Although they can make you nervous and agitated, this is unlikely. The second kind are a new sort of appetite suppressant and don't seem to have as many adverse effects on mental well-being or health.

Does it work?

A controlled trial was carried out where equally overweight women were given either Figure Trim 8 or 'pretend' pills, and they all went on a 1200-calories-a-day diet for three months. Those taking Figure Trim 8 lost more weight than those taking the dummy pills and their waist-to-hip ratios decreased more. There is no evidence that any other herbal preparation affects weight control. Kelp (seaweed) tablets have not been proved to have any effect on metabolism. Only in people with an iodine deficiency (and there are very few of them) do iodine supplements increase the production of thyroxin and so increase metabolism; there is no evidence that taking seaweed affects healthy people's metabolism at all.

As for amino acids, a study of an ornithine/arginine pill compared with other methods of weight loss found that a 'pretend' diet – eating half a carrot before meals – was just as effective. In fact, there is no evidence that amino acids taken in capsules or tablets help you to lose weight. The United States Food and Drug Administration has banned them from over-the-counter diet products because the manufacturers couldn't prove that they worked.

There isn't any scientific evidence that eating fibre before or with a meal reduces the amount you eat at the meal. Nor is there convincing evidence that cellulose affects appetite. Guar gum has been shown to make people both feel less hungry and eat less, but in quantities much greater than that permitted under British law. Other gums and fruit pectin are also supposed to be filling and reduce appetite, but there is no proof that this is so.

To test whether sugar has appetite-suppressant effects, studies of very overweight people who were given dextrose sweets to eat before a meal, on a calorie-controlled diet, were carried out. Unfortunately it wasn't clear whether the average reported weight loss – about 2 lb (900 g) per week – was the result of eating the calorie-controlled diet or of any effects on appetite. In another study, where people were given a drink with either sugar or low-cal artificial sweetener, those who had the sugary drink did say that they felt less hungry afterwards. But when, an hour later, both groups were offered as much to eat as they wanted, those who had had the sugary drink consumed significantly fewer calories; the equivalent, almost exactly, of the calories they'd had in the sugar drink.

Research has proved conclusively that starch-blockers are completely ineffective when taken by mouth – as measured by the number of calories in faeces after taking a high-starch meal and starch-blocker pills or a 'pretend pill' or by blood tests.

It is true however, that prescribed slimming pills are effective in helping people to stick to a calorie-controlled diet. A review of all the studies of two of the newer drugs showed that of a group who were on the same diet, those who took real slimming pills lost an average of 3 lb (1.4 kg) more than those who were given dummy pills, over about 12 weeks.

There is no evidence that over-the-counter pills and tablets are easier to stick to than any other method of dieting. In studies of prescribed slimming pills, it seems that people drop out because they feel unwelcome side-effects, rather than because they are dissatisfied with the amount of weight they have lost.

Keeping off the pounds

Over-the-counter pills have never been tested for lasting weight loss under scientific conditions. There is, however, some evidence to show that weight-loss lasts on prescribed slimming pills, though results from long-term trials of these pills are not yet available.

Any problems?

The British Medical Association does not recommend the use of slimming pills for anyone but the very overweight, believing that any benefits are outweighed by the health risks involved.

It is very important to read the labels on any slimming preparation, and especially so with slimming tablets. This isn't always easy, because the print is often tiny. Any seaweed preparation (described as kelp, *Fucus*, marine algae, etc.) could cause very serious problems for someone with a thyroid disorder, if it had high levels of iodine. In one reported case a Dutch woman started daily treatment with six 200-mg kelp tablets, in order to lose weight. Within two months she developed hyperthyroidism (which was cured when she stopped taking the tablets). Most preparations for sale in Britain don't contain nearly as much as this. Analysis of food supplements containing seaweed shows that the iodine levels vary widely even between different samples of the same product, with some containing hardly any. Arsenic has also been found in seaweed preparations, but in amounts too low to be harmful.

Excessive use of diuretics (preparations to make you pee more) can lead to serious health problems (see page 410).

At the moment, the medical establishment is reassessing the usefulness of bran for certain diseases of the gut. If you know that you have problems in this area, it would be best to consult a doctor before embarking on a high-fibre diet. High-fibre preparations and methyl cellulose can lead to excess wind.

In 1989 the Ministry of Agriculture, Fisheries and Food banned appetite suppressants that contained more than 15 per cent guar gum or locust bean gum, after deaths that could have been associated with their use.

None of the over-the-counter dieting methods described below seems to have any direct psychological effect. Some people have reported feelings of increased nervousness, difficulties in sleeping, irritability and anxiety on taking prescribed slimming pills. *With all the products, it's important to stick to the recommended dose.*

Tablets, pills and herbal drinks contain preservatives, anti-caking agents and so forth, and also substances called 'excipients'. Some additives are needed to facilitate processing methods; some improve the look or taste of a food; and others are needed as preservatives or anti-oxidants to stop the product deteriorating. Excipients are substances that are used as a vehicle for a drug, usually a liquid or powder it can be carried in. I haven't listed the additives and excipients contained in the products under review in this chapter, only their active ingredients, but they are all included in Appendix II, Food Labelling (p. 419).

Food Fact File

Complaints to the Advertising Standards Authority were upheld about a pair of German shoe insoles advertised as part of a weight-loss programme.

Aydslim

Diet type
Glucose tablets.

What is it?
Small cubes which you chew, with (in the larger packets) a diet programme. Two cubes contain 34 calories.

Varieties: Raspberry, vanilla and orange, packaged as 8 or 32 cubes at 92p and £3.49.

Ingredients: Glucose syrup, sweetened condensed skimmed milk, vitamins and minerals.

Aydslim is the brand leader in the appetite-suppressant market and has been on sale in Britain for more than 40 years. The product can be bought at Boots, Tesco, some chemists and health food shops.

How does it work?
The makers say that the cubes take the edge off your appetite by raising blood sugar levels and making the body feel less hungry.

The Diet
You chew two of the cubes 20 minutes or so before a meal, or between meals if you feel you want to snack, as part of a calorie-controlled diet which you have to devise yourself.

The leaflet contains guidelines on a 1000 calories-per-day plan. There are seven suggestions for breakfasts, packed lunches, lunches and dinners, and the extra daily allowance is ½ pt (285 ml) of skimmed milk and ½ oz (15 g) of low-fat spread.

Recipes aren't given, but the calorie content of the items in the diet programme is shown.

Exercise
The makers say that all diet programmes produce better results when combined with gentle exercise such as cycling, riding, walking or swimming, but there isn't a specific exercise plan.

A typical day's diet

Daily allowance	½ pt (285 ml) skimmed milk	100
	½ oz (15 g) low-fat spread	100
Breakfast	2 Aydslim tablets beforehand	34
	½ grapefruit	15
	3 oz (85 g) kipper fillets	180
Lunch	2 Aydslim tablets beforehand	34
	10 oz (280 g) can lentil soup	200
	2 crispbreads	60
Evening meal	2 Aydslim tablets beforehand	34
	3 oz (85 g) chicken	75
	Stir-fried vegetables, made with 4 oz (110 g) broccoli, 4 oz (110 g) carrots, 2 oz (56 g) onion, 1 stick celery, 1 oz (28 g) mushrooms, ½ tbsp oil	110
	Baked apple, with	70
	¾ oz (20 g) sultanas	50
	Calories (approx)	1000
	Cost	£4.26

Who shouldn't use it
Aydslim is intended for healthy people whose weight problems are caused by overeating. If you are pregnant or have a particular medical or glandular problem, you should consult your doctor before starting any diet.

Additional information
The leaflet gives nutritional advice – avoid red meats and eat high-fibre breads and pasta instead – and includes a progress chart for you to check your weight loss. The height/weight charts give the acceptable average weight for a 5ft 4in (1.63 m) **217**

woman as 8st 10lb (55.3 kg), corresponding to a BMI of 21, and the weight at which obesity can be defined as 12st 1lb (76.7 kg), a BMI of about 28, exactly in accord with medical opinion.

Expected weight loss
This is not stated, nor is there any mention of keeping off the pounds in the long-term.

They say
'Great tasting glucose cubes which take the edge off your appetite.'

You say
'They were OK. They tasted all right but they didn't work.'

'I use them to give me a lift – and they do.'

'I could have eaten half a dozen. And I did. I liked the taste.'

We say
The relationship between sugar and appetite is a very complex one (see page 213). There is no incontrovertible evidence that eating sugar before a meal makes you feel less hungry, but if you believe you will . . .

Calorie counting	√	Less than £10 to start	√
Weighing of food required	√	Personal support	×
Forbidden foods	×	Detailed 'who can't use'	√
Suit single person	√	Emphasizes fluid intake	×
Suitable for vegetarians	√		

Diet type
Detoxifying food supplement, combined with a reduced-calorie, food-combining diet.

What is it?
Bio-Light is a food supplement. It comes as a 200 ml (about 7 fl oz) bottle of brown liquid.

Varieties: Original aniseed, wild fruits, woodland fruits, citrus fruits.

Ingredients: Clove, caraway, wheatgerm, liquorice, cinnamon, kelp, juniper, boldo, cumin, ginger, sage, yeast, fenugreek, verbena, fruit and vegetable juices, flavourings and essential oils (cinnamon, orange and juniper).

Bio-Light was first marketed in France and has been sold in Britain since 1990. A three-day course costs £12.00 and is available from chemists. A daily serving (one third of a bottle) provides 50 calories.

How does it work?
Through inner cleansing Bio-Light gets your system working more efficiently to deal with fat reserves and fat assimilation, the makers suggest.

The diet
You mix one-third of a bottle of Bio-Light with 2½ pt (1.5 l) of water and drink this slowly, in small mouthfuls throughout the day, to be finished by late evening. You are also, from the enclosed eating plan, to have breakfast (this is a must), lunch and an evening meal. You do this for three days.

If you want to lose weight, rather than 'detox', for best results you are advised to take the mixture for six days consecutively followed by four days of sensible eating. You are advised not to take Bio-Light for longer than nine days consecutively, and not to drink more than six bottles in any one month. If you need to carry your daily allowance around with you, instructions are given for mixing smaller quantities.

219

The eating plan gives four choices of breakfast. Lunch and the evening meal are from the 'Bio-Light Bioblocks'. The first block has high-protein foods (e.g., lean steak, lamb, low-fat cheese); the second consists of carbohydrates (e.g., pasta, bread, potatoes); the third block is vegetables (e.g., leeks, seeds, beans), and the fourth is fruit (apple, apricot, banana and so on). For lunch you have one portion each of protein and carbohydrate and unlimited amounts of vegetables. For dinner, you have one portion of protein and unlimited quantities of vegetables: there is no carbohydrate except that gained from the vegetables. If you become hungry through the day, you may snack on small portions of fruit or vegetables.

You should remove all fat from meat and skin from poultry, and have no butter, fat, starch products, fatty cheese, sugared

A typical day's diet

Throughout the day	⅓ bottle Bio-Light mixed with 2½ pt (1.5 l) water (calorie content varies with variety)	50
Breakfast	1 diet crispbread	12
	Low-cal spread	10
	1 boiled egg	80
Snack	Celery	10
Lunch	3 oz (85 g) lean steak	200
	Asparagus	30
	French beans	50
Snack	Apple	60
Evening meal	4 oz (110 g) seafood	160
	Bean sprouts	20
	Broccoli	50
Snack	Apricots	20
	Calories (approx)	800
	Cost	£7.90

drinks, salt or alcohol. The diet as described is a high-protein, low-fat and low-carbohydrate one. No recipes are given, but there are tips on healthy cooking.

If you use Bio-Light in conjunction with food combining, you are advised not to eat protein and starch in the same meal. You should eat when you are hungry, and listen to your body rather than your mind.

Who shouldn't use it?

Bio-Light is not recommended for persons under 16 years, pregnant women, nursing mothers or people on medication, nor for the severely overweight or diabetic without first consulting a doctor. Women should not use the product just before a period, because of problems of water retention at that time.

Side-effects

To avoid side-effects you can drink 2½ pt (1.5 l) of water per day for two days before starting the programme. Side-effects are believed to be caused by the elimination of high levels of toxins, which may show themselves as headaches, spots, nausea, changes in bowel movements or bloating. Headaches may also be caused by low blood sugar, a result of a reduction in alcohol, sugar and chocolate; you are advised to have an apple if this happens. To reduce nausea, reduce the concentration of Bio-Light.

Spots are a 'good sign' that toxins are being eliminated. Bloating can be due to a temporary rebalancing of body fluids, and you should increase your fluid intake. If symptoms persist, see your doctor.

Additional information

Advice is given on using the diet as a detox rather than a weight-loss programme. There isn't a specific exercise plan, but you are encouraged to begin to introduce exercise into your daily routine when you have finished the course.

You may notice an effect from using Bio-Light on the second attempt even if you noticed no effects the first time you used it.

Expected weight loss

No potential weight loss is mentioned.

Keeping off the pounds

You are to continue to eat healthily, but in greater quantities. You are advised to use Bio-Light again every so often to give your digestive system a holiday.

They say

'In only three days it can make a real and lasting difference to the way you feel and look.'

You say

'It tasted not bad but it smelled like washing-up liquid, and it's difficult to drink that amount of stuff. I didn't notice any effects on appetite after the first day.'

'The diet plan was good but the food-combining stuff was awful. How can you have naked pasta without anything at all?'

'I didn't feel detoxified, but I lost 2 lb (900 g).'

We say

Most doctors are quite clear that the body eliminates toxins by itself, without any help, unless we are talking about poisons. It's good that Bio-Light give such a comprehensive list of side-effects and strongly advise you to drink plenty of water. The side-effects may be due to hunger as much as detoxification; this diet is very low in calories because it is so low in carbohydrates. Doctors don't advise anyone to diet on less than 1000 calories per day without medical supervision. You must eat as many vegetables as possible to keep up your calorific intake on this diet. In view of the low calorie level, heed the makers' advice: you really *must not* follow the programme for more than the recommended six days.

Calorie counting	√	Less than £10 to start	×
Weighing of food required	√	Personal support	×
Forbidden foods	√	Detailed 'who can't use'	√
Suit single person	√	Emphasizes fluid intake	√
Suitable for vegetarians	√		

Diet type
An appetite suppressant.

What is it?
A high-fibre food supplement in the form of a drink, soup or tablets, with enclosed leaflets detailing diet and slimming plans.

Varieties: Drink: hot chocolate (30 calories, 6 g fibre). Soup: tomato (40 calories, 6 g fibre). Tablets (6 calories, 2.68 g fibre each).

Ingredients: Drink: skimmed mild powder, vegetable fibre, cellulose, corn bran, gum, aspartame and vitamins. Soup: cellulose, vegetables, starches, sugar and vitamins. Tablets: wheat bran, sugars, corn starch, gum, honey and flavouring.

Drinks cost £7.99 for six, soups cost £3.99 for six, and tablets are £5.29 for a packet of 100. All these products are made by the Thompson Medical Company and can be bought at chemists.

How does it work?
People don't stick to diets because they get hungry. If you eat enough fibre, you will feel full and then you will eat less, eat more healthily and lose weight, the makers say.

The diet
The Bran-Slim slimming plan enclosed with the tablets suggests that you take two Bran-Slim tablets before breakfast, lunch and at mid-afternoon, and whenever you feel hungry. These are to be chewed thoroughly and followed by two glasses of water, and they should be taken 15–30 minutes before a meal. You can have a Bran-Slim drink mid-morning and as an evening snack, again with two glasses of water. Drinks and soups are made up with water.

There are meal plans described for seven days. The meal plans are high in carbohydrate and fibre but low in fat. There are no forbidden foods, and you are advised to eat more fruit.

Recipes are not included, as all the menus are for simply prepared meals. Meat or fish are in all the daily meal plans given.

A typical day's diet from the Bran-Slim slimming plan

Breakfast	2 Bran-Slim tablets with water	12
	½ grapefruit	40
	4½ fl oz (125 g) natural yoghurt	75
	2 oz (50 g) wholemeal muffin with 1 tsp fruit jam	120
Snack	Bran-Slim drink with water	30
Lunch	2 Bran-Slim tablets with water	12
	9 oz (225 g) can of baked beans in tomato sauce	200
	Slice toasted wholemeal bread	60
	Diet yoghurt	50
	Banana	90
Mid-afternoon Snack	Bran-Slim drink	30
Evening meal	2½ oz (60 g) lean roast shoulder of lamb	150
	7 oz (175 g) boiled potatoes	140
	3 oz (75 g) boiled carrots	50
	3 oz (75 g) steamed broccoli	20
	3 oz (75 g) steamed cauliflower	25
	Diet yoghurt	50
Snack	Bran-Slim drink with water	30
	Calories (approx)	1200
	Cost	£5.81

Variations

Men should aim to eat 1500 calories per day when trying to lose weight.

Exercise

There isn't a specific exercise plan, but the value of increasing activity levels and so energy output is stressed. You are told that exercise will help to suppress appetite.

Who shouldn't use it?

No one who is pregnant, nursing, has a health problem or wants to lose more than 40 lb (18.2 kg) or more than 20 per cent of body weight should start this diet without a doctor's advice.

Additional information

The leaflet with the Bran-Slim tablets includes a very detailed calorie and fibre counter for all sorts of common foods. This shows you how many calories you get from a certain amount of the food and whether the fibre content is high, medium, low or zero.

You are advised on ways to change your habits – not keeping biscuits or cakes in the house, trying to eat more slowly and on sensible food choices when eating out of the house.

The height/weight table in the leaflet shows a 5ft 4in (1.63 m) woman's recommended weight to be between 8 st 1 lb (51.3 kg) and 9 st 6 lb (59.9 kg), representing a BMI of between 19 and 23, a little lower than current medical opinion recommends.

Expected weight loss

A user is quoted in the leaflet that goes with the soups as saying that she lost 12 lb (5.4 kg) in four weeks. That's 3 lb (1.4 kg) a week, slightly above the recommended weekly weight loss.

Keeping off the pounds

Apart from continuing to use Bran-Slim products and following a healthy diet, there's no specific plan.

They say

'Welcome to successful weight loss without hunger . . . you can lose weight the natural way – with real food . . . without going hungry.'

You say

'The tablets are incredibly sweet, with a kind of cereal taste.'

'I didn't notice any effect at all, except on my bowel movements!'

'I've never been on a calorie-controlled diet, I'm too lazy. But I lost a couple of pounds in a week on these, I think they did make me feel full.'

We say

The Bran-Slim slimming plan contains sensible and informative advice about nutrition and healthy eating. This is one of only a few over-the-counter diet products which gives advice (in the leaflet you get with the Bran-Slim drink) about adapting the diet to meet the needs of non-dieting family members. There's no clear-cut scientific evidence that exercise can suppress appetite, though.

This is a well-balanced diet, but you would need to keep up your intake of zinc, iron and vitamin B6 to maintain recommended levels. You might well lose weight following the suggested reduced-calorie diet, but the effects of the fibre complement aren't scientifically proven.

Calorie counting	√	Less than £10 to start	√
Weighing of food required	√	Personal support	×
Forbidden foods	×	Detailed 'who can't use'	√
Suit single person	√	Emphasizes fluid intake	√
Suitable for vegetarians	√		

Diet type

An appetite suppressant tea.

What is it?

A leaflet and 100 g (about 3½ oz) of tea leaves from the Yunnan tree. It appears that fifth-century BC Chinese scripts recorded that the dried leaves of the Yunnan tree helped digestion. You can obtain the product by mail order from Nature Plus, La Ramee, St Peter Port, Guernsey GY1 2EU. Call 01481 710981 for credit card orders. There is a 12-day trial pack for £7.95, going up to £25.95 for 60 days' supply, with an added £1.50 for postage and packing. You can get your money back if you do not lose 10 lb (4.5 kg) in 12 days.

How does it work?

The tea attacks unhealthy excess weight with its 'bio-dynamic fat-burning' qualities, according to the makers. It activates the digestive system to reduce fat, they say.

The diet

The leaflet tells you to make the tea in the ordinary way (without milk) and to drink two cups before breakfast, lunch and dinner. You don't have to limit the size of your meals and you don't have to take exercise. However, later on the leaflet says that a 'weight-loss course' with Yunnan Chinese tea 'along with regular exercise' *is* a very efficient way to lose weight. Presumably a 'weight-loss course' means a diet. No recipes are given.

Exercise

There isn't a specific plan, but you are advised that taking exercise will speed weight loss.

Who shouldn't use it?

There are no warnings against anyone using this as a weight-loss product.

227

A typical day's diet

Breakfast	2 cups Yunnan Herbal Infusion Normal meal	(variable)
Lunch	2 cups Yunnan Herbal Infusion Normal meal	(variable)
Evening meal	2 cups Yunnan Herbal Infusion Normal meal	(variable)
	Calories (approx)	Whatever you choose
	Cost	£4.36

Additional information
The rest of the leaflet gives users' case-histories of their success with the tea.

Expected weight loss
You can get your money back if you don't lose 10 lb (4.5 kg) in 12 days, so presumably you are expected to lose that much. That is more than 5 lb (2.3 kg) per week, well above the recommended rate. However, it says in the small print on the back of the leaflet that after an initial weight loss you will lose 2–4 lb (0.9–1.8 kg) per week.

They say
'Shed weight effortlessly . . . this slimming herb . . . guarantees weight loss of up to 30 lb (13.6 kg) or more.'

You say
'I enjoyed drinking it – it was very refreshing. I didn't feel so hungry, but then I don't usually drink two cups of tea just before a meal.'

228 'I lose 5 lb (2.3 kg) and I started to feel full quickly.'

'I did stick to a calorie-controlled diet, so if it works it's not pricey.'

'I lost 4 lb (1.8 kg) but that was because I was so sick of it.'

We say
There isn't a plan for keeping the weight off in the long term. I would feel happier if the company promoting the tea could spell 'calory' and 'excercise' (*sic*). If there is scientific evidence that the tea has any effects on weight loss, the makers should state this explicitly.

Calorie counting	√	Less than £10 to start	√
Weighing of food required	×	Personal support	×
Forbidden foods	×	Detailed 'who can't use'	×
Suit single person	√	Emphasizes fluid intake	×
Suitable for vegetarians	√		

Diet type
An appetite suppressant.

What is it?
It is a food supplement in the form of soft capsules. The ingredients are sterculia (a plant fibre), safflower oil, soya lecithin, apple pectin, kelp, phenylalanine, vitamin B, boldo extract, juniper berry oil and potassium. It has negligible quantities of protein, carbohydrate and fat, and has virtually no calorific value. It is not suitable for vegetarians as the capsules are made of gelatine.

Figure Trim 8 has been on the market for over 20 years worldwide, since when several million people have used it. A 14-day supply costs £5.95; a five-day trial course costs £2.19. You get it at chemists and health food shops.

How does it work?
The manufacturers say that Figure Trim 8 contains a herbal appetite suppressant that swells in the stomach to take the edge off your hunger, making it easier for you to eat less.

The diet
You are to take one of the capsules with a full glass of water 30 minutes before each meal, while following a calorie-controlled diet you will need to devise yourself.

Who shouldn't use it?
The product is not recommended for children or during pregnancy.

They say
'A concentrated health food supplement . . . helps you to control your eating and slim more easily.'

You say
'I thought it was working at first because I lost 5 lb (2.3 kg) by the third day, but then I lost confidence in it as an appetite suppressant.'

'My nails improved fantastically, so I'd recommend it as a vitamin supplement.'

'One month later I'm still trying to finish the course.'

A typical day's diet

Breakfast	1 Figure Trim 8 capsule Calorie-controlled meal	(variable)
Lunch	1 Figure Trim 8 capsule Calorie-controlled meal	(variable)
Evening meal	1 Figure Trim 8 capsule Calorie-controlled meal	(variable)
	Calories (approx)	Whatever you choose
	Cost	£3.99

We say

This is the only over-the-counter product in this chapter to have independent evidence from a controlled study of its effectiveness in promoting weight loss (see page 212). The scientists who carried out the study are now analysing the data to try to discover which of the ingredients are active in suppressing appetite.

Calorie counting	√	Less than £10 to start	√
Weighing of food required	×	Personal support	×
Forbidden foods	×	Detailed 'who can't use'.	√
Suit single person	√	Emphasizes fluid intake	√
Suitable for vegetarians	×		

Slimist Dietary Mouth Spray

Diet type
An appetite suppressant.

What is it?
A spray containing enough of the product to last for 30 days, if you use it eight times a day.

Varieties: chocolate, peppermint and grapefruit.

Ingredients: fruit juice, flavouring, pyridoxine hydrocholoride, cyanocobalamin, chromium picolinate, aspartame, the amino acids phenylalanine, glycine, lysine, ornithine and arginine with traces of vitamins B6 and B12. (Pyridoxine hydrochloride is vitamin B6 and cyanocobalamin is vitamin B12, so it is puzzling that these are mentioned twice.) There is no indication of how much of any ingredient is supplied.

Originally marketed in the USA, the product has been available in Britain since 1994. It is advertised in the press, and you can call the credit card line on 01483 268888 to place an order. Slimist costs £9.95 for one container, but you can get two for £18.95, including post and packing. If within seven days of receipt you don't think that Slimist is helping you to lose weight, you can have a full refund if you return the product within 14 days.

How does it work?
No theory is given. It is simply stated that the product is an appetite suppressant.

The diet
You are supposed to spray Slimist into your mouth every time you feel the urge to snack and 15 minutes before you have a meal, but the makers advise that it can help weight loss only in conjunction with a calorie-controlled diet that you will need to devise yourself.

Who shouldn't use it?
You are supposed to keep it out of children's reach unless under adult supervision.

Expected weight loss

This is not mentioned, but a user in an advertisement claims to have lost 2 st (12.7 kg) in eight weeks, implying a weight loss of 3–4 lb (1.4–1.8 kg) a week, which is above the rate recommended by current medical opinion.

They say

'Spray away the snack attack ... a delicious-tasting appetite suppressant.'

You say

'It's quite bitter-tasting – I had the chocolate. I can't say I noticed any effects.'

'If you liked sweet things it might put you off, but I didn't notice any effect on my appetite.'

We say

There is no scientific evidence that the ingredients in this spray affect appetite or have any other effects on weight loss, nor is there evidence that sugars (in the fruit juice) and aspartame act as appetite suppressants when used in mouth sprays. Still, Slimist is new and if you believe in it and follow a calorie-controlled diet, you could lose weight. But if you did, I'd think the diet was more likely to be working than the product.

Don't make my mistake, though – at first I thought this was a nasal spray.

Calorie counting	√	Less than £10 to start	√
Weighing of food required	×	Personal support	×
Forbidden foods	×	Detailed 'who can't use'	×
Suit single person	√	Emphasizes fluid intake	×
Suitable for vegetarians	√		

Slimming Clinics

Diet type
Appetite suppressants and low-calorie diets.

What is it?
Private slimming clinics provide a course of prescribed anorectic (appetite-reducing) drugs, which you take under a doctor's supervision. They have been around since the 1930s at least, but there was an increase in their number following the discovery of amphetamine-type drugs in the 1960s. Now another expansion is underway as a new generation of slimming drugs becomes available.

Advertisements for slimming clinics offering medication appear in the national and local press, and in women's magazines. Prices vary in different parts of the country, and on special offers, but you can expect to pay £40–60 per month, which includes initial consultation, weekly weigh-ins and prescribed drugs. There are sometimes special offer periods when rates are as low as £20 per month.

How does it work?
Appetite suppressants in themselves will not make you lose weight, but according to the suppliers, because you will not feel hungry, it will be easier to stick to a diet.

The diet
At the first consultation, you will be weighed, your blood pressure will be measured and a medical history taken. If the doctor thinks that you are a suitable case for treatment, you will be prescribed one of a number of tablets which cause you to feel less hungry. You take these tablets preferably with a glass of water in the mid-morning.

You should take extra care when driving or using machinery. You must not give your medication to anyone else, and you must keep it out of children's reach. You will also be given a diet sheet, usually of the sort which has different foods colour-coded into ones you can eat a lot of, ones you can eat a little of and so on. Your diet will probably be restricted to 1000–1200 calories per day. You may also be given vitamin pills.

234

It depends very much on the clinic as to whether or not you would be given any general dietary advice.

A typical day's diet

Breakfast	*Tablets* *Calorie-controlled meal*	*(variable)*
Lunch	*Tablets* *Calorie-controlled meal*	*(variable)*
Evening meal	*Tablets* *Calorie-controlled meal*	*(variable)*
	Calories (approx)	1000–1200
	Cost	£5.00

Who shouldn't use it?
A doctor examines each patient and decides whether he or she should be treated.

Side-effects
The common side-effects of the prescribed drugs include head-aches, agitation, tremor, restlessness, stomach upsets, sleeplessness, dry mouth and increased nervousness.

Expected weight loss
Some clinics suggest that you will lose 4 lb (1.8 kg) per week, which is higher than the medically recommended rate.

Keeping off the pounds
Any programme to keep weight off in the long term depends on your personal circumstances and the types of treatment offered by the clinic.

They say
'The most hunger-free, the most successful, easiest diet you have ever tried.'

235

You say

'They put me on these pills and I couldn't sleep and had terrible mood swings. They gave me vitamin pills, but I swear they were diuretics because I was never out of the loo. I smoked like a train and started drinking coffee all the time. You lose weight but you feel like hell.'

'I've been on it for a couple of weeks and the pills do take off the hunger. I have cut down on all my portions, and I've no side-effects – just a bit dry-mouthed.'

'The clinic I went to didn't seem to care what size I was so long as I paid the money. I'm 5 ft 9 in (1.75 m) tall and I lost 2½ st (15.9 kg). I was down to 9 st 2 lb (58.1 kg) but no one ever said, "That's enough". They made me feel very ill.'

'I was still just a teenager. I was taking bran tablets and diuretics at the same time, I don't know why – I know it was daft and I wasn't even fat. My mother took me to the doctor and he gave me these pills. Great for a night out – they made you want to drink, because you were thirsty, and dance, because you had so much energy. I lost 3 st (19.1 kg) in six months and put it back in the next six months.'

We say

The appetite suppressants prescribed nowadays don't have the dreadful side-effects that the old amphetamines used to have, but they are still powerful drugs. Some people will experience quite severe side-effects. If this happens to you, it's important to contact the clinic that supplied you with the drugs – don't just stop taking them suddenly. The General Medical Council insists that there is no justification for the use of these drugs, because any possible benefits are outweighed by the risks.

There has been criticism of some slimming centres which apparently take on anyone as a client, even if they are actually underweight. This would be very wrong, as these drugs are specifically for people who are at least moderately overweight, that is who have a BMI above 30.

Calorie counting	√	Less than £10 to start	×
Weighing of food required	×*	Personal support	√
Forbidden foods	×*	Detailed 'who can't use'	√
Suit single person	√	Emphasizes fluid intake	√
Suitable for vegetarians	√		

* Depending on the clinic.

Food Fact File

Nowhere in the world has anyone ever been allowed to eat what they like, where they like, when they like and with whom they like. Every culture has taboo food. The reason is often religious: Muslims and Jews prohibit pork, Seventh Day Adventists and Buddhists prohibit meat, Hindus beef and Mormons coffee and tea. However, taboos can also apply to particular groups – many traditional communities have special food taboos for pregnant women, mostly against meat, and for hundreds of years it was thought that children should only be given insipid and tasteless fare. Other taboos may be superstitious in nature: until the early part of this century in Britain, it was believed pregnant women shouldn't eat strawberries, in case their child should be born with a birthmark.

Diet type
Amino acid capsules.

What is it?
A 15-day course of capsules containing amino acids. The ingredients are 250 mg each of ornithine and arginine, with 25 mg of carnitine. The capsules are made with gelatine so they are not suitable for vegetarians. The company presently producing Slim-Nite tell me that they have sold nearly 70 000 items since 1992. You can buy Slim-Nite in health food shops and from some chemists. A course costs £9.99.

How does it work?
The amino acids ornithine and arginine play an important role in the body's metabolism, the makers suggest, and carnitine helps to convert fat into energy in the body. No claims are made for this product.

The Diet
You take three capsules with a glass of water or juice before going to sleep at night. You mustn't take them with protein. No further information is provided, so a typical day can't be detailed.

Who shouldn't use it?
There aren't any restrictions on use. The product says that it is suitable for adults on a calorie-controlled diet.

They say
No claims are made.

You say
'I don't know if they worked or not – I was cutting down because I was trying to slim, so I stopped eating so much.'

We say
You might assume from its name that this product has some effect on weight or eating, but no claims are made for it. There

is no justification for a claim anyway, as there is no scientific evidence that these amino acids affect your metabolism when taken like this. In fact, the amino acids in these capsules are banned from over-the-counter diet products in the USA, because no one could prove that they work. No additional information such as height/weight charts, exercise routines and so on is provided.

Calorie counting	×	Less than £10 to start	√
Weighing of food required	×	Personal support	×
Forbidden foods	×	Detailed 'who can't use'	×
Suit single person	√	Emphasizes fluid intake	×
Suitable for vegetarians	×		

Food Fact File

'A woman should never be seen eating or drinking, unless it be lobster salad and champagne' – Byron.

Diet type
Vegetable protein tablets.

What is it?
A 30-day course of tablets containing vegetable protein concentrate. The ingredients are: Phaseolamin, *Cicer arietinum*, *Pisum sativum*, *Pisum hortenese*, *Lens esculenta*, *Phaseolus angularia*, *Vigna anguiculate* (mainly beans, peas, lentils) and guar gum.

You can obtain Speed Slim by mail order and from specialized stockists − call 0181 503 1040 for credit card orders. One course costs £13.95.

How does it work?
No explanation is given of the theory behind these tablets.

The diet
You take one tablet with a glass of water before up to three meals a day. The product will help with slimming or weight control only as part of a joule (calorie) controlled diet, the makers say, but there's no guidance given as to what that is. Speed Slim has negligible quantities of protein, carbohydrate and fat, and has virtually no calorific value. It is suitable for vegetarians.

A typical day's diet

Breakfast	1 *Speed Slim tablet with water* *Calorie-controlled meal*	*(variable)*
Lunch	1 *Speed Slim tablet with water* *Calorie-controlled meal*	*(variable)*
Evening meal	1 *Speed Slim tablet with water* *Calorie-controlled meal*	*(variable)*
	Calories (approx)	Not known
	Cost	£4.56

Who shouldn't use it?

People who are allergic to legumes (fruits, their pods, or vegetables), beans or nuts should not take Speed Slim, nor those with stomach disorders or ulcers. Pregnant women, nursing mothers and those on medication should consult a doctor before using this product. It is not recommended for children under 16 years of age.

They say

No claim is made.

We say

'I didn't notice any effects,' one of my dieters told me. Bean proteins were once thought to act as starch-blockers and so prevent absorption of energy from foods, but research has shown conclusively that starch-blockers are ineffective when taken in this way. There may be an effect from an increase in fibre intake, but at these minute quantities that would be unlikely. No additional information is provided, such as a long-term weight plan, menus, height/weight charts or exercise suggestions.

Calorie counting	√	Less than £10 to start	×
Weighing of food required	×	Personal support	×
Forbidden foods	×	Detailed 'who can't use'.	√
Suit single person	√	Emphasizes fluid intake	×
Suitable for vegetarians	√		

Swiftrim

Diet type
Seaweed tablets.

What is it?
A food supplement consisting of a 30-day course of seaweed extract tablets. The only ingredient is *Fucus* (seaweed). Swiftrim can be obtained by mail order and from specialized stockists. One course costs £13.95.

How does it work?
No information on how Swiftrim works is given.

The Diet
You are told to take two tablets three times per day with water, and that the product can aid weight control only as part of a calorie-controlled diet. There is no guidance as to what that is.

A typical day's diet

Breakfast	2 *Swiftrim tablets* *Calorie controlled meal*	*(variable)*
Lunch	2 *Swiftrim tablets* *Calorie controlled meal*	*(variable)*
Evening meal	2 *Swiftrim tablets* *Calorie controlled meal*	*(variable)*
	Calories (approx)	Not known
	Cost	£4.00

Who shouldn't use it?
You should not exceed the recommended dosage. If you have, or suspect you have, a thyroid disorder you must not use this product. Pregnant women, nursing mothers and persons on medication should consult a doctor before using Swiftrim. It is not recommended for children under 16 years of age.

They say
'Anti-fat tablets.'

You say
'They didn't work for me. They made no noticeable difference to anything.'

'It says nothing much on the box and what it does say is in very small lettering. Maybe this improves your eyesight? I didn't lose any weight.'

We say
Although Swiftrim simply call these 'anti-fat tablets', any sea-weed preparation would normally contain iodine. The body uses iodine to make thyroid hormone and thyroid hormones can alter our metabolism. However, only in people with an iodine deficiency do iodine supplements actually increase metabolism (an increase in metabolism can burn up more energy). Seaweed contains a lot of iodine, but there is no evidence that taking seaweed powder affects healthy people's metabolism in any way.

Many doctors believe that tablets of this kind should not be sold as slimming aids because there is no medical justification for their use. Swiftrim offer no additional information such as height/weight charts, menus or a programme for keeping off the pounds in the long term.

Judge for yourself whether you think these tablets are worth the money.

Calorie counting	√	Less than £10 to start	×
Weighing of food required	×	Personal support	×
Forbidden foods	×	Detailed 'who can't use'	√
Suit single person	√	Emphasizes fluid intake	×
Suitable for vegetarians	√		

Overview

It is not possible to say that a slimming product doesn't work, because human beings are complex creatures and someone somewhere will always lose weight using a particular method, especially when combined with a low-calorie diet.

Even so, it still makes sense to consider what the scientific credibility of any product is, and whether or not any research evidence has shown a dieting aid to be effective.

Key features of appetite suppressants, pills and supplements

Name	Theory scientifically proven	Promotes long-term healthy eating	Suggests new habits	Exercise plan	Weight-loss maintenance plan
Aydslim	✕	✓	✕	✕	✕
Bio-Light	✕	✕	✕	✕	✕
Bran-Slim	✕	✓	✓	✕	✕
Chinese Yunnan Herbal Infusion	✕	✕	✕	✕	✕
Figure Trim 8	✓	✕	✕	✕	✕
Slimist Dietary Mouth Spray	✕	✕	✕	✕	✕
Slimming Clinics	✓	✕	✕	✕	✕
Slim-Nite	✕	✕	✕	✕	✕
Speed Slim	✕	✕	✕	✕	✕
Swiftrim	✕	✕	✕	✕	✕

Chapter 12

Food Intolerance and Allergy Diets

What's the theory?

There are really two theories in this chapter: the theory of food intolerance and allergy, and the theory of food combining developed by Dr William Hay in the 1930s. (The diet resurfaced in a similar form as the Beverly Hills Diet in the 1980s.) Everything we eat, according to Dr Hay, is either acid- or alkaline-forming. Acid-forming foods (like meat or cereals) should be cut down and the intake of alkaline-forming foods (fruit, vegetables) increased.

Dr Hay believed that the way to health was to eat only one food of a particular type – starch, protein, fruit, etc. – at each meal, and that with the help of a daily enema this would keep the body free from poisons and toxins which could lead to acidosis and the formation of fat. In fact, despite what Dr Hay believed, there are very few foods which are not a mixture of protein and starch, and which do not combine acid and alkali.

Food intolerance and allergy was recognized more than two thousand years ago in Ancient Greece. However, recent research in Britain and the Netherlands has shown that although about 20 per cent of the population *believe* they are intolerant of or allergic to certain foods, only about one-tenth of that number actually are. Where people are found to be intolerant of food-stuffs they are more likely to suffer from other allergic reactions as well – hay fever, asthma, eczema. The study found that migraine was the most common complaint, with chocolate blamed as the main cause.

Intolerance of additives in food is also much less frequent than people think. Studies have shown that although 7 per cent of people think they are intolerant of additives, probably only one in a hundred people is.

Do these diets work?

There has been no published scientific evidence as to whether these diets work. Some people do prefer very rigid diets, which you get with food combining because you don't have to spend time thinking about what you are going to eat. I haven't found any scientific evidence about the ease of following these methods, although the authors of many of the books quote from testimonials to the effect that they are easy to follow.

Keeping off the pounds

There is no independent evidence that any of the diets in this chapter promote long-term weight loss.

Any problems?

There may be physical problems on any diet if you don't follow the instructions. Nutritionists have expressed concern that, depending on what you are found to be intolerant of, you could find it very difficult to maintain adequate nutrition if the variety of your diet has been drastically reduced.

I am concerned that the books on food combining seem to imply a much higher rate of intolerance or allergy to foods than has ever been found scientifically. People who believe that certain foods disagree with them may worry unnecessarily that they are damaging their health when they find they can't stick to their supposed 'safe' items. Similarly, people who find that they can't stick to very controlled diet regimes can feel ashamed of their lapses, and blame themselves rather than the diet. It is believed people are much more likely to binge when they try to stick to very restrictive diets.

Diet type
Food intolerance, detoxification and food combining.

What is it?
A diet programme by Harvey and Marilyn Diamond describing their almost vegan diet and covering such topics as 'The Natural Body Cycles', 'Proper Food Combining', 'The Theory of Detoxification' and 'The Principle of Correct Fruit Consumption'. There are sections on exercise, a question-and-answer chapter, the diet programme itself and recipes.

Fit for Life was first published in the USA in 1985, since when 4 million copies have been sold worldwide. The book is 320 pages long, costs £5.99 and is published by Bantam.

How does it work?
Because we process food by cooking it, the Diamonds suggest, we aren't biologically adapted to digesting the result and this creates toxins. If the toxic waste builds up, we put on weight. With enough vital energy, the argument goes, we will be able to eliminate this waste. The stomach should be kept as alkaline as possible, because eating more than one type of food with another will result in overproduction of acid, resulting in putrefaction of food in the stomach, fermentation and the possibility of liver damage, gas, flatulence, heartburn and acid indigestion.

The diet
There are two main principles to the Fit for Life Diet. The first is that because our bodies are 70 per cent water, our diet should be 70 per cent fruit and vegetables, since these foods are made up mainly of water. Only 30 per cent of our intake should come from 'concentrated' items, which is everything else – carbohydrate, protein and fat.

The second basic principle is that foods taken in the correct combination are easier to digest. Only one concentrated food should be eaten at any one meal. If this advice is followed, no undigested food passes through the body and so the energy

247

levels stay high. If you eat two proteins simultaneously, as say bacon and eggs, the theory is that these will rot in your system, slowing up digestion and causing energy loss. Fruit must be eaten on an empty stomach.

A typical day's diet

Breakfast	14 fl oz (400 ml) fresh orange juice 2 bananas	140 180
Lunch	8 fl oz (225 ml) carrot juice Salad, made with 3 cups lettuce, 1 cup raw spinach, 1 cucumber, 1 tomato, 2 cups alfalfa sprouts, carrots, celery, with dressing made from garlic, 1½ tbsp olive oil, ½ tbsp lemon juice, ¼ tsp sea salt	60 300
Evening meal	Vegetable juice cocktail, made from 8 carrots, 1 stalk celery, ¼ small beetroot, 1 tomato, 1 red pepper, raw spinach	90
	Cauliflower soup, made from ½ tbsp butter, ¼ tbsp olive oil, onion, scallions, garlic, ½ stalk celery, ½ cauliflower, salt, curry powder	100
	Potato boat, made with 1 potato, 4 oz (110 g) butter squash, ⅛ cup butter, cumin, salt, ½ tsp butter	400
	Garlic string beans, made with ½ tbsp olive oil, garlic, 1 cup string beans, thyme, salt, stock, lemon juice	100
	French green salad, made with ½ lettuce, ½ cup aragula, 1½ tbsp olive oil, ½ tbsp lemon juice, salt, pepper	200
	Calories (approx)	1500
	Cost	£3.57

Coffee, tea and soft drinks should be cut out of the diet and if possible you should avoid sugar, sweets and salt. If you must drink wine, you should do so on an empty stomach. It will take less to 'loosen you up'.

The book does not concern itself with calories, and says that the diet does *not* work because it is low in calories. Lowering calorie intake will not reduce weight if you are eating toxic foods. The Diamonds maintain that in the rich countries of the world many people eat far more protein and dairy produce than they need to for their health. Meat, eggs and dairy foods do not have to be eaten on a daily basis, they suggest. Humans aren't physically or psychologically equipped to eat meat; dairy foods apart from butter are to be cut back, because they are acid-forming; eggs stink, and are not required. None of the daily menus contains meat, fish, eggs or dairy foods, apart from butter.

Exercise plan
The programme will not work unless you do some exercise, the Diamonds maintain, and aerobic exercise is essential every day. Rebounding – mini-trampolining – is recommended, but in any case you must go for a brisk walk or take some other form of aerobic exercise for at least 20 minutes every day.

Learning new habits
There's a complete page covered with the admonition 'Do not overeat' written 100 times.

Who shouldn't use it?
A disclaimer at the beginning of the book states: 'In the event you use this information [the author's advice] without your doctor's approval, you are prescribing for yourself, which is your constitutional right, but the publisher and authors assume no responsibility.'

Side-effects
You may experience bloating, gas, flatulence, an increase in mucus, headaches, diarrhoea and nausea; these are apparently signs that toxins are being washed out of your body. Brittle nails and minor hair loss may occur as you cut down on dairy consumption.

Expected weight loss

You may be able to lose 10 lb (4.5 kg) in 10 days. This is well above the medically recommended rate of 1–2 lb (450–900 g) per week.

The Diamonds say

'The internationally acclaimed weight loss plan that proves it's not *what* you eat, but *when* and *how*!'

You say

'I lost 5 lb (2.3 kg,) but it wasn't easy to stick to. It's for people who don't go out or socialize.'

'I liked the principle, but I found it very difficult to do it properly.'

We say

You would have to like vegetables a *lot* if you wanted to go on this diet, and you would be advised to live near a greengrocer, because the required quantities are so enormous. The authors acknowledge that many of the fruits and vegetables recommended may not be easily available. In Britain they would also be quite expensive at certain times of year.

If you did stick to the diet, you might well lose weight. However, you would be likely to do so because the suggested daily calorie intake is less than what most people need, not because you are clearing toxins from your body. In addition;

- Some doctors and nutritionists believe that this diet is unscientific and may be potentially harmful to health. There isn't any evidence that having bacon and egg or beans on toast is bad for you!
- The diet as it stands could be nutritionally inadequate in the long term. There is a serious shortage of vitamin B12; the protein, calcium and niacin levels are low; and almost half of the calorie content comes from fat.
- The book suggests that the diet is all right for pregnant women. No one who is intending to get pregnant or who is pregnant should go on a diet without consulting a doctor.

All in all, it is hard to take seriously a book that contains a sentence like, 'Many people eat melon incorrectly.' The authors don't mean eating it with chopsticks but, shock horror, *with other food.*

Calorie counting	×	Less than £10 to start	√
Weighing of food required	√	Personal support	×
Forbidden foods	√	Detailed 'who can't use'	×
Suit single person	√	Emphasizes fluid intake	√
Suitable for vegetarians	√		

Food Fact File

US doctors are concerned that if an effective appetite-suppressant drug free of long-term side-effects is found, the cost implications will be enormous; a quarter to a third of the American population, perhaps 60 million people, would want to be treated with it.

The Food Combining Diet

Diet type
Food combining.

What is it?
Kathryn Marsden has devised a 28-day plan modifying Dr
William Hay's theory that mixing different kinds of food causes
a build up of toxins in the body.

Her husband recovered from cancer surgery using the Hay
System, she says, and she then became interested in using it to
help people with other medical problems. Some of them also
lost weight, and her 192-page book is intended both for those
who do and those who do not want to lose weight. The diet is
also said to help those who are underweight to balance their
weight. She covers topics such as 'Why Dieting Doesn't Work',
'The Dieter's Nightmare – Hypoglycaemia' and 'The Importance
of Detoxifying and Cleansing'.

The Food Combining Diet first appeared in 1993, since when
it has sold 180 000 copies. It is published by Thorsons and costs
£4.99.

How does it work?
The Hay System was devised by Dr William Howard Hay in the
1930s, as a cure for illnesses of all kinds. Dr Hay believed that
ill health resulted from the accumulation of toxic wastes in the
body, partly caused by mixing starches with protein in the same
meal, and thus not providing the alkaline environment he
considered essential to good digestion. The Hay System as an
aid to weight loss is intended to be not so much a diet but more
a way of life, according to Kathryn Marsden.

The diet
In *The Food Combining Diet* the different food groups – the
proteins, starches and neutral foods – are explained, and lists
given of foods which you can combine at protein, starch and
neutral meals. There is also a quick reference chart to show you
whether a food is compatible with other foods or should not be
eaten in conjunction with them.

252   You must drink at least 2 pt (1.1 l) of water a day over

and above tea, coffee, etc., though you are advised to cut down on the amount of tea and coffee you drink anyway. No foods are forbidden, if eaten in the right combinations, but bread, wheat products, milk, sugar, factory-farmed meat or meat products, refined, processed and rich foods are to be avoided as much as possible. Pulses are only to be eaten in small amounts.

There is a four-week plan of breakfasts, lunches and evening meals. The first two days of the diet, which you are to start on a Friday, are called the Detox Diet, and you eat only fresh fruit and salads. On the third day, a Sunday, the diet is high in protein and could be high in fat if you didn't use low-cal versions of the yoghurt dessert (see below).

A typical day's diet

Throughout the day	*2 pt (1.1 l) water, black tea and coffee*	
Breakfast	*Fruit ciabatta, served hot with butter*	*210*
Pre-lunch aperitif	*1 glass of white wine*	*100*
Lunch	*Organic roast lamb*	*200*
	Peas, broccoli and parsnips	*200*
Evening meal	*Apple coleslaw, made with 1 chunk white cabbage, 1 carrot, apple, stick of celery, 1 tsp chives, lemon juice, spring onion, Brazil nuts, dressed with yoghurt and herbs*	*175*
Dessert (to be eaten at least one hour after evening meal)	*Yoghurt sweetened with a little honey*	*100*
	Calories (approx)	1000
	Cost	£3.57

Recipes are given in imperial measures and American cups, for one serving, as part of the daily plans. They are coded as to whether they are to be eaten alone, or suitable for vegetarians, and are protein, starch or alkaline-forming. A number of 'Master Recipes' for salads are included at the end of the book.

Exercise
You should aim to exercise for 15–20 minutes per day, Kathryn Marsden says, and you don't need to overdo things to keep healthy. Swimming, rebounding, walking, dancing, yoga, stretching and deep breathing are all beneficial types of exercise.

Who shouldn't use it?
If you are concerned about your health or are taking any medication you should consult a doctor before starting the diet.

Side-effects
You may experience a 'Healing Crisis' as toxins are eliminated, apparently. The symptoms of this may be headaches, nausea, bowel disturbance or skin irritation.

Expected weight loss
A patient of the author's is described as having lost 2 st (12.7 kg) in three months, about 2 lb (900 g) a week, which is in line with current medical opinion about safe rates of weight loss. You are warned not to expect any rapid weight loss – in fact you are advised to forget about your weight as the looseness of your clothes will let you know that you are becoming slimmer.

Keeping off the pounds
This is a diet for life, so there isn't a weight maintenance plan.

Kathryn Marsden says
'This book shows you how you can lose weight happily and healthily without cutting or counting calories ever again!'

You say

'If you did it properly you'd have a lot more energy and not feel so bloated.'

'You had to really analyse it, and it wasn't easy if you had to go out for a meal.'

'I've lost 21 lb (9.5 kg) in three months, so far, but it's not a diet, it's a way of life. I still eat sweets and biscuits and I do have blow-out days when I don't combine. You can't go out for a meal and do it. You really have to learn about the proteins and starches and things. I've learned to use more herbs.'

We say

If you stuck to this diet you would probably lose weight, but not necessarily because you were eliminating toxins from your body. By cutting down on fat, sugar, bread, dairy products and meat, you are cutting down on your calorie intake. The symptoms of 'healing' described in this book are very similar to symptoms of hunger.

Kathryn Marsden acknowledges there is no scientific evidence that food combining causes toxins or that toxins cause obesity. This is not as restrictive a regime as some food-combining diets, but it is still very constraining. In addition:

- It is hard to see how any diet can promote both weight loss and weight gain.
- People tell me that sometimes they can't remember what they're not supposed to eat with what when they're out socially and on food-combining diets, so they don't eat at all. This would not be good for anyone, let alone someone trying to put on weight.
- This diet could be low in iron, zinc and calcium, the last because of a reduction in dairy products.
- The exercise plan does not stress, as it should, that aerobic exercise is best for improvements in long-term health and in calorie burn-off. I am sure that 20 minutes a day of yoga could help to tone up the body, and may well lead to a reduction in stress, but it wouldn't help weight loss.

Food Intolerance and Allergy Diets

Calorie counting	×	Less than £10 to start	√
Weighing of food required	√	Personal support	×
Forbidden foods	×	Detailed 'who can't use'	×
Suit single person	√	Emphasizes fluid intake	√
Suitable for vegetarians	√		

Food Fact File

One of the reasons that people in Britain may be reluctant to adopt the 'Mediterranean' style diet may be because it's popularly thought that the people who live there may be fitter but are also fatter than Britons. This is in fact true, as women in France, Italy and Spain tend to have a bigger BMI than British women of similar age. Any diet, even a Mediterranean one, can make you fat if output is less than input.

Diet type
A food intolerance diet.

What is it?
A blood test, a diet and a book.

The NuTron Diet involves first having a blood test to identify to which of approximately 100 common foods you are intolerant. You use this information to devise a personal diet plan. The 'Vacutainer' kit for taking the blood is available from the Individual Diet Company, The Old Mill, The Street, Albury, Surrey GU5 9AZ, or call 01483 203555 for one. You must make a booking for analysis of the sample.

You can ask your doctor or practice nurse to take the blood samples, or the Individual Diet Company can arrange for them to be taken at their laboratory in Surrey or at clinics with whom they have arrangements in London. The Individual Diet Company can also arrange for your blood sample to be taken privately by a clinic near you, if you wish. If your own doctor takes the sample you must send it to the laboratory before 12.30 midday (blood samples must be fresh). Clinics specializing in chiropractic, acupuncture, beauty, slimming, or health and fitness also arrange for the blood test through the Individual Diet Company.

The cost of the blood test is £135. Some doctors may charge you for taking the blood test, but there is no fee for having the sample taken at the Individual Diet Company's laboratory.

The NuTron Diet was launched in 1993, and the Individual Diet Company inform me that so far some 13000 people have had their blood analysed for food intolerances. Dr Patrick Kingsley developed the theory, and Ian Stoakes was responsible for developing the analysis methods. Their book describing the theory and the diet, *The NuTron Diet*, costs £4.99 and is published by Penguin.

How does it work?
Ideas about allergic reactions to foods have been around for a long time, but Dr Kingsley and Mr Stoakes claim in their book that there are differences in time of reaction between allergies

257

and intolerances, with the former showing themselves more rapidly after ingestion of the suspect food. The theory behind their dietary method is that most overweight people aren't fat, they are waterlogged. If foods to which the person is intolerant are removed from the diet, then fluid is no longer retained and weight loss occurs. Much of the weight most people need to lose is fluid and not fat. Every woman who has 'cellulite' has food intolerance. The food to which you are intolerant allows your intestine to leak, letting partly digested food enter the blood-stream and attack a certain type of blood cell, which makes the cells leak toxins.

Dr Kingsley and Mr Stoakes believe that a blood test can determine to which of approximately 100 foods you are intolerant. The efficiency of the intestine is improved, less fat is absorbed from all foods and cravings for, say, carbohydrates disappear when these foods are removed from the diet.

The diet
After the blood analysis you will be sent a 'red' list of the foods to which you are intolerant, in order of severity. On average, the lists show people to be intolerant of between 10 and 15 foods, although some people are intolerant of only one or two. No one is given a list of more than 20 foods to which they are intolerant. You must cut out foods to which you are intolerant completely for a month.

You are also sent a 'green' list of foods which you can eat without any ill-effects and are given guidance on how to construct your individual diet. For example, one of the most commonly found intolerances is to baker's yeast. This means that you can't eat bread, cakes or pizza, but you can eat rice cakes.

Having cut out all the foods you are intolerant to for a month, and eaten only those to which you are not intolerant, you can start to introduce other foods. You begin with ones which are not on either the 'red' or 'green' lists, that is, foods for which you were not tested. Then, if no adverse symptoms appear, you can start to eat some of the foods at the bottom of your list of banned foods, the ones to which you aren't *very* intolerant. (You can do this because, according to the NuTron Diet, your immune system has had a rest and you may not now be intolerant to the banned food.)

You are to introduce the foods gradually, one at a time for three to four days, and then another one and so on. You will know if you are intolerant because you will get blinding headaches, a feeling of bloating or general malaise, or you will gain weight. You must then stop eating the food, and if it wasn't already on, add it to your banned list. Otherwise, you can eat as much as you like of non-banned foods.

A typical day's diet can't be given, because each individual works out their own diet. No guidance is given on calorie control, because the theory is that calorie counting is not effective; Dr Kingsley believes it to be 'dangerously simplistic'. You are advised to cut out alcohol for a month at least, and to eat as much fresh food and as little processed food as you can. You are to reduce sugar and fat.

Variations
If you are going on holiday, having been on the diet and cut out all foods to which you are intolerant, you can ask your doctor to prescribe sodium cromoglycate for you. It is a treatment for food allergy. This is intended to prevent a reaction to foods you may be eating while abroad which are not on your safe list.

Who shouldn't use it?
Vegans are advised not to use the diet. Special dietary advice is given to pregnant women. A doctor's written permission is required before the blood test can be made for anyone with an eating disorder, or who has had treatment for cancer, or who is an insulin-dependent diabetic. Anyone with a history of any kind of medical treatment would be individually advised.

Side-effects
The first sign that the diet is working is that you may feel unwell, the makers say. These are withdrawal symptoms from the foods you are intolerant to. Symptoms last only a few days. Headaches seem to be the most common problem.

Additional information
Eliminating foods to which you are intolerant may also alleviate arthritis, eczema, cystitis, PMS and irritable bowel syndrome among other complaints. Dr Kingsley and Mr Stoakes state that **259**

the NuTron Diet can reduce hyperactivity in children and make it very unlikely for a young person to develop anorexia nervosa.

Forms for ordering *The NuTron Diet* book are included in the information you get from the Individual Diet Company. The book has a foreword by Nina Myskow, who lost 1 st (6.3 kg) on the diet, describes the background to the development of the test and the theory behind it, gives case-histories and has a section where common questions are answered, and includes a postal booking form.

The special report of foods to which you are intolerant comes with supportive notes with lists to help in building a healthy eating pattern.

There's a Nurse Help Line available from Monday to Friday for personal advice; call the number given above.

Expected weight loss

It is claimed that 70 per cent of users of the diet lose 7 lb (3.2 kg) or more in the first four weeks, and 10 per cent lose 1½ (9.5 kg) to 2 st (12.7 kg) in eight weeks, which is above recommended rates of weight loss.

Keeping off the pounds

Weight loss is maintained by the gradual reintroduction of non-diet foods. If weight gain occurs, that particular food must be discontinued.

They say

'Makes every other weight-control method obsolete ... no calorie counting ... you're hard-pressed to realize you're on a diet!'

You say

'You've got to want to believe in it, but I've cheated, and when I do I feel terrible, so I know it works. I used to like bread but I don't miss it now ... they advised me not to have refined sugar, mushrooms or melon. I've lost 14 lb (6.3 kg) and I'd like to lose more. I changed to soya milk but they advised me to blend it half and half with [cow's] milk because it is so high in fat.'

'I didn't lose any weight because I just couldn't stick to the list they sent me. Everything I liked I couldn't eat.'

We say

Dr Patrick Kingsley acknowledges that the theory of food intolerance is not accepted by the medical profession as a whole. It is clear that you could lose weight on this diet, but it doesn't follow that you would do so simply because you had cut out foods to which you were intolerant. Anyone who is told that up to 15 per cent of the foods they eat are disagreeable to them will lose weight if they stop eating those foods and so reduce their overall intake.

Most people drink, and will lose weight if they cut out alcohol for a month, as the diet advises. Most people eat processed food, so a shift to fresh food means that more effort is needed to obtain the same calories. The average diet is high in sugar and fat, and so any reduction in the amount of these you eat will cause weight loss too.

Dr Kingsley states that you can gain weight on a diet providing just over 500 calories per day. This is theoretically true, but only if you lie in bed all day and weigh less than 40 lb (18.2 kg) to begin with. People *think* they eat very little and so report very low calorie intakes, but the evidence shows that for adults of normal height a diet of 1000 calories per day will invariably cause weight loss.

Calorie counting	×	Less than £10 to start	×
Weighing of food required	×	Personal support	√
Forbidden foods	√	Detailed 'who can't use'	√
Suit single person	√	Emphasizes fluid intake	×
Suitable for vegetarians	√*		

* But not vegans.

The Vitality Diet

Diet type
A food intolerance diet.

What is it?
Maryon and Alan Stewart noticed in their work at the Women's Nutritional Advisory Service that when making dietary changes to maintain health some people lost weight without even trying, and they developed their diet from their observations.

The diet is contained in a 240-page book, *The Vitality Diet*. This includes chapters on understanding obesity, controlling your appetite, and food allergies and how to detect them, and goes on to describe the ten-week Vitality Diet itself. There are case-histories, questionnaires about health and exercise, and facts about nutrition and the problems of sticking to diets generally.

In order to test the theory that some substances can interfere with the nutrients in the body, Alan Stewart became a guinea pig for the analysis of vitamin and mineral changes while taking his normal diet, but with the addition each day of 4 cups of tea, 2 cups of coffee, 3 alcoholic drinks, ½ can cola, 12 teaspoons of sugar, half a large Mars bar and 6 cigarettes per day, for 6 weeks. He could not continue for the 8 weeks originally envisaged as his usual enthusiasm for sex had waned, he felt ill all the time and he was falling asleep at work. In fact levels of many vitamins had fallen alarmingly by the end of the experiment. We are not told whether he gained or lost weight.

The Vitality Diet costs £4.99 and is published by Optima. About 25 000 copies have been sold to date.

How does it work?
To lose weight you need to know what your body needs, the Stewarts believe. If you have failed at dieting before, it may be because you are allergic to or intolerant of certain foods. You need to become a nutrition detective and work out which foods are bad for you.

The diet
The Vitality Diet is divided into several stages. In the first part, you eliminate all the foods that might not suit you. Meat and

fish, vegetables and fruit are allowed, but dairy produce, grains, additives, sugar, alcohol and foods containing yeast are not allowed. There is a chart which shows you what to eat for every day of the diet, and another chart on which to record any symptoms you have had. You can choose alternatives to any of the foods if you don't like them. You stick to Stage 1 of the diet for four weeks, completing extra charts at the end of each week, and then move on to Stage 2, which lasts for another four weeks.

For each week of Stage 2 there is a specific diet to follow. Again, you get a daily diet sheet and a chart to record symptoms. In the first week, wheat, oats, barley and rye are reintroduced; in week three alcohol and yeast, and so on for four weeks. If you experience side-effects during the reintroductions, (a reaction could occur after anything from a few minutes to a day or two later) you must then immediately eliminate from your diet the food you suspect might be giving you problems. Symptoms include depression, puffy eyelids, headaches and so on.

At the end of the first eight weeks you move on to Stage 3, your long-term diet. First, you complete a review of your progress, which will show you exactly which foods agree with you and which do not. If you haven't reached target weight yet, you continue with the diet, adding 'safe' foods and avoiding 'suspect' ones. If you have reached target weight, you increase your calorie intake and continue eating 'safe' foods only. Although this is a two-week stage, it is recommended that, having worked out what does and does not suit your body and your lifestyle, you can stay on the diet for life. You are advised how to calculate your own needs if they are higher than 1000 calories a day and then adjust the diet accordingly, so you do have to count calories.

Detailed recipes are given at each stage of the diet. Servings are for two to four people, and there are vegetarian dishes, packed lunches and desserts. Some convenience foods are included in lunch menus.

Variations
Men should have 1500 calories per day.

A typical day's diet

Breakfast	2 size 3 boiled eggs	160
	2 rice cakes	55
	1 tsp low-cal margarine	25
Snack	3½ oz (100 g) low-cal yoghurt	40
	1 chopped apple	60
Lunch	5 oz (140 g) canned salmon	220
	Bean sprout salad	65
Snack	2 oz (56 g) raw carrot	13
	3 oz (85 g) stick of celery	6
Evening meal	Cumin chicken, made with 4 oz (110 g) chicken breast, onions, ¼ red pepper, ½ tsp oil, cumin, ginger, cornflour, ½ pt (285 ml) stock	145
	4 oz (110 g) broccoli	20
	4 oz (110 g) carrots	20
	4 oz (110 g) potatoes	90
	Fruit salad	100
	Calories (approx)	1000
	Cost	£3.57

Exercise

The Vitality Diet describes how and when people of different levels of fitness and fatness should begin to increase the amount of exercise they take. You are advised to choose an activity you enjoy, to build up gradually and to exercise every day.

Learning new habits

The Stewarts suggest that you plan for your diet before you start, which will increase your chances of success. You should begin by getting your life into a regular and ordered pattern, so that you have time to make the necessary changes to your diet and shopping habits without becoming stressed. Having made a list of positive and negative consequences you expect from dieting, you should carry this around with you and look at it several times a day, before meals or if you feel tempted to cheat. Ways to change your habits when shopping and eating – such as not shopping when you are hungry, or using a smaller plate – are given, but there's no overall plan for a complete change of lifestyle.

Who shouldn't use it?
You shouldn't use this diet if you have a serious medical condition without first consulting your doctor, particularly if you have had allergic food reactions which have caused ill-health in the past.

Side-effects
The Stewarts note that some people do experience slight side-effects, including headaches, irritability, bowel disturbances, wind and skin rashes. They believe many of these to be withdrawal symptoms as caffeine is removed from the diet, but some may have been the result of an allergy or food intolerance showing itself when a particular food was reintroduced.

Additional information
You are advised that although you may wish to diet for cosmetic reasons, being slightly overweight carries hardly any medical risks. The height/weight charts are in line with current medical opinion.

Expected weight loss
People on whom the Stewarts tested the diet lost on average about 11 lb (5 kg) over seven weeks, which at 1–2 lb per week is the rate doctors recommend for permanent weight change.

Keeping off the pounds
To maintain weight loss you simply stay on the diet for the rest of your life, having worked out how to avoid foods to which you are intolerant.

The Stewarts say
'Increase your vitality ... improve your health ... enjoy delicious and nutritious food *and* lose weight and keep the pounds off.'

You say

'I found it very interesting, not gimmicky. It was full of straightforward facts. It gave you credit for having some brains. The exercise bit was the same as them all. The recipes seemed to be enjoyable, though I never cooked them.'

'People might get carried away about allergies. If you think your mouth ulcers are because of allergies, you could get obsessional. You could stick to the diet because it wasn't too low-calorie. I know this stuff because I read a lot of health magazines, but with this I think you could get hooked on thinking about food all the time.'

We say

Another diet which gives correct weight charts, for which full marks, but I'm not happy about diets which might make people think they have food intolerances when in reality food intolerance is rare.

As with other diets in this chapter, you may lose weight simply because of the number of foods you could cut out, such as sugar, cakes, sweets, chocolate, butter, milk, cheese, cereals, yeast-rich foods, fried foods and salt.

Without care, the number of daily calories on this diet may be too low and the diet as it stands is also low in calcium and iron. Many of the side-effects noted above could also be signs of hunger. In any case, if you eat a tiny bit of butter and three hours later come down with a headache, does that necessarily mean you are intolerant of butter and should stay off it the rest of your life? Possible, but not very likely.

Calorie counting	✗	Less than £10 to start	✓
Weighing of food required	✓	Personal support	✗
Forbidden foods	✓	Detailed 'who can't use'	✓
Suit single person	✓	Emphasizes fluid intake	✗
Suitable for vegetarians	✓		

I cannot recommend diets which are without any scientific validity. None of these diets has been proven to have any theoretical backing and there are no published reports of any controlled studies. Doctors pour scorn on them. I don't deny for one moment that the testimonials the authors have garnered are true, and as you will see from dieters' comments, people have lost weight using these methods. But if these diets do cause you to lose weight it is because you are eating fewer calories and/or expending more energy. *There can be no other reason.* If you do sincerely believe that you are suffering from a food allergy or intolerance, you should consult your doctor and never try to treat yourself through diet.

Key features of food intolerance and allergy diets

Name	Theory scientifically proven	Promotes long-term healthy eating	Suggests new habits	Exercise plan	Weight-loss maintenance plan
Fit for Life	✗	✗	✗	✓	✗
The Food Combining Diet	✗	✗	✗	✓	✗
The NuTron Diet	✗	✗	✗	✗	✗
The Vitality Diet	✗	✗	✓	✓	✗

Chapter 13

Therapies

Therapists are not licensed to practise in the way that doctors are. You can become a therapist after years of intensive academic study or after just a weekend course. You can call yourself a hynotherapist or acupuncturist any time you like, and you don't need any training at all before setting yourself up as a reflexologist, dream analyst or Bach Flower Remedies Person.

Qualified therapists are trying to have the law changed in this area, to prevent untrained and sometimes unscrupulous quacks calling themselves therapists. The professional bodies will give you free advice about choosing a therapist in your local area, and the Institute for Complementary Medicine (PO Box 194, London SE16 IQ2) offers completely independent advice about all kinds of 'alternative' therapies. They maintain the British Register of Complementary Practitioners.

Psychologists are not allowed to call themselves psychologists unless they have a degree in psychology, and most are registered with the British Psychological Society (tel: 01533 549568).

There are big bucks in overweight people's fears. Don't sign up for any kind of therapy until you know exactly what is involved and what you will get for your money. Ask for proof of professional qualifications.

What's the theory?
The theories behind the different therapies are all to do with changing behaviour. Their approaches are very different and are described in the sections dealing with the different methods of weight loss.

Does it work?
Behaviour therapy is well-established as an effective method of inducing weight loss. More than a hundred scientific studies of the technique have been published. A review showed that on average patients lost 1 lb (450g) in weight per week. There is no

evidence that behaviour therapy techniques can be easily learned without professional help. For people who binge eat, behaviour therapy may be less effective than other forms of weight control.

There is some evidence that hypnosis is an effective therapy for weight loss, but much of the evidence is contradictory or based on a small sample of people. In one study of hypnotherapy, as many people gained as lost weight; in another study, where people were randomly assigned to hypnotherapy or no treatment at all, those given hypnotherapy lost an average of 7 lb (3.2 kg) over a month, while those who got nothing lost an average of ½ lb (225 g).

A review of studies concluded that hypnotherapy was about as effective as behaviour therapy, and if behaviour therapy was incorporated into the hypnosis sessions then the results would be better. Most hypnotherapists now always include behaviour change as part of treatment, but very recently the effectiveness of hypnosis was still being questioned.

In the second study just decribed, the therapists gave some of the clients autohypnosis tapes to listen to at home; the tapes were designed to reinforce what the therapists had been saying, and keep up the weight loss. But the clients who were given tapes didn't lose any more weight than those who were not given them, so the therapists concluded that the use of audio-tapes 'as a form of auxiliary autohypnosis' was a waste of time.

The usefulness of acupuncture in alleviating pain in certain conditions is no longer questioned by orthodox Western science, but its effectiveness in treating overweight people is not so clear-cut. In China acupuncturists have a professional training, but in Britain anyone with a couple of spare embroidery needles can set themselves up as an acupuncturist; fully qualified acupuncturists in Britain are very keen to see the rules tightened up to prevent such abuses, and regulation of this profession is expected to be made mandatory in the near future. It is possible to buy 'acupressure' ear-rings which you are supposed to stick on particular points on your ears, in order to suppress your appetite. In the USA, the Food and Drug Administration has said that the effectiveness of such ear-rings has yet to be proven.

Most of the studies of the effectiveness of acupuncture are published in Chinese journals, and I am not equipped to evaluate **269** their findings. One British review has suggested that the studies so far have been of poor quality, and that no definite conclusions can be made.

Keeping off the pounds

In the hypnotherapy study cited above, weight loss averaged nearly 18 lb. (8.1 kg) six months after the sessions had ended so clients had continued to lose weight. Other studies have failed to show any maintenance of weight loss.

Long-term weight-loss maintenance following behaviour therapy has been extensively investigated. Results are very variable, but it has been shown that five years later people on average had maintained a loss of about 7 lb (3.2 kg). As yet, there is no long-term evidence for weight loss using acupuncture treatments.

Hypnotherapy seems to be enjoyable, which would imply it is easy to stick to, but there is no scientific evidence that this is so, nor any for the drop-out rate from acupuncture. Behaviour therapy seems to have drop-out rates of about 10 per cent when practised by professionals, which is a very low rate when compared with other forms of weight-loss management.

Any problems?

For people who attend unqualified acupuncturists, infection from unsterilized instruments has occasionally been a problem. I can find no evidence of any physical problems associated with other therapies.

Usually, the only psychological problems are disappointment and anger when the therapy doesn't work.

Treatment type
Chinese medicine.

What is it?
Acupuncture is a system of specific techniques and dietary recommendations designed to bring the body back to a balanced state of health. It has been practised in China for more than 3000 years. Its use as a way of returning the patient to good health, which in turn leads to losing excess weight, began in Britain in the 1960s.

If you contact the Council for Acupuncture, at 179 Gloucester Place, London NW1 6DX (tel: 0171 724 5756), for £2 they will send you a directory of fully qualified acupuncturists.

It would cost about £25–50 for a first consultation, and then £15–40 for subsequent treatments, depending on locality – charges might well be much higher in London. Reduced-rate treatments are available at some clinics where students are taught, such as the Northern College of Acupuncture (tel: 01904 785120).

How does it work?
Traditional Chinese theories of anatomy and physiology are very different from those of Western medicine. Chinese medicine holds that there are 12 channels running over the body, each representing an internal organ. Vital energy runs along these channels, and at acupuncture points on the channels the insertion of a needle can alter the flow of energy. In all traditional Chinese medicine the aim is to get the body back to a balance between yin and yang, passivity and activity. It is when either yin or yang is seriously deficient or excessive that illness results.

The acupuncturist will ask you for your full medical history and will then give you a complete physical examination. He or she will examine your tongue and take your pulse, and will also look at your spine, abdomen and other parts of the body, depending on what the acupuncturist thinks is the cause of your ill-health.

Treatment consists of electrical or manual stimulation of very fine needles in one or both ears, with or without general acupuncture to other sites on the body, particularly the arms and legs. You may be treated on your first appointment or be asked to return for treatment. The acupuncturist will ask you about your eating habits, attempts to lose weight and current diet, and you may be given questionnaires to complete or asked to keep food diaries. Dietary advice varies from patient to patient, depending on what the acupuncturist thinks the cause of the problem is.

The colour of foods and the nature of their growth is also important in traditional Chinese medicine. Red foods are considered to be yang, and foods tending towards the violet end of the spectrum are more yin. Green foods are considered neutral. Of growing things, roots are more yang and shoots and leaves are yin. Cooked or very spicy food is more yang; uncooked or cooling foods such as salads are more yin. Meat is generally warm or hot in energy, but different meats have different properties. It is believed that too much red meat has a clogging effect and can contribute to weight gain. If the acupuncturist believes that you have an imbalance between yin and yang, you will be encouraged to eat more cooling or heating foods, more cooked or uncooked foods, as appropriate.

Dairy products should be avoided; it is believed that these have mucus-forming properties which encourage fat deposits.

Variations
There are basically three variations to acupuncture: 1) electrical or manual stimulation of the ear of other parts with needles which are then removed; 2) the implantation of very small needles, a stud or beads, which are replaced regularly; 3) moxibustion – the burning of moxa, the herb *Artemesia vulgaris*. A small amount of the herb may be formed into a cone, placed on the body and set alight, or the herb may be wrapped in paper to make a cigar-like moxa roll, which is lit and held about an inch away from the skin. The client is not burned; when the heat is felt, the moxa is removed and re-applied to the same or to a different site.

Exercise
The acupuncturist should discuss your current level of activity and make recommendations where appropriate. He or she will

advise on all problems to do with weight, or any other health problems you may have.

Learning new habits
Traditional Chinese medicine places emphasis on where and how you eat, in order to control weight. You should eat three times a day, and in general you should try to be as relaxed as possible when you do eat. For example, if you watch television while eating, it is thought that energy is diverted to your eyes and mind which you should be using for digestion.

Who shouldn't use it?
A qualified acupuncturist will take a full medical history, and only then decide whether your condition is amenable to treatment by acupuncture. If it is not the acupuncturist will refer you elsewhere.

Side-effects
A possible side-effect is infection, but a qualified acupuncturist will sterilize all instruments properly, so this should be unlikely.

Additional information
You should be given a diet sheet and specific advice about altering your lifestyle, as well as more general ideas about healthy nutrition. Height/weight charts are not used, as far as I can discover.

Expected weight loss
It is unlikely that you will be told how much weight you will lose.

Keeping off the pounds
A qualified acupuncturist would encourage you to stick to the recommendations you have been given in order to maintain physical health and avoid putting the weight back on.

They say
'Acupuncture by itself can't make you lose weight unless you want to. You must follow the dietary advice given as well as undergoing treatment.'

You say

'It does relieve hunger, but a lot of it is psychological.'

'I had this thing I was supposed to twiddle about in my ear if I felt hungry. I can't say I noticed any effect.'

'I lost a stone (6.3 kg) in three months, but it was very expensive.'

We say

'Many people find acupuncture very soothing and relaxing, suprisingly enough, and the relief of stress may make it easier to follow a sensible eating plan and consequently you might lose weight. Acupuncture is not magic, and the treatment by itself will not make you any thinner. It is *very important* to check that the acupuncturist you visit is qualified.

Personal support	√	Dietary advice	√
Available on the NHS	×	Less than £10 to start	×

Food Fact File

One kiwi fruit contains as much vitamin C as an adult requires per day.

Treatment type
Psychological therapy.

What is it?
Behaviour therapy has developed from a psychological technique that was originally devised to help people overcome problems through permanently altering their behaviour. It works by teaching you how to alter your environment and to change the way you 'reward' yourself.

In the 1960s, psychologists believed that obesity was primarily the result of faulty eating habits, and that behaviour therapy could help overweight people. At first it was hailed as a major breakthrough, and now almost all weight-loss techniques include elements of it. However, the early euphoria has worn off a bit. Behaviour therapy is much more common in the USA than in Britain.

Seven principles of behaviour modification have been identified.

The first of these is stimulus control. You learn behaviour habits such as shopping for food only after you have eaten, or shopping from a list, to avoid buying things you shouldn't.

The second is to learn to modify your eating behaviour in ways that will tend to make you eat less, by for example putting down your knife and fork between mouthfuls and chewing thoroughly.

The third is to reward yourself for your new good behaviour and thus 'reinforce' it. You can do this by asking friends to praise you for example, or by using food diaries as the basis for rewarding yourself with some special treat.

The fourth principle is to monitor your behaviour at all times so that you are less likely to overindulge and are able to recognize the 'triggers' that set off overeating. You are less likely to eat a cream cake if you have to write the fact in a food diary, and if you realize that you always turn to biscuits when you have a row with your partner, you can learn to avoid such situations.

Nutrition education is another principle of behaviour therapy. You can use your daily diary to identify particular problem areas around food and avoid or minimize these. For example,

275

you may find it impossible not to have an alcoholic drink without a packet of crisps. You have to unlearn this behaviour, either by not having a drink or by substituting something less fattening for the crisps.

The sixth principle of behaviour therapy for obesity is to increase physical activity. You set yourself a small routine task, for example always taking the stairs instead of getting the lift, and build up from there, keeping records of your increasing level of activity.

The final principle is that of 'cognitive restructuring'. This means altering your mind-set so that you aren't setting yourself completely unreasonable goals – I'll lose a stone by next week – and thus always failing and feeling guilty. In fact, you shouldn't use words like 'always' or 'never' at all.

This is a short description of what can be a very long process. Everything we know about eating is learned, apart from how to suck, and if you have been punished in childhood for not eating up everything on your plate, or have learned that you can make yourself feel better with a chocolate bar, these can be difficult habits to unlearn.

Many slimming techniques now incorporate parts of behaviour therapy. You will need to be referred to a clinical psychologist or to a hospital-run obesity clinic by your doctor if you wanted to avail yourself of professional help on the National Health Service, and there would almost certainly be a long waiting list. Alternatively there are private therapists, not all of whom are qualified. *The Directory of Chartered Psychologists* lists qualified psychologists. Details of the library nearest you which holds a copy of a directory can be obtained from the British Psychological Society (tel: 01533 549568).

Treatment is free on the National Health Service, but private practitioners would charge you between £40 and £60 an hour, although it could be as much as £100 an hour.

How does it work?
Through learning to modify your behaviour in specific ways, you can learn to alter your eating patterns and control your food intake. You learn how to change the 'rewards' you give yourself for behaving in a particular way.

You would meet with the therapist either on your own or in a group and talk together for about 20 minutes to an hour, generally once a week or perhaps more frequently at the beginning. Dietary advice will be given as an integral part of the therapy.

Who shouldn't use it?
You would need to demonstrate that your weight problems seriously affected your happiness and your ability to live life to the full, and that other methods of losing weight had failed.

Side-effects
There haven't been any adverse reports of side-effects using these techniques.

They say
'Self-control is a skill which can be learned; new habits can be acquired and the old ones discarded.'

You say
'I went once a week for four or five months. I didn't lose a lot of weight, but I did start exercising and I stopped overeating. It was better than that other thing, which did my head in, where you couldn't lose weight until you'd met God.'

'My problem is that I'm 68 and I'm just beginning to realize the damage I've done to my body with overeating, and I am trying to stick to what they say. I'm a diet-controlled diabetic, but I love to bake. The thing is, when I feel sorry for myself I eat, but if I'm happy I want to celebrate by eating too.'

We say
The principles of behaviour therapy are scientifically proven, but sticking to the advice you are given is always the dieter's problem. The sort of practical advice you would be given – calorie counting, weighing or cutting out foods – would depend on the practitioner's view of your particular problems. The focus is not on the food itself, but on your behaviour around food.

Personal support	√	Dietary advice	√
Available on the NHS	√	Less than £10 to start	√*

* On the NHS.

Hypnotherapy

Treatment type
Therapy through hypnosis.

What is it?
In a therapeutic or 'trying to help' situation, the therapist suggests to the client ways in which the client can do something about whatever problems he or she has. Using hypnosis the therapist can help motivate the person towards a better view of themselves and of their decision-making powers. Hypnosis as a treatment (hypnotherapy) for weight loss has been used since at least the 1950s. Recently there has been an interest in the use of audiotherapy (autohypnosis) tapes (see page 268).

The Centre Training School of Hypnotherapy and Psycho-therapy (tel: 01772 617663), The National Register of Hypnotherapists and Psychotherapists (tel: 01282 699378) and The National School of Hypnosis and Psychotherapy (send an SAE to N-SHAP, 28 Finsbury Park Road, London N4 2JX) all offer a referral service by phone or by post, and will supply you free of charge with a list of hypnotherapists in your area who have been trained, adhere to a code of ethics and carry appropriate insurance. You can also contact the Institute for Complementary Medicine (PO Box 194, London, SE16 IQ2). A number of different kinds of training are offered in hypnotherapy, and it is important to secure the services of someone whose training is recommended by the Institute for Complementary Medicine.

The cost can vary quite substantially. Some hypnotherapists would make the first consultation free; others would charge perhaps £25–50. Subsequent sessions would be £25–50 a time, but these prices would vary round the country. You should expect to be charged more in London.

How does it work?
Hypnosis causes relaxation, and in a relaxed state a person is much more open to suggestion. Ideas about weight of which the client is not conscious can be explored, and it is thought that discovering what these are will make them easier for the client to resolve. Finally, suggestions about specific weight-loss practices can be hynotically planted in the client's mind such as

278

increasing exercise, planning meals ahead of time, avoiding potentially stressful situations where overeating might occur or dealing with problems instead of resorting to food as a comfort.

On your first visit, the hypnotherapist will ask you about your general health and about the history of your weight problem, the methods you have used in the past and so on. The therapist will explore the reasons behind your eating patterns and their development in order to build up a profile of your problems: are they related to traumatic incidents in childhood, general family eating patterns, a lifelong history of solving emotional problems by overeating, current relationship problems? If the therapist thinks that you could benefit from hypnotherapy, treatment will begin then or at another appointment.

The therapist will ask you to adopt a relaxed pose, in a chair or on a couch. Treatment consists in the therapist putting you in a light hypnotic trance. Then the therapist will explore the issues brought up in the discussions you have had and will seek to assist you towards a new way of dealing with your problems which doesn't involve overeating. Suggestions about ways to alter your behaviour will be implanted. Sessions usually last for about one hour.

During treatment practical solutions might well be offered, with advice about the best kind of diet to follow. It is stressed that hypnotherapy isn't magic – you can lose weight only if you eat less and exercise more. You may be taught self-hypnosis or given an audiotape to listen to at home. Unlike commercially produced tapes, these are individually produced for each client.

Your goals for attempting to lose weight will be investigated, too. Are you dieting for yourself or for others, for your appearance or your health? Are your goals realistic? What fantasies do you have about what life will be like when you are thinner? Could you cope with being thinner?

The hypnotherapist will as a matter of course investigate all the other areas of your life and try to help with any problems. Hypnotherapists stress how important it is to allay any fears clients may have about the process of hypnosis. You will be assured that the client always remains completely in control of the situation; you will not find yourself barking like a dog or eating raw onions, as some stage hypnotists persuade their audiences to do.

279

Variations

Different hypnotherapists have different approaches to the treatment of their clients, depending on their particular training, and the hypnotherapist will explain his or her ideas about how best to help you.

Exercise

An exercise plan will sometimes be given, and suggestions might be implanted about how best to set and reach some goals.

Learning new habits

The whole purpose of hypnotherapy is to help you to alter your behaviour by exploring the underlying reasons for your overeating.

Who shouldn't use it?

People with serious medical or psychiatric problems will be referred elsewhere.

Side-effects

No side-effects should be expected from treatment by a fully qualified hypnotherapist.

Additional information

You could be given help in coping with any other emotional problems you may have. Height/weight charts of the kind found in diet books are not often used.

Expected weight loss

Not all hypnotherapists would state how much weight could be lost. You might well be encouraged to decide on your own target weight.

Keeping off the pounds

Any long-term plan would depend on the kind of treatment you are receiving and on the nature of your problems.

They say

'Hypnotherapy could assist your motivation, your will-power and the clarity with which you could hold your goal of slimness in front of you. It is a strategy for life, bringing you knowledge and information.'

You say

'I went for two months and I lost 2 st (12.7 kg). It was good for the short term but too expensive for the long term.'

'After a month I hadn't lost any weight and the hypnotherapist said the treatment just wasn't for me. I tried it again later but the result was the same.'

'She wanted me to tell her what the matter was, and then she talked to me about what I should and shouldn't eat. She never mentioned the word "diet" and she told me to throw my scales away. I wasn't sure about it at first but it was very pleasant, going under − I lost a lot of weight. I don't know how much because I still don't weigh myself.'

We say

Some hypnotherapists are beginning to specialize in weight-loss management. If you feel that you could benefit from treatment of this kind, make sure that you choose a hypnotherapist who is experienced and fully trained. Hypnotherapy is not cheap, so it is doubly important to see someone who really does know what they are doing.

Hypnosis is currently being re-evaluated, both as a technique and as a treatment, by professional psychologists.

Personal support	√	Dietary advice	√
Available on the NHS	×	Less than £10 to start	×

Treatment type
Self-help therapy.

What is it?
Thin-Think is a book by Jane Walmsley, illustrated with cartoons by Gray Joliffe. It claims to have a strategy for weight loss that will help you to succeed on any diet you go on. The basic idea is that most women and many men *must* diet because, although most people aren't naturally slim, society thinks that only slim people are successful and desirable. Of course dieting is depressing, the argument goes, but you will be less miserable while you lose weight than you will be spending years hating yourself for not doing it. People are often good at dieting, but usually they put the weight back on again. To keep it off, you have to adopt a whole new set of attitudes. You have to THIN-THINK instead of FAT-THINK. Sensible eating and a change of attitude is the only way to lose weight permanently.

Jane Walmsley emphasizes that you have to suffer to lose weight. It isn't easy, and often doctors don't help. It is all very well being told by your doctor to stick to sensible foods and eat as much as you like of them, but the fact is that if you confine yourself to 1200 calories a day you are bound to feel hungry. Nor is it helpful to be told to stop worrying about dieting and simply eat normally. Jane Walmsley thinks that this is a real put-down, implying that worrying about your weight is self-indulgent and petty. The reality is that most people no longer know what eating 'normally' is.

The book is amusingly written, informative and full of examples of how FAT-THINK can be changed into THIN-THINK. It is 304 pages long, was published by Penguin in 1994 and costs £4.99.

How does it work?
Food is fattening and dieting is hell, in Jane Walmsley's view. You should face the fact that it isn't easy to diet, and take control of your life by using psychological tricks to change your mind-set from FAT-THINK to THIN-THINK. That way you

will be more likely to lose weight and keep it off in the long term.

Techniques to overcome hunger include 'grazing', or having several small meals per day, and 'spoiling your appetite' on purpose – people who are hungry eat more, so you should have a snack an hour before a meal. In addition, make all your meals as boring as possible but don't forbid yourself things – just limit yourself to two bites of that favourite creamy cake.

In this book, healthy eating means a diet low in fat but high in carbohydrate and fibre, with sugar and alcohol cut right down. However, few details are provided of how to go about this, and there are no eating plans or recipes. There is advice on feeding children, about cravings during the menstrual cycle and about staying slim while feeding a family.

Learning new habits

Charts show you how to find out whether you are a 'natural fatty' or a 'natural skinny'. Fatties, for example, always eat all the food on their plate, prefer to eat alone and salt their food before they've even tasted it. Skinnies, on the other hand, find preparing food a bore, can't eat when they are upset, and fidget all the time. Having determined which type you are, you are to modify your behaviour accordingly.

Who shouldn't use it?

Any dieter not in good physical or mental health should consult a doctor before attempting to lose weight.

Additional information

It is suggested that a healthy woman of 5 ft 4 in (1.63 m) should weigh between 7 st 6 lb (47.2 kg) and 10 st (63.5 kg), representing BMIs of 18 to 24. This is in line with current medical opinion. On the other hand, another height/weight chart for the fashionably thin woman who wants to look good in clothes indicates that a 5 ft 4 in (1.63 m) woman should weigh from 7 st 7 lb (47.7 kg) to 8 st 2 lb (51.7 kg). This represents a BMI of between 18 and 19, which is on the low side of what is medically considered healthy.

Keeping off the pounds

Many people will consider her maintenance plan stupefyingly dull, according to Jane Walmsley. Basically you eat more or less the same thing every day, a method that has enabled her to maintain a weight of 8 st (50.8 kg) for many years. As she is 5 ft 4 in (1.63 m) tall, this represents a BMI of 19.

Jane Walmsley says

'Achieving the shape you want means reprogramming your attitudes along with your eating habits.'

You say

'If I had to live on the maintenance diet for the rest of my life I'd kill myself. It's so boring.'

'I can't work out how to do this and it isn't that clear just what you are supposed to do. The endless jokes annoyed me. She tends to go for extremes. This book doesn't seem to be for ordinary fat people like me.'

We say

This book doesn't pull any punches. Losing weight, Jane Walmsley implies, is painful and distressing but then so is being fat. She is rather dour overall, though the cartoons are cheering and the book is funny in parts. There are a few points:

- The height/weight chart for the fashionably thin woman is unrealistic in suggesting a desirable target BMI of between 18 and 19. Insurance companies have found women with BMIs lower than 20 to be higher than average risks.
- Pointing out how silly many of the ideas about weight loss actually are isn't the same as showing you how to take control of your life.
- You are told that to make the successful move to THIN-THINK you must develop a sense of humour, confidence and the ability to relax. Unfortunately, there's no advice as to how to go about this. I've never heard of anyone developing a sense of humour — you've either got one or you haven't.

There is a danger here that overweight readers might end up feeling even worse about themselves.

Personal support	×	Dietary advice	√
Available on the NHS	×	Less than £10 to start	√

Food Fact File

The most frequent reason women give for putting on weight is getting married; the next is taking the contraceptive pill; followed by having children, getting older and stopping smoking. Men most frequently say they put on weight when they give up exercise or stop smoking.

It is important to ask about the qualifications of any therapist you use, and any reputable one will gladly supply evidence. Call up and ask about the therapy before you decide to go along.

All the therapies described in this chapter (except for *Thin-Think*) are expensive and none of them will provide easy answers to weight loss. Hypnotherapy and behaviour therapy won't work unless you reduce your calorie intake. Acupuncture might help you to lose weight, especially if you are asked to eat unusual combinations of foods or foods that you don't normally have, but again the crucial factor is reducing your intake of calories. It is not easy to follow general advice given in books, but *Thin-Think* might help you to identify your particular problems, which is half-way to dealing with them.

Key features of therapies

Name	Theory scientifically proven	Promotes long-term healthy eating	Specific behaviour change plan	Specific exercise plan	Weight-loss maintenance programme
Acupuncture	×	√*	×	×	√
Behaviour therapy	√	√	√	√	√
Hypnotherapy	×	√**	√	×	×
Thin-Think	×	×***	√	×	√

* If every diet is different it can't be said they are all necessarily healthy.

** Depending on the therapy.

*** Nutritionists recommend a wide variety of foods be eaten.

Chapter 14

Slimming Clubs

About 3 million people in Britain are members of a slimming club. More than 10 per cent of those trying to lose weight attend one. About 3 per cent of all the people *not* trying to slim attend them, presumably to maintain weight loss. Women outnumber men by about three to one in membership, and older people (those over 35) are more likely to attend than younger ones.

Clubs are generally held in community or church halls, or in hotels, and although most meetings are in the evening, all clubs will offer some daytime meetings. There are some non-commercial slimming clubs or groups, run by health visitors, nutritionists, dieticians or other health professionals, but the quality varies hugely and it is not possible to review them here.

Professionals tend to approve of slimming groups. Britain's leading expert on obesity, Professor John Garrow, thinks that one of the best things the government could do to combat obesity would be to set up 'affordable slimming groups, open to the public who want sound advice about dieting'.

What's the theory?

Nutritionists agree that the advice slimming clubs give about dieting is scientifically correct. Being overweight can isolate people socially, whereas in a group you can share your experiences with others and enjoy going out. Being in a group is also supposed to give people extra motivation, as they compete with each other to lose weight. It's reassuring to know that you are not alone with your problem, and because the adviser, counsellor, leader or whoever will herself (and it's usually a she) once have been fat, she will understand the difficulties of losing weight and will have plenty of experience of motivating people and advising them on the best ways to change their eating patterns.

Exercise is encouraged in some clubs. Some people may find it easier to begin by exercising with others who are concerned about their weight, rather than attending aerobics classes full of fit young things.

Does it work?
Slimming clubs can be very effective in helping people to lose weight. The clubs themselves won't give out information on success rates – it's 'commercially confidential'. However, a survey of 350 women who joined Weight Watchers, Slimmer Clubs UK or Slimming Magazine Clubs found that they lost an average of 20 lb (9.1 kg) each.

A poll of viewers of the TV programme 'That's Life!' found that slimming clubs were much more effective (dieters lost an average of about 10 lb (4.5 kg) over six weeks) than a herbal tea, a 'Grapefruit Pill', or a 'pretend' diet. (On the 'pretend' diet you were told to take a half a raw carrot before meals, and this did work for some people.) A Swedish study found that a slimming club was more effective than a very-low-calorie diet or seaweed tablets, and worked even better than their government's own recommended reducing diet!

The number of people who drop out from slimming clubs is very high (they usually say that it's because the club is too expensive or is not convenient). In general, about half the people who start a course stay for six months, though it's not known whether this is because they have failed or succeeded in losing weight.

Keeping of the pounds
In the survey of 350 women mentioned above, most said a year later that they had regained some, but not all, of the weight they had lost. A study of Weight Watchers who had reached target weight found that 15 months later 70 per cent were within 10 lb (4.5 kg) of their goal or had lost even more weight. In Norway only 15 per cent of users of a slimming club had put back all the weight they had lost after four years.

Any problems?
Slimming clubs rely on the advice of expert nutritionists, so there shouldn't be any problems as a result of attending one. If you are pregnant, have a mental or physical illness, are under 16 years of age or are very heavy, you must consult your doctor

before attending any slimming club. If you fall into any of these categories, most clubs will refuse you membership unless you have a doctor's certificate, anyway. All slimming clubs will refuse anyone who has an eating disorder, although some will accept people who have recovered from one, if they have a doctor's letter.

Very-low-fat diets, however, can be as bad for you as very-high-fat diets. Don't be tempted to cut down on the levels of fat recommended by a slimming club diet; these are carefully balanced to provide the full range of daily nutrients, and you shouldn't cut down any further in an attempt to speed weight loss.

Some years ago there were worries that a few slimming clubs (those covered in this chapter are not among them) were taking the motivation aspects of their programmes too far. They were upsetting people, putting them into 'pig-pens' if they had failed to lose weight, making them cry and humiliating them in public in an attempt to shame them into doing better. There is no evidence that such extreme practices continue today – in any case it is hard to imagine they would be effective.

Having a role model who has lost weight on the same programme can be useful in helping you to lose weight. If the person leading the class has shared your problems, you can feel more confident about any advice she or he gives, which is why slimming clubs, alone among diet-aid suppliers, insist that their counsellors have themselves experienced problems in controlling weight. Doctors, nutritionists, dieticians, psychologists, therapists and so forth rarely have personal experience of the problems of overweight people. Nevertheless, slimming club counsellors vary in approach, even in the same club; some are tougher, some more sensitive. Try before you buy.

Diet type
A reduced-calorie diet combined with a slimming club and an exercise and fitness programme.

What is it?
These clubs are part of a diet and fitness programme based on Rosemary Conley's Hip and Thigh Diet or Flat Stomach Plan (see pages 361 and 366) and an exercise session. You are given dietary advice and follow an exercise programme conducted by instructors who have been trained by Rosemary Conley and her team.

The clubs are run as franchises and began in 1993. Since then more than 100 franchises have opened, operating over 1000 classes a week, and more are scheduled to open all over Britain in 1995. Before opening a Rosemary Conley Diet and Fitness Club, all franchisees must attain the Royal Society of Arts Basic Certificate in Exercise to Music qualification.

On joining you are given a diet pack, with a book containing details of the diet, record charts and details of classes. The book sets out the diet principles, and gives nutritional information and daily requirements, advice for vegetarians and on weight-loss maintenance generally.

There are press advertisements on local club meetings, or you can call 01509 620222 for details of a class near you. It costs £6 to join and £3.50 each week to attend (these fees may vary slightly, as it is up to the franchise holder how much to charge). You will still have to pay something if you don't attend a class, unless you have contacted your instructor in advance and explained why it is impossible for you to do so.

How does it work?
The idea behind this club is that with weekly support and encouragement people can lose weight, tone up and become fitter by following a nutritious diet plan and taking part in safe and effective exercises.

Classes begin with a weighing session, where each member is weighed and personal advice given. The time taken will depend on how many members there are, but will average about half an hour or so. There is an award for the Slimmer of the Week, and for anyone else who has lost 1 st (6.3 kg) or reached their target weight. There is then a short talk from the instructor on diets and food-related topics, during which recipe cards may be handed out, and after that there is the exercise programme, which lasts for about 45 minutes.

The diet
The diet is based on Rosemary Conley's Hip and Thigh Diet. Every day you must choose one meal from each of the breakfast, lunch and dinner menus in the diet booklet. Breakfasts include cereals, fruit and cooked foods; lunches can be cold, hot or packed, or just consist of fruit; dinners include starters, main courses and desserts. Eating between meals is strongly discouraged.

Each day you are allowed ½ pint (285 ml) of skimmed milk, one alcoholic drink, and 4 fl oz (110 ml) of unsweetened fruit juice. Unlimited vegetables, including potatoes, are permitted so long as they are cooked and served without fat. Red meat is allowed only twice per week, and all high-fat foods, sugar and refined carbohydrates are to be avoided. There is a list of forbidden foods, including butter, oil, cakes, nuts, meat products and crisps.

Recipes are given for some of the meals; they are taken from two of Rosemary Conley's books. Servings are for one and are marked where suitable for vegetarians – there is no separate vegetarian diet.

Variations
Men are allowed two alcoholic drinks per day.

Exercise
The programme of activity consists of a warm-up, followed by aerobic exercise and a toning session, then a cool-down stretch session. Very overweight people are not expected to join the full exercise programme straight away. They can watch until they

291

A typical day's diet

Throughout the day	½ pt (285 ml) skimmed milk	95
	1 alcoholic drink	100
	4 fl oz (110 ml) unsweetened fruit juice	40
Breakfast	1 oz (28 g) cereal with milk from allowance	100
Lunch	Jacket Potato, with	150
	8 oz (225 g) baked beans	200
Dinner	Grapefruit segments in natural juice	40
	6 oz (170 g) skinned chicken with unlimited vegetables	400
	1 piece fresh fruit, say banana	90
	1 diet yoghurt	50
	Calories (depending on amount of vegetables)	1300
	Cost	£4.10

feel able to join in, when they will be encouraged to start with the warm-up and stretch parts of the programme before moving on to the aerobics and toning sessions.

Franchisees are given special training in, for example, the prevention of osteoporosis (brittle bones), or exercises for the very overweight, and will advise members accordingly.

Who shouldn't use it?

You should confirm with your doctor that you are in a fit condition to diet and exercise before trying to join the club. You will be given a screening form to complete, which covers such questions as your recent medical history, your current weight and whether or not you have exercised before. Depending on your answers, you will be allowed to join the club. Children under 16 are allowed to attend classes if accompanied by a parent, but not to diet.

Additional information

Rosemary Conley videos, books, clothing and equipment can be purchased through the club. There are no height/weight charts to monitor. Instead, personal weight targets are set with advice from the instructor, and no one is allowed to set themselves an unrealistic or unhealthy target. The instructor suggests attainable goals in terms of achieving a target loss of a stone or so at a time.

Rosemary Conley says

'Never before has slimming been so much fun – you've got absolutely nothing to lose but everything to gain.'

You say

'I went because it was just round the corner – I'd only tried my own diets before and I never kept the weight off. This time I've lost 2 st (12.7 kg) in eight months. I enjoy the exercise now and it's so much easier since I lost the weight. We all eat the recipes now, my husband has lost a stone as well and nobody has suffered.'

'I liked it because you weren't just wasting money getting weighed – you were getting the exercise as well. I never stuck to the recipes, just cut out fat, and I lost weight.'

We say

The Hip and Thigh Diet has proved to be one of the most successful diet plans ever devised (see page 361), and if you felt that you needed extra support to follow it or to follow Rosemary Conley's Flat Stomach Plan (see page 366), this could be the club for you. Whether you do or not, for those who want to exercise while on a diet, but in a supportive and definitely non-embarrassing atmosphere, this club would suit many tastes.

However, the programme doesn't mention any expected weight loss, there isn't a specific plan for keeping off the pounds in the long term and there isn't a plan for vegetarians.

Slimming Clubs

Less than £10 to start	✓	Exercise obligatory	✓
Free visit before joining	✓	Diet requires weighing foods	✓
Have to stay for talk	✓	Forbidden foods	✓
Asked to leave if you don't lose weight	✗	Diet requires calorie counting	✗
Suit single person	✓		

Food Fact File

A woman in Glasgow paid £200 for a block of wood she was supposed to put on top of the TV, where it would give out ions to make her thin; it didn't.

Diet type
A slimming club and reduced-calorie diet programme.

What is it?
This slimming club started in 1968, as Silhouette, and became Slimmer Clubs UK in 1989, since when thousands of people have achieved their ideal weight attending the classes.

Group support and motivation is provided at weekly meetings, and a wide variety of eating plans is detailed in a booklet which you are given. There is also a chart on which to record your weight loss. The club's new 1995 programme includes advice on learning new habits, with advisers who will explain about the psychology of dieting and of overeating.

It costs £6.50 to join and £2.95 to attend each week, though you may attend the first meeting for free and see what the club is like before committing yourself to join. Senior Citizens get special rates. You are allowed three weeks' holiday per year, but you must pay half the fee for any other meetings you miss. Having paid for one week you can attend as many more meetings that week as you like without paying again, but without being weighed.

Slimmer Clubs hold 750 classes each week all over Britain, led by 450 advisers. There are advertisements in the press, or you can call 01235 550700 for information about a class near you.

How does it work?
According to the company, this is a calorie-controlled dieting system, with no forbidden foods, which aims to help you lose weight and keep off the pounds by changing your eating habits.

At the weekly meetings everyone is weighed, and you can leave after this, although you will be very strongly encouraged to stay. The programme for the rest of the meeting was updated and revised in April 1995.

The emphasis is on group discussion, which lasts for about 45 minutes, with an adviser who will herself have successfully overcome a weight problem. Members share their problems and are encouraged to come up with useful and supportive answers. Although the adviser will provide information where required,

295

she is really there to act as a facilitator so that members can exchange experiences. She will ensure that the discussion centres on changing behaviour, whether in terms of increasing motivation to succeed or the practical aspects of altering eating habits permanently. The adviser will give you her telephone number, and you are invited to call her during the week between meetings if you have any problems.

The adviser helps you to choose which level of the diet to start on, having worked out your ideal weight using BMI height/weight charts. This is called your Gold Star weight – when you achieve it you will be awarded a gold star. The booklet you are given contains details of the diet, the rules of membership and Lifestyle cards with tips on how to diet when travelling, ideas for entertaining and for family meals, and so on. You receive one of these cards monthly.

Slimmer Clubs UK say that it is too difficult for overweight people who may well have been eating 3000 or 4000 calories per day to switch straight to a very-low-calorie diet. It makes them want to binge. They suggest that the heavier you are, the more calories you should eat at the beginning of your diet. As you lose weight, you move on to different plans and you eat fewer calories.

The diet

There are five different diet plans, which provide a low-fat, high-carbohydrate, calorie-controlled diet of between 1050 and 1600 calories per day – the Free 'n' Easy Diet. Each day you choose one item each from lists of breakfast, light meals and main meals. In addition you are allowed a certain number of 'extras', depending on which diet you are on. Extras include alcoholic drinks, sweets, biscuits, high-calorie vegetables and the like.

You have to weigh portions carefully, though much of the calorie counting has been done for you. The menu plans are sorted into sections depending on the number of calories in them and you then choose foods which add up to your daily calorie allowance. There are convenience food options, and no foods are forbidden. You can save up your extras and have a special treat or a meal out.

Lists of low-calorie vegetables are given which you can eat in unlimited quantities. Tea and coffee are also allowed in unlimited quantities, but if you have milk it must come from your daily skimmed milk allowance.

A typical day's diet for average women with 1–2 st (6.3–12.7 kg) to lose

Throughout the day	½ pt (285 ml) skimmed milk for tea, coffee	100
	½ oz (15 g) low-fat spread or 1 tsp oil	50
Breakfast	1½ oz (40 g) cereal	200
	5 oz (140 g) fruit	
Snack	Small slice of bread, with spread from allowance and 1 tsp jam	70
Light meal	Sandwich, made with 2 slices bread, 2 oz (56 g) lean ham, unlimited salad 1 diet yoghurt	300
Main meal	4 oz (110 g) chicken 6 oz (170 g) potato Vegetables 5 oz (140 g) fruit	400
Snack	1 fun-size chocolate bar	75
	Calories (approx)	1200
	Cost	£4.00

The diet includes basic recipes. Additional recipes are given on the Lifestyle cards, and in the leaflets (see below) describing diet variations, and are for one, two or four servings.

Variations

Men and teenagers should follow the plans for 1500 or 1650 calories a day.

Apart from the basic diet plans the club will also provide leaflets describing other diets: the Plateau Breaker Diet, the Little **297** and Often Diet, the Asian Alternative and a vegetarian diet. There is a Slimmer by Post plan for those who cannot or do not want to attend in person.

Exercise plan
On your fifth week you will be given a 'Step Out' card, with details of how to start taking more exercise. Although the adviser will brief you on the benefits of taking more exercise, there isn't a specific plan.

Who shouldn't use it?
No one with an eating disorder or under the age of 16 can become a member without a doctor's permission. Anyone who has or has had diabetes or high blood pressure, or who is pregnant, is advised to see a doctor before starting the diet. There are no weight restrictions.

Additional information
The height/weight charts used by Slimmer Clubs UK are BMI ones. You will be encouraged to aim for a weight representing a BMI of 23, with a range from 21 to 25, which is in accord with best medical practice.

You can buy *Slimmer* magazine for £1.75. This is published in association with Slimmer Clubs UK and contains club news and stories, with recipes and articles about slimming. You can also buy the *Slimmer Guide to Calories and Fat* calorie-counter, which costs £1.75, and you will be recommended to do so, so that you can calculate the exact value of extras not included in the Free 'n' Easy Diet plans.

Expected weight loss
Members usually lose 3–5 lb (1.4–2.3 kg) in the first week and 1½–2 lb (675–900 g) per week thereafter, according to Slimmer Clubs UK.

Keeping off the pounds
On reaching your Gold Star weight you are given the option of continuing in the club and following the maintenance eating plan, the Hold Your Gold Plan. You continue to attend the club, but with the adviser's help increase your calorie consumption

until you start to put on weight, at which point calorie consumption is reduced again. It generally takes between four and eight weeks for people's weight to stabilize. If after four weigh-ins on the Hold Your Gold Plan you are still at or around Gold Star weight, you will be made a Lifelong Member which means that you can attend classes for free. If subsequently you put on more than 3 lb (1.4 kg) you will be asked to pay the class fee again, but you don't pay a rejoining fee.

Slimmer Clubs UK say
'The easy, healthy way to slim.'

You say
'I found it easy to stick to, and I lost a stone.'

'The biggest obstacle is accepting that you're only going to lose 2 lb (950 g) a week. I'm a secret crash dieter, but I know it's better this way because I always put the weight back on before. I like the food.'

'It's very calorie-orientated – they say it's easy but you do have to measure things. I did lose weight, though.'

We say
On this diet you are encouraged to eat anything you like in moderation. There are lots of different types of diet and there should be something for everyone. The emphasis is very strong in this club on support and mutual encouragement, and its attitude is tender rather than tough.

Slimmer Clubs UK's new 1995 programme is too recent for me to have had reports of it, but psychologists believe that group discussion is an excellent way to help people to alter their way of going about things. It is often easier to understand what other people are talking about than listening to a lecture on 'behaviour modification' or reading lists of tips.

It is very sensible not to encourage people who have been eating a lot to go on a very-low-calorie diet that they will never be able to stick to, and the method of moving through diet plans and reducing calories as you lose weight also seems very reasonable.

Slimming Clubs

Less than £10 to start	√	Exercise obligatory	×
Free visit before joining	√	Diet requires weighing food	√
Have to stay for talk	×	Forbidden foods	×
Asked to leave if you don't lose weight	×	Diet requires calorie counting	√
Suit single person	√		

Food Fact File

A rapidly growing boy of 15 may need more than 4000 calories per day just to maintain weight.

Diet type
A slimming club with a reduced-calorie diet.

What is it?
These slimming clubs were established in 1971, two years after *Slimming* magazine started. A million pounds in weight is shed each year by Slimming Magazine Club members.

At the meetings, a group leader who has overcome a personal weight problem encourages discussions on all aspects of slimming and tries to help members understand the causes of overeating. Members are encouraged to help and support each other in the group. On joining the club you are given a new member's wallet containing an introductory leaflet, fully illustrated booklets describing the different diets, weight record charts and vouchers for friends which let them join the club for free. Company surveys show the typical member is a working married mother who attends the club for three months and heard of it through a friend.

There are now over 600 clubs, with approximately 30 000 people attending every week. Call 0171 225 1711 for information about a class in your area or watch for local press advertisements. It costs £5 to join and £3.80 to attend each week. You can attend your first meeting for free and pay the fee only if you decide to join. You must pay for all missed weeks and there are no free holiday periods. Instead you are encouraged to take up the 'Holiday Weight Loss Challenge'. If you can lose even half a pound (225 g) while on holiday, then on returning you need only pay a rejoining fee rather than for missed weeks (it's cheaper), and Slimming Magazine Clubs will issue you with vouchers for free classes to the value of £4.

How does it work?
The overall message is that to get slim you must eat less food. Slimming Magazine Clubs maintain that this need not mean drastic calorie reduction; many people can lose weight on 1500 calories per day.

Everyone is weighed at the beginning of each weekly meeting **301** and privately told their weight. Each member is then given advice about, say, changing to a different diet plan should that be appropriate, or overcoming any particular problems. The group leader then talks for about 20 minutes on different aspects of dieting and encourages members to discuss issues raised and share experiences. You must stay for this part of the meeting unless you have an exceptional reason not to.

Afterwards in some clubs there may be a short exercise session, but only for those who want to take part.

The diet

A new Flexi Diet was introduced in January 1995, bringing the Slimming Magazine Clubs' choice of diets to 23: all provide more than 1000 calories a day and the emphasis is on low-fat, high-carbohydrate foods.

You eat one breakfast, one light meal or packed lunch and one main meal per day from lists you are given. You must weigh all portions, though each diet is already calorie-counted for you. In addition you are allowed extra items from lists supplied (fruits, drinks, sweets, cakes and so on); your group leader will tell you how many of these you can have. There are also 'free' choices — low-calorie vegetables — to be eaten raw or cooked and served without oil or butter. You will be allowed 250 calories' worth of these if you have 1 st (6.3 kg) to lose, 500 if you have 2 st (12.7 kg) to lose and so on; the free choices are calorie-counted to make this easier. If you want a particular food that's not listed, the group leader will fill in the calorie values for you in the diet plan.

Each diet plan contains simple instructions on how to cook menu items where applicable, but there are no elaborate recipes. There aren't any forbidden foods, and you can eat convenience, take-away and ready-made meals.

You may have unlimited tea and coffee, provided that any milk comes from the daily allowance of 1 pint (570 ml) of skimmed milk.

Variations

There are Asian, Jewish, Men's, Slim for Summer, Christmas, Human, Low-Fat, Little and Often, F-Plan, Young Person's, Penance, Vegan, Social Slimmer's, Feast and Fast, 6 Week

A typical day's diet

Daily allowance	1 pt (570 ml) skimmed milk Tea and coffee, with milk from allowance	190
Extras	1 apple	60
	1 fun-size Mars bar	85
	1 glass wine	100
Breakfast	1 oz (28 g) breakfast cereal, with milk from allowance	100
	1 small banana	70
Light meal	2 fish fingers, grilled	100
	5.3 oz (150 g) baked beans	115
	1 tomato	15
	1 tbsp tomato ketchup	15
Main meal	5 oz (140 g) trimmed lamb chop, grilled	300
	6 oz (170 g) baked potato	150
	2 tbs fat-free fromage frais	15
	Unlimited low-calorie vegetables	50
	Calories (depending on amount of vegetables)	1250
	Cost	£4.00

Family Favourites, Back to Basics, Slim Track, Maxi, Chocolate Lover's and 6 Weeks Summer Diets.

The Flexi Diet is also available in braille and in Welsh.

Exercise
Some clubs offer a planned course of light exercise at the end of the weekly meeting, for those who wish to take part.

Who shouldn't do it?
Children under 16 may attend only if accompanied by a parent. No one who is an injecting diabetic or who has had an eating

disorder is permitted to join, and pregnant women will be accepted only with a doctor's written permission.

You will not be permitted to join if you have less than 7 lb (3.2 kg) to lose, and you must lose 5 lb (2.3 kg) per month to stay in the club.

Additional information
At meetings *Slimming* magazine (£1.60) and the *Slimming Magazine Guide to Calories* (£1.70) will be offered for sale.

Expected weight loss
Your group leader will set you a target weight of BMI 21–23 if you are a woman, 21–25 if a man. Members may be able to lose 7–8 lb (3.2–3.6 kg) per month, which is in line with current medical opinion.

Keeping off the pounds
Members who reach target weight become Honorary Members and are given the Target Weight Package which includes advice about staying slim. They can continue to attend the club for free unless they put back 7 lb (3.2 kg) or more, in which case they must start to pay fees again, though they won't be asked to pay a rejoining fee.

Privilege Membership is available to those who complete the Target Weight maintenance plan. This is a series of weekly diets, rising by about 200 calories per week – if your weight goes up by a pound then you stick on that level. If no further weight increase takes place, then that is your maintenance level. The fee is the same as for ordinary classes, but on completion of the course the new Privilege Member pays no further fees so long as the weight loss is maintained.

They say
'It's where you'll fit in.'

You say
'There wasn't enough information about exercise.'

'I did lose weight but I didn't like having to think about food and weigh it all the time, and think about what I was going to eat at the next meal. I felt restricted and sat and read recipe books.'

'I lost 1 st 3 lb (7.7 kg) over six months. It was effective, and because I went with friends the commitment was there. I got into a pair of size 12 jeans but then I went to America and put it all back on.'

'I liked the group leader and I got on quite well. I lost 1 st 7 lb (9.5 kg) and I'm happy.'

We say

This is a sensible and healthy plan. It has the biggest range of diets of all the clubs and the only plan for vegans that I've seen. The diet programme seems to be easy to follow, and nothing is forbidden.

Slimming Magazine Clubs steer a middle ground between firmness and sympathy. This club is not as tough as some, but those who are only interested in the social side and who don't even try to lose weight will be advised that the club doesn't want money for nothing.

Less than £10 to start	√	Exercise obligatory	×
Free visit before joining	√	Diet requires weighing food	√
Have to stay for talk	√	Forbidden foods	×
Asked to leave if you don't lose weight	√	Diet requires calorie counting	×
Suit single person	√		

Diet type
A slimming club and reduced-calorie diet programme.

What is it?
Slimming World is a slimming club started in 1969 by Margaret Miles-Bramwell, who had had weight problems all her life, and she still runs the business. To date it has helped 20 million people lose 50 million pounds in weight.

The club works on the basis of weekly meetings organized by a consultant. New members are issued with a booklet which contains two eating plans, food lists, facts about nutrition, advice on dieting from a clinical psychologist and charts on which to record progress.

Slimming World's consultants hold approximately 3000 classes per week nationwide, attended by more than 300 000 people. Call 01773 521111 for information about classes in your area or watch for adverts in the local press.

It costs £6.95 to join a Slimming World class and £2.95 per week thereafter, though you may sit through the first session for free and see how you like it before deciding to join. There is a money-back guarantee, payable within the first four weeks if you haven't lost any weight at all.

You pay for Slimming World classes whether you attend or not. You are allowed to miss four weeks in any one year before having to pay all back fees or rejoin. Shift workers do not have to pay for classes they cannot attend because of their rotas, if the consultant is notified in advance.

How does it work?
The message in this club is that overweight people suffer from guilt, self-criticism and poor self-esteem as well as excess weight. A twofold approach is necessary to help them slim: an eating plan with group support, and advice from a trained consultant who has or has had personal weight problems.

At the beginning of the weekly meeting everyone is weighed, their progress is briefly discussed and, privately, they are told their weight. It usually takes about half an hour to weigh everyone, depending on how many are in the class.

It is not compulsory to stay after the weigh-in, but you are encouraged to do so. Next there is half an hour or so of IMAGE therapy (Individual Motivation and Group Experience) – designed by Slimming World, this is a group support system to improve self-esteem, raise self-awareness and help modify behaviour.

The consultant makes sure that everyone receives help with problems, is praised for achievements and is encouraged to plan for the coming week. Specific advice on ways to help members avoid breaking their diets – staying out of the kitchen as much as possible, coping with social occasions – are covered in this last part of the IMAGE therapy.

'Team Fun Tech' involves group members in humorous discussions designed to promote friendly competition. Members will be divided into teams and will compete with other teams to see which one has lost the most weight, attended most frequently and so on, depending on the consultant's preferences.

The consultant will contact individual members between meetings, if she or he feels that a person needs extra support. Members are asked to make lists of their 'Lifelines' – people to call when they feel tempted to stray from their diet, and they are also encouraged to contact other members or to call their consultant if they feel the need.

The diet

This comes in the form of the Sin-a-Day eating plan, which is divided into the Original and the Green plans. The Original plan is for meat-eaters; the Green plan is for vegetarians or for those who want to reduce the amount of meat they eat. Both diets are high in fibre and low in fat, but the Green plan is higher in carbohydrate than the Original and lower in protein. You do not have to count calories, but certain things must be weighed.

Both plans divide food into three categories. First, there are Free Foods – all kinds of meat, fruit and vegetables. These must have all visible fat removed and be cooked without the addition of any fat; you can eat unlimited quantities of them. Second, there is an Extra allowance of dairy foods, of which you may have one a day. Third, there is a '2 for You' section featuring such items as breads, crackers and high-calorie fruits – you may have two of these per day. Food choices are flagged if they are good for quick weight loss and for their fibre content.

In addition, you can have between 5 and 15 Sins per day. These are precise amounts (shown in lists) of thousands of high-calorie foods: meat, sweets, cereals, desserts, yoghurts, drinks, fish, pizza, sauces, snacks and so on. The number of Sins you may have each day depends on your general level of activity, how much weight you have to lose and your sex. Most women will be advised to have 10 Sins and most men 15 Sins per day.

No recipes are given in the booklet. It is up to you how you prepare your meals.

A typical day's diet from the Original Sin-a-Day Plan

Breakfast	*Grilled lean bacon*	*160*
	1 fried egg	*100*
	Grilled tomatoes	*30*
	Poached mushrooms	*20*
Snack	*1 apple*	*60*
Lunch	*Sandwich, made with 2 slices of Vitbe Hi-Bran bread, corned beef, tomatoes and a mixed salad*	*280*
Snack	*1 small banana*	*70*
Evening meal	*Roast lamb*	*200*
	Carrots	*30*
	Green beans	*30*
	Cauliflower	*30*
Snack	*1 treat-sized Wispa*	*125*
Snack	*1 packet of Quavers*	*100*
	Calories (approx)	1200
	Cost	£4.00

Variations

Slimming World run five men-only classes and 21 of their consultants are male; they take both mixed and men-only classes. There is a postal course for those who are unable to attend meetings.

The Countdown Plan is available for those who want to make an extra commitment to losing weight – 14 lb (6.3 kg) in five weeks or 28 lb (12.7 kg) in ten weeks. You pay for the plan in advance.

Who shouldn't use it?

No one who has medical problems, is pregnant or under the age of 16 may join Slimming World unless they have written permission from a doctor.

Additional information

Height/weight charts can be used to help you find your target weight, called your Personal Achievement Target (PAT), but you are strongly encouraged to set your own target. You are allowed to change it if you like, or to put off setting it until you feel up to it. Slimming World's charts indicate that a 5 ft 4 in (1.63 m) person's health is not in jeopardy between a weight of about 7 st 10 lb (49 kg) and 10 st 8 lb (67.2 kg), corresponding to a BMI of between 19 and 25. This is in line with current medical opinion. You aren't allowed to set yourself a PAT below a BMI of about 19, which is also exactly as would be recommended. Expected weight loss isn't mentioned.

Keeping off the pounds

Once you have reached your PAT you can attend Slimming World free for the rest of your life, although there isn't a specific weight-maintenance plan. The consultant will encourage those who have met their PATs gradually to increase the number of Sins they are allowed per day, while checking for weight gain. If their weight remains stable, they can continue to introduce more Sins. As soon as their weight increases, they must cut back again.

They say

'You will never feel hungry when dieting again.'

You say

'There was too much counting up for me – I couldn't be bothered.'

'It is a good diet and a good approach – it's not cut out this and cut out that. The attitude is "there's nothing you can't eat".'

'I've never been really fat but I can look six months' pregnant in a straight skirt. Slimming World has been the best club I've tried because there is no good-food and bad-food stuff, it's good diets and bad diets.'

We say

This is an excellent plan. Because it allows you to eat absolutely everything, it will help to prevent the, 'I'm so deprived I've got to have a cream cake' response that so often leads to disaster. You will need to be careful, though. For example, on this plan you are allowed as much grilled chicken as you want whereas fruits are restricted, so you could inadvertently put too much protein in your diet.

In line with their emphasis on building self-esteem, Slimming World take a gentle, easy-going approach. Part of their philosophy is that successful slimming is strongly linked with the subconscious mind (though some might argue that there isn't much evidence either for this, or for the subconscious mind). There is evidence, though, that setting targets, meeting goals and being rewarded does help some people to stick to their diet. These aspects are strongly emphasized in this slimming club, together with friendly competition between dieters.

Less than £10 to start	√	Exercise obligatory	×
Free visit before joining	√	Diet requires weighing food	√
Have to stay for talk	×	Forbidden foods	×
Asked to leave if you don't lose weight	×	Diet requires calorie counting	×
Suit single person	√		

Diet type
A slimming club and reduced-calorie diet programme.

What is it?
Weight Management, which is called Scottish Slimmers in Scotland, is a weekly slimming club where class managers teach the group about food and how to adopt a new way of eating which is to be followed for life.

Each class manager has herself lost weight successfully. New members are not permitted to join until they have sat through a class. After completing a medical questionnaire, they will be told about the club's rules and the principles of the club's Eating Plan.

The club started in 1980, and now a club member reaches Target Weight every 82 minutes. There are 350 classes per week in Scotland and 200 classes per week in England, mainly in the North, but the company is expanding. Call Freephone 0800 36 26 36 for information.

It costs £7 to join and £3.75 per week. You must pay for weeks you miss, but if you miss more than two weeks you can pay a rejoin fee rather than all your back fees.

How does it work?
This club allows you a huge range of food, which means that the whole family can follow the Eating Plan, and you can eat out or entertain. In this way, the argument goes, you won't feel isolated, starved or deprived – the main reasons why other diets don't work.

Those who have reached target weight are weighed at the start of each weekly meeting and, if they wish, may leave at this point. Everyone else must stay. There is then a short session of about 20–25 minutes, during which the class manager will talk to members about a different aspect of dieting each week. Some of this will be purely informative, but most of it will concentrate on the pitfalls of slimming and how to avoid them. Then everyone is weighed and their progress noted, targets are set and **311** personal advice is given, with the emphasis on increasing motivation and working towards change.

Badges and a choice of Eating Plan card are awarded for every 7 lb (3.2 kg) lost.

The diet

Essentially, this is a low-fat, low-sugar, high-fibre diet; you don't have to count calories and there are no forbidden foods.

The basic Eating Plan menus are described on four cards which you are given on joining (there is a vegetarian version). This set is divided into four different categories of foods: breakfasts and suppers, quick meals, main meals and snacks. There are a further 14 sets of recipe cards to collect, covering topics such as fast food, exotic Eastern cuisine and soups and starters. A very wide variety of convenience and fresh foods is suggested, including Pop Tarts, Twiglets and tofu, for example, and the recipes are for one or two servings. Recipes are marked as suitable for entertaining, microwaving, packing or freezing.

Members are given a simple guide to using the plans. Women are allowed to choose one breakfast or supper dish, one quick meal, one main meal and four snacks per day, plus an allowance of skimmed milk for use in tea or coffee. Quantities are spelled out – for example, eggs must be size 3. Snacks include sweets, alcoholic drinks, starters and desserts. You can save up your snacks for special occasions if you want, and you are permitted unlimited low-calorie vegetables if they are served raw or cooked without any fat.

Variations

A postal course is being planned, and short courses can be arranged for companies or rural communities.

Exercise

The club emphasizes that you don't have to exercise to lose weight. Neither do you have to don a leotard and head for the gym: simple increases in activity – going for walks, climbing stairs instead of taking lifts – will help to speed weight loss, if you feel that you can manage it.

A typical day's diet

Throughout the day	½ pt (285 ml) skimmed milk	95
Breakfast	1 oz (28 g) cereal with 5 fl oz (140 ml) skimmed milk	150
Snack	1 apple	60
	1 orange	60
Lunch	Golden soup, made with ½ medium potato, onion, carrot and turnip, and ½ small tin of tomatoes	75
	5–6 oz (140–170 g) baked potato	100
	Small tin tuna	70
	Salad	20
Main meal	5 oz (140 g) lean steak, grilled	250
	Unlimited vegetables	50
	Tropical fruit salad, made with strawberries, melon and 1 kiwi fruit	75
	1 glass wine	100
	Calories (approx)	1100
	Cost	£4.00

Who shouldn't use it?

No one with an eating disorder can join this club. There are no age or weight restrictions, but children under 15 would only be accepted after the child's parent had consulted with the class manager.

Additional information

The class manager helps you to decide your target weight. The Metropolitan Life Insurance Company's tables are used to work this out, but the club doesn't use the lower extreme of the range given on that chart. The target weight of a 5 ft 4 in (1.63 m) woman is about 9 st 5 lb (59.5 kg), corresponding to a BMI of about 22, which is in line with current medical opinion.

Expected weight loss
You are expected to lose between 1½ and 2 lb (675–900 g) per week, or 6–8 lb (2.7–3.6 kg) per month, although you may lose more in the first week: all in accord with current medical opinion.

Keeping off the pounds
The club's weight-maintenance programme has recently been altered. Now, when you meet your target weight, you can become either a Target or Diamond Member. Target Members can attend meetings as frequently or infrequently as they like, so long as they remain no more than 7 lb (3.2 kg) above their target weight. If they go above this, they must pay to rejoin the club and attend classes as before.

To become a Diamond Member, you pay an annual fee of £12 and receive a lapel pin and membership card. This entitles you to attend as many meetings as you like for free. If you go more than 7 lb (3.2 kg) above your target weight you must pay to attend classes again, but you won't have to pay a rejoining fee. Diamond Members get a free quarterly newsletter with features of interest, special offers and so on. The Diamond membership card entitles you to discounts on a wide range of services, including beauty treatments, hotel stays and sports equipment.

They say
'Everyone who follows our superb Eating Plan loses weight successfully.'

You say
'I lost 1 st 7 lb (9.5 kg) and it really worked. I liked our class manager – she was quite abrasive, which doesn't suit everyone if you're paying for it.'

'I lost a stone in a month – I didn't like the teacher, she shouted at me if I put on a pound after that. There's no chat, no blather, it was like being in a classroom.'

'The class manager went to a lot of trouble, she was very professional. The food was easy to stick to. I never ate all the chocolate and treats you were allowed, but I still lost weight without being hungry.'

We say

This club's Eating Plan is well thought out and very varied. Their claims are justified: you could easily feed a family on this kind of food, go out for an evening or entertain.

The club does insist that you stay for the part of the meeting devoted to increasing motivation and changing your eating patterns, because they consider this essential to successful weight loss. Their class managers have a reputation for being among the toughest of slimming club leaders. If you have a genuine reason for backsliding they will be very sympathetic, but pathetic excuses will not be tolerated and you'll quickly be told to pull your socks up.

The weight-loss maintenance plan is too new for me to have had any dieters' verdicts. However, it's a well-known fact that people like to get their money's worth when forking out hard-earned cash, and this plan does have financial benefits if you don't put on weight.

Less than £10 to start	✗	Exercise obligatory	✗
Free visit before joining	√	Diet requires weighing food	√
Have to stay for talk	√	Forbidden foods	✗
Asked to leave if you don't lose weight	✗	Diet requires calorie counting	✗
Suit single person	√		

Weight Watchers

Diet type
A slimming club and a reduced-calorie diet programme.

What is it?
Bernice Weston, a lawyer who had had weight problems, set up Weight Watchers in Britain in 1967, six years after the organization was founded by Jean Nidetch in the USA. The company has been owned by H. J. Heinz Company Ltd since 1976. Some 150 000 people attend Weight Watchers classes each week in Britain, and it has been estimated that 37 million people have passed through their doors worldwide.

Weight Watchers' new programme, Slim & Trim, was launched in January 1995. It consists of a menu plan based around meal cards and food lists for different stages of a diet, a self-management plan to help you control your eating by understanding more about situations in which you are likely to overeat, an exercise plan and group support to help you maintain weight loss.

In Britain, a network of group leaders organizes about 3700 Weight Watchers meetings each week. Local classes are advertised in the press, or you can call 01628 777077 for information about a class near you. It costs £9 to join a Weight Watchers class and £3.95 per week thereafter. Those over 60 and young people aged 10–16 pay a reduced rate of £2.95 per week. You can attend your first meeting for free before deciding whether you want to join, at which point you will be asked to complete a short medical questionnaire. You are allowed four holiday weeks per year, if you inform your group leader in advance, but otherwise you must pay for missed weeks unless you have a very good reason for failing to attend.

On joining, new members receive a small ring-binder containing an introduction to the club and the diet, your group leader's telephone number and stickers you apply to each day of the week of the preliminary four-week diet, if you stick to the diet for that day. You will be given cards and booklets to add to the ring-binder as you go through the programme.

How does it work?

Weight Watchers believe that it is difficult for people to change their bad eating habits and maintain weight loss permanently. People need to understand the 'triggers' that may make them eat the wrong kinds of foods, and avoid such circumstances.

At the weekly meeting everyone is first weighed and told their weight privately, by the group leader, who will herself have overcome a weight problem. This takes about 30 minutes, and members are then given additional cards to add to their diet programme, depending on the stage they are at. Members can leave at this point if they wish.

The majority of members stay on for another half hour or so, during which the group leader may talk about an aspect of dieting, demonstrate recipes or start a general discussion.

The diet

Slim & Trim is a low-fat, high-carbohydrate, low-cholesterol eating plan. Each day you are allowed one breakfast, one light meal and one main meal, plus 1 pt (570 ml) of skimmed milk, or 2 oz (56 g) of dried milk, or ½ pint (285 ml) of natural yoghurt, or 1 pt (570 ml) of buttermilk. For the first week the meals from which you can choose are detailed on meal cards. On subsequent weeks you are also given meal cards, but you can start to make up your own menus from the second week if you wish.

Each week you are given the next week's diet, and you do this for four weeks, after which you stick to the guidelines of the Slim & Trim diet until you reach your target weight. There are also planners to help you make sure that you don't exceed weekly allowances of eggs (7), offal (7 oz, 200 g) or meat and cheese (14 oz, 450 g).

Slim & Trim uses a system of Selections, which are lists of foods in six different categories, all of similar nutrient content. If you decide to make up your own meals after the first week of the diet, then you use these Selection lists to plan them. You may swap Selections from a range of equivalents: for example, swaps listed for chicken with jacket potato and vegetable include swapping the chicken for beef, pork or lamb and swapping the potato for bread, pasta or rice. You don't have to count calories but you do have to weigh things accurately.

Every member's diet will vary depending on their age, sex and how much weight they have to lose. You will be allocated particular amounts of food in particular categories, all expressed as a number of Selections per day. You may also be allowed a number of optional extra calories per week from a list of items including alcohol, cakes, biscuits, sweets, snacks, desserts and sauces.

Recipes, which you are given every week, come on cards for your ring-binder. These are marked as economy, quickly prepared, family, salad, packed, and suitable for entertaining; recipes suitable for vegetarians are indicated. All recipes are for one person. Some Weight Watchers From Heinz products are included in the menus for meals (see page 205), but you don't have to have these.

You are encouraged to drink plenty of fluid every day.

A typical day's diet

Throughout the day	2 Milk	1 pt (570 ml) skimmed milk	200
Breakfast	1 Fruit	½ medium grapefruit	20
	1 Protein	1 boiled egg	75
	1 Carbohydrate	1 thin slice toast	50
Lunch	1 Protein	1 oz (28 g) ham	50
	1 Carbohydrate	4 oz (110 g) baked potato	100
	1 Fat	1 tsp margarine	25
	1 Vegetable	Salad vegetables	20
	1 Fruit	4 oz (110 g) apple	40
Dinner	2 Protein	Bean stir-fry, made with 6 oz (170 g) beans	150
	1 Fat	1 tsp oil	40
	2 Vegetables	vegetables	60
	2 Carbohydrate	6 oz (170 g) cooked rice	200
	1 Fruit	4 fl oz fruit juice	40
	Calories (approx; not including optional calories)		1100
	Cost		£4.13

Exercise

The exercise plan consists of cards which you are given on Weeks 2 and 7 of the programme. These detail three types of exercise – Fat Burners, Lean Builders and Stretches, designed to burn extra calories, improve muscle tone and increase flexibility. Later there are charts showing the benefits of various forms of exercise.

If they wish, members can work out with the 'Mr Motivator' Weight Watchers video.

Learning new habits

This aspect is boosted with an audiotape you are given. You are to play the tape when you feel that you need a little extra help. The first side includes all sorts of tips to prevent overeating: what to do if you feel hungry although you know you aren't; how to avoid temptation at the shops; ordering food when eating out; dealing with negative emotions; taking more exercise without doing anything strenuous, and so on. There's a section at the end especially for people who know they binge.

The second side of the tape gives advice on using the meal cards and food lists to fit in with your lifestyle, and on using the Selection system in general.

Variations

A Weight Watchers By Mail scheme is available for those who can't or don't want to attend meetings; call 091 296 2200 for details. The programme is the same as the Slim & Trim.

Pregnant women (with their doctor's approval) can follow a different food plan, and men and teenagers are given higher allocations of Exchanges.

Who shouldn't use it?

You must be 10 lb (4.5 kg) over the lowest healthy weight for your size (about BMI 19) before being allowed to join this club, and you must want to lose at least 7 lb (3.2 kg) or more. If your weight falls below the acceptable weight range your membership will be suspended. No one with an eating disorder is accepted.

Weight Watchers will not accept children under 10. Those aged 10–16 must have written permission from a doctor before joining, and they must attend with a parent to confirm parental agreement. Anyone with a history of medical problems, who is pregnant or who is currently under a doctor's care must have their doctor's written approval before using the diet.

Additional information

As Weight Watchers is owned by Heinz, members may receive special offers for their products, although there is no pressure to buy. You can buy the *The Weight Watchers Complete Diet Book* at a reduced rate (see page 185), as well as other cookery books, scales and measuring spoons. There is also *Weight Watchers* magazine (£1.35) and exercise videos (£9.99) made specially for Weight Watchers, featuring 'Mr Motivator' from GMTV.

There are special plans for pregnant women and nursing mothers, if they have their doctor's permission, and Weight Watchers offer advice on diet after giving up smoking and for anyone who starts hormone replacement therapy.

Expected weight loss

Weight Watchers expect a higher weight loss, perhaps 3–6 lb (1.4–2.7 kg), in the first two weeks of the programme after which the typical weekly loss would be 1–2 lb (450–900 kg). Your group leader would be concerned if you consistently lost weight faster than this, and having asked you to keep a food diary would go through with you exactly what you had eaten to ensure that you understood the importance of eating enough.

Weight Watchers' height/weight charts show the healthy weight range for a 5 ft 4 in (1.63 m) woman aged 26–45 to be 8 st 2 lb to 9 st 8 lb (51.7 to 60.8 kg), corresponding to a BMI of between 20 and 23, which is fully in line with current medical opinion.

To begin with you choose a temporary goal weight and later, in discussion with the group leader, you decide on a permanent goal weight within the bounds of the chart. You are not allowed to choose a goal weight which is less than 3 lb (1.4 kg) above the bottom of the scale. You can set your own personal target weight; this must be above the highest level in the Weight Watchers' chart and it must be at least 7 lb (3.2 kg) less than you currently weigh. It is called your Personal Target Weight.

Keeping off the pounds

Weight Watchers have a maintenance plan, Staying Slim, which you can follow after reaching your goal weight. The programme costs £19.75 and runs for at least five weeks and possibly longer, depending on how long it takes for your weight to stabilize. Your group leader will give you special booklets, help and advice at this time. Essentially, the programme involves gradually increasing or decreasing the number of Selections from the diet plan until you find that your weight is stable to within 2 lb (900 g) either way. Charts show you how to monitor the changes in weight.

On purchasing Staying Slim, you become a Gold Member. You are entitled to attend Weight Watchers free for the rest of your life if you remain within 5 lb (2.3 kg) of your weight at the end of the Staying Slim programme and attend one meeting a month to be weighed; even if you put on more than this, you don't have to pay to rejoin the club.

Alternatively, on reaching your Personal Target Weight you can become a Silver Member, and you are given a card. A Silver Member pays only for meetings he or she attends. If the Silver Member's weight goes more than 5 lb (2.3 kg) *below* their Personal Target Weight, on three successive weigh-ins, or if he or she fails to attend for more than three months, the membership is revoked. A Silver Member can become a Gold Member by setting a new goal weight and then reaching it and purchasing the Staying Slim plan.

They say

'You needn't be hungry . . . the safest and most successful weight-loss programme in the world.'

You say

'I lost over a stone. I really liked it and the group leader was nice. She would whisper "try better next time" if I put on weight.'

'I was seriously concerned that if I got any fatter I'd never be slim again. Weight Watchers worked for me, and I'm very pleased, but I didn't like the way they went on and on about being fat as if it was a crime. Still, I am determined never ever to put on weight in the future. It's not worth it when it is so hard to take off.'

'I couldn't follow the exchange ideas. The group leader kept telling me I had to drink the milk but I couldn't use it up.'

We say
Weight Watchers is the market leader, but with their tie-in to Heinz I was concerned that members might find they were steered towards Heinz products. However, nothing I've discovered suggests that this is so: although new Weight Watchers products are mentioned, no one is under pressure to buy. Otherwise, this programme is based on healthy eating, there is plenty of variety and you can eat convenience foods. Weight Watchers have been criticized in the past because their diets were thought too complicated, but the 1995 revision has made the Selection swap system much easier to understand.

Because they have been around so long, Weight Watchers seem to feel that they have a reputation to defend. In terms of strictness, they are on the firm side rather than the soft. But this extends to staff as well – group leaders who can't keep their weight within set limits will lose their job! The exercise plan is good, and the advice on learning new and healthy habits is in line with best practice.

Less than £10 to start	✕	Exercise obligatory	✕
Free visit before joining	✓	Diet requires weighing food	✓
Have to stay for talk	✕	Forbidden foods	✕
Asked to leave if you don't lose weight	✕	Diet requires calorie counting	✕
Suit single person	✓		

Slimming clubs are great if you are the gregarious sort who likes company, and there's no doubt that people get on better when they go with friends. You can go along on your own, of course, and you don't have to stay for the talk at all the clubs. At some you can just be weighed and go home again.

However, it is important that you don't get upset at the prospect of being weighed and starve yourself for the whole day beforehand, as some people do (and they're usually the ones who go off to the pub afterwards). Some clubs encourage you to save your treats and go out with other members for a meal after the meeting; others strongly discourage this kind of behaviour.

Clubs vary in attitude, with some being much 'tougher' than

Key features of slimming clubs

Name	Scientifically credible	Promotes long-term healthy eating	Suggests new habits	Exercise plan	Weight-loss maintenance plan
Rosemary Conley Diet and Fitness Clubs	✓	✓	✗	✓	✗
Slimmer Clubs UK	✓	✓	✓	✗	✓
Slimming Magazine Clubs	✓	✓	✓	✓*	✓
Slimming World	✓	✓	✓	✗	✗
Weight Management/ Scottish Slimmers	✓	✓	✓	✗	✓
Weight Watchers	✓	✓	✓	✓	✓

* In some.

others. It is up to you whether you feel you need a tough or tender approach. Even in the same organization there are differences between leaders. Some shout, some don't. Some people swear by a tough group leader who keeps you in line and brooks no argument; others find being lectured at very annoying. It's a personal thing, and if you like the idea of a slimming plan but not the idea of trailing out with a lot of other tubby people to a church hall every week, you can always take up one of the postal plans.

The menu ideas for all the clubs are well thought out and well-balanced nutritionally. There may be an emphasis on buying convenience foods, but there are usually plenty of alternatives. How well your family fit in to the diet is something to bear in mind before selecting your club.

Choosing a club comes down to convenience, atmosphere, style of diet and the amount of exercise you want. Remember that with most clubs you can attend the first session for free to see whether it is the right place for you.

Food Fact File

The National Food Survey reported in 1994 that 35 per cent of all food eaten at home is convenience foods.

Chapter 15

Health Farms

Diet type
A combination of reduced-calorie diet, exercise and therapy.

What are they?
Health farms developed out of the eighteenth-century habit among the rich of 'taking the waters' at places famous for mineral springs, in the belief that drinking or bathing in these special waters would cure them of bodily and mental ills. Today, health farms are usually well-appointed large houses set in rolling countryside. Your room will have tasteful furnishings, an *en suite* bathroom, mini-bar, safe, satellite TV, a direct-dial telephone and, if you pay for them, optional extras such as a sitting room, a waterbed, private sauna and jacuzzi. The atmosphere is relaxed. You can hang about all day in a tracksuit or dressing gown, though you must dress for dinner. Some smaller health farms specialize in weight loss for women; the accommodation is less spacious but you get more individual attention.

You can choose how long you would like to stay in a health farm, depending on your finances. Some offer one day stays, or you can stay as long as your money lasts. In Britain the cost varies. You could pay upwards of £80 per night for a shared standard room, but there are sometimes special offers. There is usually no extra charge for using the gym, swimming pools, tennis courts, etc. Treatments vary in price from about £5 to £40 each – budget for £20 as an average – though some health farms include treatment costs in the overall price. Health farms overseas can cost upwards of £1000 per week, and of course there's the air fare as well.

Health farms in Britain are advertised in magazines and newspapers. There is a central reservations and enquiry service which also offers free advice: call Healthy Venues on 01203 690300. For the incredibly expensive and luxurious health farms in the United States, South America and Switzerland you should consult a travel agent.

What's the theory?
The theory is that if you are taken out of your normal stressed environment into one where all your needs are catered for, you will be able to relax into a healthy routine which promotes fitness.

How do they work?
On arrival you will be given a health check, probably by a nurse. If you request it, she may also be able to check your level of fitness or metabolic rate and measure your cholesterol level. You will also be weighed if you are staying for longer than a few days. Your needs will be identified, and you will be given a personal programme of supervised activities, treatments and periods of relaxation. Most of these will last for about half an hour to an hour, running from 8 a.m. to 5 p.m. or so in the afternoon. Consultants will be on hand to advise you on nutrition, beauty and fitness.

The diet
The food during your stay will be prepared by chefs for maximum nutrition and minimum calorie content. Vegetarian meals are always available. Some health farms serve meals on a buffet basis where the items are colour-coded or otherwise marked to designate low-calorie foods. Others operate on the traditional 'two-room' model, where those who want to lose weight and those who don't are placed in separate dining-rooms with separate menus.

Additional information
Whether you want to throw yourself into activities all day or simply laze around at a health farm is entirely up to you. Most of them, however, do offer a huge range of treatments, sports and diversions:

- You can generally play most kinds of sports, use a variety of fitness machines in a gymnasium, take aerobics classes, have

hydrotherapy, use steam rooms, saunas, toning tables and jacuzzis.
- Beauty treatments will include hair styling, manicure, pedicure, tanning, ear-piercing, upper lip bleaching and leg waxing.
- Therapies may include aromatherapy, reflexology and flotation therapy.
- Body treatments on offer will include blitz jets, mud baths, seaweed wraps, salt scrubs, bust firming treatments, anti-cellulite treatments and faradic (electrical) stimulation.
- Some foreign clinics may offer injections of cells from animal foetuses supposed to slow down the ageing process.
- During the day you will be offered a choice of all sorts of activities from creative art and flower arranging, to yoga.
- In the evenings there may be lectures on interesting topics, cookery demonstrations, a course of beauty tips and so on.

Who shouldn't use them?
Children under 16 years of age are not usually permitted to attend health farms. You won't be able to take your pets, but you may be able to board them in a local kennels.

Expected weight loss
Weight loss is not guaranteed.

Maintaining weight loss
You will be given advice if you ask for it.

They say
Nothing very specific about losing weight, usually – more along the lines of gracious living, toning your body and revitalizing your life.

You say
'I lost more £££s than lbs.'

'The one I go to is excellent. I only go for three days at a time; it's all I can afford, but I don't expect to lose much weight in that time. The food is delicious, though the portions are small. They discuss your eating with you. You're told how many calories you can have and then you choose what you like from the menus.'

We say

Health farms are only a dream for most of us, I'm afraid. You can't really afford to lose weight at a health farm unless you are seriously rich, though by all means go for a relaxing, away-from-it-all weekend. Most of the extra treatments on offer have not been shown to induce permanent weight loss, but if you stuck to the diet most health farms prescribe then in the long term you would lose weight.

The old image of health farms as virtual prisons, where the inmates kept trying to break out and run to the shops for a bar of chocolate, is long gone. If you wanted to cheat you could at most of the establishments, although at these prices you would be daft to do so. Some health farms are much stricter than others, so if you really want to lose weight it makes sense to choose one that suits your style as well as your purse. With the publicity given to them by celebrity slimmers such as Oprah Winfrey, health farms can probably expect to do even better in the future. They are a multi-million pound business worldwide.

Chapter 16

Spot Reduction, Body Shaping and Exercise

Spot reduction, which is sometimes known as body shaping, means losing fat from one part of your body but not from others. Methods claiming to achieve this include the use of special diets, the surgical removal of fat, electrical stimulation and increased exercise.

An early form of spot reduction for the stomach used electrical stimulation and was called the 'obesity belt'; it made its appearance in 1892. By 1900 there were special chairs you could sit in while your muscles were passively exercised by 'galvanic' or continuous currents. (This treatment is still available at some health farms and spas, though nowadays it is described as an aid to muscle toning, because there's no scientific evidence it can aid weight loss). Machines using a different form of electricity to stimulate the muscles can be bought for home use or tried in beauty salons.

Pressure and sweating have been used as methods of redistributing subcutaneous water and inducing apparent weight loss since the fourteenth century, when poor Princess Isabeau of Bavaria shut herself in her special chamber, applied cups to herself and stoked up the fire in an attempt to reduce her stoutness; not an effective method, apparently, since she kept it up for years.

I haven't included here any methods of achieving 'inch loss' – understood by dieters, but not by the manufacturers of toning tables, thigh creams, seaweed wraps and so on, to imply weight loss – unless it's made clear that they can only work when combined with a reduced-calorie diet.

Exercise has a long history as a method of weight control. The Greek philosopher Socrates made a point of dancing regularly every morning to stay slim. The different theories about how spot-reduction can be brought about are dealt with under the specific diets.

Does it work?

Doctors are adamant that you cannot diet to reduce fat deposits at specific sites on the body. When people diet they tend to lose fat from all over the body, but there are different amounts of fat deposited in different areas. You are most likely to notice fat loss first from the waist, then from the face, then from the top of the back, then from the hips and thighs, and then from the bust or chest.

This is a generalization, and you could be the person who will appear to lose fat first from the bust or chest and last of all from the hips, not a welcome prospect for most women. How you lose the fat is determined by your genes. It is easier to lose weight from the stomach area than from the hips and thighs, which may be why men are said to be 'better' than women at losing weight. There is some evidence that women, after the menopause, find it easier to lose weight from the hips, and thighs than do younger women, which would tie in with what is known about the function of fat deposits in women of reproductive age.

There's no evidence that a low-fat or indeed any other kind of diet will change the shape of one part of your body without altering the rest of it. Women, apparently, lose as much weight on low-calorie as on low-fat diets, but they find it easier to stick to the low-calorie diets. And although specific exercise can build up muscle in particular areas, you can't remove fat from one site using exercise.

Although some years ago it was thought that electrical stimulation could reduce fat deposits at specific sites on the body, women on whom the theory was tested went on a diet at the same time, and so the effects were not clear-cut. The US Food and Drug Administration don't believe that electrical muscle stimulators are effective in promoting weight loss and body toning, and think they could be dangerous and cause electric shock and burns.

You can, however, lose weight by taking more exercise. Walking is considered one of the best forms of exercise, but unfortunately it's a slow process unless you diet as well. Exercising while dieting seems to reduce by half the amount of lean body tissue that is lost, compared with dieting alone, which means that you end up with a leaner and more toned body if you exercise and diet at the same time. Unfairly, there's also evidence that it's easier for men to lose fat through exercise than for women to do so; women tend to 'defend' their fat deposits more than men.

How easy it is to stick to the diets in the books outlined in this chapter is a matter of personal inclination. Most of the books contain testimonials from readers saying that they found the diet or method easy to stick to, but we'll never know how many other readers didn't find things so easy to stick to.

Keeping off the pounds

There's no independent evidence that weight loss lasts with most of these methods, but people who exercise tend to keep the pounds off better than people who don't.

It seems that being cosseted and pampered in a beauty salon is very relaxing, and lying at home watching TV while machines massage you can be as well, which is why so many women enjoy the experience and repeat it as frequently as they can afford.

Any problems?

A variety of different methods are reviewed in this chapter, and there are potential problems with some of them:

- You may suffer slight skin irritation if you are allergic to rubber and use electrical stimulation while dieting. Manufacturers will advise on how to avoid this.
- With all low-fat diets it is important to remember not to reduce your fat intake too far. Nutritionists' recommendations vary, but it's estimated that for good health fat should contribute approximately 25 per cent of your total daily calories.
- With diets in books it is very important to follow the plans as described. Most have been designed by expert nutritionists to provide all essential nutrients when followed properly, even at low levels of calorie intake.
- The benefits of exercise to health cannot be overemphasized, but don't try to do too much too soon and follow any instructions carefully. Exercise is often promoted as a way of making you feel cheerier about life, but there isn't any strong

evidence to support this. If you do feel better after exercising, it may be because you got out of the house and had a good laugh with friends, or simply because you knew you were doing something that was good for your health. What makes dieters happiest is losing weight, unsurprisingly.

Food Fact File

Mothers who breast-feed their babies exclusively or partially have significantly slenderer hips and are less above their pre-pregnancy weights at one month after the birth than are mothers who bottle-feed their babies.

Exercise has been around as long as history. Dancing about, chucking things in the air, kicking them on the ground, poking them in various ways with various kinds of sticks – all have been deemed fun recreational pastimes even when chasing and killing animals or grubbing in fields was an all-day, every-day necessity. Generally you wear more revealing clothes and do a lot more posing when you are leaping around – in the original Olympic Games 2000 years ago all the contestants were naked, and in many sporting events today contestants might as well be, which brings in a bit of sexiness as well. Nowadays many of these thrills can be experienced sitting on your backside viewing other people doing them on television, or in an arcade pressing buttons. Lack of exercise is believed to be a major contributor to the increasing number of people who are overweight.

You can walk quickly round the block, join a health club and use their machines, take up roller-skating or trampolining, or exercise at home to a video. It's up to you, your lifestyle and your purse.

How does it work?

Exercise is known to increase energy expenditure and reduce the health risks of obesity. Overweight people tend to take less exercise than thinner people do, but they may use more calories just by doing ordinary things with such a heavy body. Weigh 8 st (50.8 kg) and run for a mile and you'll use up 85 calories; but run the same distance at 11 st (69.9 kg) and you'll use up 119 calories.

There has been a lot of controversy about whether the increase in metabolic rate during exercise is maintained afterwards, but it now seems clear that within 40 minutes of concluding a period of exercise your energy output levels have returned to normal. In any case, any such effect would be very small: one study found that 30 minutes of moderately intense exercise raised the energy expenditure over the next three hours by only 14 calories.

A recent review of studies of the effects of exercise on weight loss showed that over three months women lost an average of about 3 lb (1.4 kg), through aerobic exercise alone, without dieting. Could this be explained by changes in appetite rather

333

than by increased expenditure of energy? The relationship between appetite and activity isn't clear, and seems to depend to some extent on what sex you are – women are less likely to feel hungry after exercising. It is known that although thin people tend to increase the amount they eat as they increase activity levels, overweight people don't, and so the effects of exercise on weight loss would seem to be more likely to result from a change in energy output than food intake. There is no evidence that exercise can change your proportions selectively, so that for example you can lose more weight from your stomach area than from your hips.

All this sounds like good news for some of us, as it reinforces our suspicions about exercise of any kind – and frankly there's nothing worse than to have to face the sneers of teenage boys, or worse, teenage girls, down at the swimming pool. So if exercise isn't going to have much effect on your shape or your weight, why bother? Well, there are some excellent reasons.

Exercise, if maintained long enough, is known to have beneficial effects on *health* in overweight people. It is a good preventative strategy against heart disease, reduces the risk of diabetes and can reduce high blood pressure even if you don't lose weight. And if you do lose weight, the risks of these problems are reduced even more. So if you can increase your general level of activity – and I don't mean forcing yourself to run half a mile every day, but just generally getting off your bum and doing more – there's every chance that you might feel better. You will know that exercise is doing you good, and there is some evidence that you'll find it easier to keep off any pounds you lose through dieting. Then you can show off your new *svelte* self down at the pool.

Who shouldn't use it?
If you haven't done anything strenuous for years then you should follow a carefully graded programme, starting off with mild exercise and progressing slowly to more demanding routines. If your BMI is over 30, you should take a doctor's advice on the best programme to follow.

Side-effects
There are no adverse effects when exercise is taken in a controlled manner.

Experts say
'There's no better way to improve your health.'

You say
'I know it makes me feel better. It can be hard to get started, but afterwards you can eat and feel it's OK, and you do get a kind of buzz.'

'I went to classes for two years and actually put on weight, but I felt a million times better – fat but fit. When I went on a diet as well I was staggered at how much easier the exercise was having lost weight.'

We say
Go for it.

Calorie counting	×	Suit single person	√
Weighing of food required	×	Suitable for vegetarians	√
Forbidden foods	×	Less than £10 to start	√

A Flat Stomach in 15 Days

Diet type
Body shaping combined with a reduced-calorie diet.

What is it?
A six-step exercise programme to flatten the stomach, and a diet, the Positive-Neutral-Negative Diet, in a book written by Judith Wills. This eating plan, she says, works for both people who do want to lose weight and for those who don't.

A Flat Stomach in 15 Days is 224 pages long and was first published in 1988, since when 150 000 copies have been sold worldwide. The publisher is Warner and it costs £4.50 from bookshops.

How does it work?
As the title suggests, through a series of exercises and by following a special diet you can quickly reduce the size of your stomach, according to Judith Wills.

The diet
Judith Wills is adamant that no diet can reduce fat from a particular area. She advises you first to find out if your large stomach is due to excess fat, by consulting height/weight charts. If you are overweight or your big stomach is caused by fluid retention or gas from eating the wrong things, you should go on the diet and the exercise programme. If you are not over-weight and your big stomach is caused by poor posture or weak stomach muscles, you should use the exercise programme alone.

The diet is designed to be low in starch and salt, to produce the minimum of gas, and to help avoid constipation, reduce fluid retention and aid digestion. You don't need to count calories. You design your own diet to suit your likes and dislikes round three lists of foods.

You can eat as much as you like from the list of fruits, salads and low-calorie vegetables. One or two of these are to be eaten with every meal. You make up the rest of your meals from the list of meat, fish, low-fat dairy products and vegetables that are high in carbohydrates. You are allowed only specified numbers or moderate portions of, for example, bread and potatoes. Another list includes items of which you are to eat as little as possible. These are white bread, white rice, cakes and foods high in fat. You are also to avoid foods high in salt, and you must drink 3 pt (1.7 l) of water a day. There aren't any forbidden foods but alcohol isn't listed.

A typical day's diet

On rising	*1 cup of lemon tea*	
Breakfast	*1 glass orange juice*	*50*
	Small bowl strained Greek yoghurt with 1 banana chopped in	*200*
Snack	*1 rye crispbread with 2 oz (56 g) cottage cheese*	*80*
Lunch	*2 oz (56 g) brie*	*180*
	2 rye crispbreads with low-fat spread	*50*
	Salad made with tomato, lettuce, red pepper, cucumber, basil and oil-free dressing	*20*
	1 peach	*50*
Snack	*2–3 oz (56–85 g) sunflower seeds*	*100*
	1 cup herb tea	
Evening meal	*Medium portion grilled chicken*	*200*
	3 oz (85 g) new potatoes	*60*
	Salad made with 1 stick celery, ½ apple, ½ oz walnuts, mixed with low-cal mayonnaise, natural yoghurt, lemon juice and parsley	*150*
	8 oz (225 g) slice of melon	*40*
	Calories (approx)	1200
	Cost	£3.57

You can make up your own diet using these guidelines, but if you find that too hard, a 15-day plan is given. On this plan you **337** eat five times every day, and there are main meal and vegetarian options. Simple recipes, most for two servings, are given after the day plans.

If you find at the end of the 15-day period that you still have a big stomach and/or are still fat, you continue on the diet and doing the exercises until you are the size you want.

Variations

Two sizes of portion are given in the plans. The first is for women wishing to lose weight; the second and bigger size is for women who want to maintain their weight loss or who don't need to lose weight, and also for men who want to lose weight.

There are also sections for mothers, pregnant women and men, with specific advice about diet and exercise.

Exercise

In the stomach exercise programme illustrated you move through three grades of difficulty for each of the six exercises over the 15-day period. You are to do the exercises for not more than 40 and not less than 30 minutes each day. There is a warm-up period beforehand and a cool-down period afterwards.

Who shouldn't use it?

Pregnant women should not go on a calorie-reduced diet without consulting a doctor.

Side-effects

You may find that eating too much fruit gives you diarrhoea, in which case you should cut down your intake.

Additional information

Judith Wills suggests how to make the most of your figure, by dressing to suit your body, trusting your own judgement and concentrating on style rather than fashion. There are shopping tips and advice on fabrics, patterns and styles which flatter the figure.

The height/weight charts give the acceptable weight range for a person of 5 ft 4 in as 108–138 lb (49–62.6 kg), a BMI of 18–24.

Expected weight loss

Men and women are expected to lose 5–7 lb (2.3–3.2 kg) over 15 days.

Keeping off the pounds

When you have got down to the weight you want to be, you move on to the larger portions detailed in the diet, but it is recommended that you work out your own diet in the long term by using the food lists. To maintain your flat stomach, you should continue with the exercise programme at least twice a week.

Men are allowed 14 units of alcohol per week on the maintenance plan designed for them.

Judith Wills says

'The Positive-Neutral-Negative theory is a healthy way to eat for always. Now everyone can beat that bulge forever. It's easy when you know how!'

You say

'It's good because it deals with real problems like beer bellies and constipation. I liked being allowed seven pints of beer a week on the maintenance plan.'

'It didn't work for me – it was so rigid.'

We say

This is a good exercise programme on the whole, but Judith Wills tells me that she intends to revise it in future editions: the diet is nutritionally well-balanced, but rather complicated to remember at first. There are just a couple of points to bear in mind:

- The typical day's diet shown above is a little low in iron, but other daily plans from the book would make up for this.
- On a calorie-reduced diet you are likely to notice weight loss around the waist area first. So your stomach looks thinner, but it will still be flabby unless you exercise as well.

Calorie counting	✗	Suitable for vegetarians	✓
Weighing of food required	✓	Less than £10 to start	✓
Forbidden foods	✗	Detailed 'who can't use'	✓
Suit single person	✓	Emphasizes fluid intake	✓

Food Fact File

Probably one of the reasons the Mongol hordes were so successful as they raped and pillaged their way across Asia was that they didn't have to weigh themselves down with provisions on their long journey from the steppes. They could survive entirely on the blood of their horses, and each man had 18, which was quite sufficient if each was bled of half a pint every ten days. As Marco Polo pointed out, this method of feeding had another advantage – you didn't have to waste time running around to find fuel for building fires, and the enemy was less likely to know of your approach.

Diet type

Body shaping and metabolism speeding, and a reduced-calorie diet.

What is it?

Five different diets, on a sliding scale of calorific content, for those who want to lose weight quickly. They are in a 144-page, large-format book by Judith Wills. This has topics such as 'Speed Slimming', 'Fast Weight Loss' and 'How Much Weight Do You Need to Lose?', a question-and-answer section, diet programmes and fat-burning and body-shaping routines. A chapter covers weight maintenance.

First published in 1993, *Judith Wills' Complete Speed Slimming System* is published by Vermilion at £8.99.

How does it work?

A reduced-calorie diet which speeds up metabolism combined with exercise is the best way to achieve rapid weight loss safely, Judith Wills believes.

The diet

Diet 1 is for those with 3 st (19.1 kg) or more to lose, Diet 2 is for those with 2–3 st (12.7–19.1 kg) to lose, and so on to Diet 5, for those with only half a stone (3.2 kg) to lose. Depending on where you start, you gradually move through the diets as you lose weight so that by the time you only have half a stone to lose you move on to Diet 5. You stay on each diet until you have reached the threshold for the next one.

Each diet shows exactly what you should eat each day. However, if you'd prefer the flexibility of choosing what you want to eat, there is a Flexi Diet for each main diet, from which you can choose from a range of breakfasts, lunches and evening meals. Alternatively, you can mix any particular diet about, having set meals one day and choosing from the Flexi Diet on other days.

On all the diets there is a daily allowance of skimmed milk, and **341** you can eat from a list of 'unlimited' foods, all of which are low-calorie vegetables. You can have one, two or three snacks a day from a list, depending on whether you have rated low, medium or high in terms of metabolic rate in the book's question-and-answer section. Snacks include fruit, low-fat drinks, crisps and bread. All provide about 100 calories. Essentially this is a high-carbohydrate, low-fat diet – there aren't any forbidden foods.

Daily calorie intake varies, depending on the diet and your metabolic rate. If you are more than 3 st (19.1 kg) overweight, have a high metabolic rate and are on Diet 1, the figure is 1500

A typical day's diet from Diet 3

Daily allowance	*4½ fl oz (125 ml) skimmed milk*	40
Breakfast	*3 whole apricots*	50
	1 oz (28 g) bran flakes with 4 fl oz (110 ml) skimmed milk, not from allowance	150
Snack	*1 banana*	90
Lunch	*15 oz (420 g) can of lentil soup*	150
	Wholemeal roll with low-fat spread	120
	Unlimited salad	40
	1 clementine	50
Snack	*1 muesli bar*	80
Evening meal	*Fish parcel, made with 9 oz (250 g) white fish, carrot, celery, lemon juice, seasoning and fresh herbs*	225
	9 oz (250 g) new potatoes	180
	4½ oz (125 g) broccoli	30
	Calories (approx)	1200
	Cost	£3.57

calories each day. This drops down to 900 calories if you have a low metabolic rate and are on Diet 5.

You don't have to count calories, but you do have to weigh portions. It isn't so important to do this properly for the vegetables and other low-cal items, but it is for high-calorie foods such as meat. Convenience foods are included in the set plans and in the Flexi Diet, but on the Flexi Diet you are advised not to have more than two ready-made dishes per week.

Recipes are for two or four and are calorie counted. The recipes are also suitable for non-dieters. There is a vegetarian main meal section in the recipes.

The sample daily menu plan is from Diet 3, for people who have between 1 and 2 st (6.3–12.7 kg) to lose and who have an average metabolic rate.

Variations

Very tall or active men add extra snacks and increase the quantities of certain carbohydrates where these are mentioned in recipes.

The Speed Plus Plan is a short-term diet of 800 calories a day for times when you have gone off your diet for some reason and need a physical and psychological boost to get you back on course. You follow the diet for one or two days usually, and never for more than five. There are four lists of foods and you choose a mini-meal from each list per day.

Judith Wills suggests that you can speed up your metabolism by being happy, eating a high-carbohydrate diet, eating frequently, eating raw, cold and spicy foods, taking exercise, lowering the temperature of your environment and sleeping less.

Exercise

The body-shaping plan consists of a basic routine to which you can add supplementary exercises depending on your answers to questions in the book about your present shape. The basic routine is a warm-up followed by strength and toning exercises, and then cool-down stretches. All the exercises are illustrated, and you are told exactly how many times to do each one. If your shape analysis indicates that you should do supplementary exercises – on bust or chest, upper back and arms, thighs and calves, etc – these come before the cool-down stretches.

The fat-burning routine emphasizes that to lose body fat you must exercise aerobically for sustained periods, at a steady pace, regularly. First, you answer a number of questions about yourself, and if you answer 'yes' to any of them then you should see your doctor before starting the programme. Having assessed your present state of fitness – after answering questions in the book on resting, exercise and recovery pulse rates – you move on either to walking or cycling or to more challenging activities. You fill in charts to monitor your progress and move up the programmes as you reach new levels of fitness.

Learning new habits
Judith Wills points out that you can change your lifestyle to help keep the pounds off in the long term by, for example, analysing when and how you overeat. She shows how to control such situations and minimize their effects.

Who shouldn't use it?
You are told that if you are under 18 years of age, pregnant, breast-feeding, suffering from or convalescing from an illness, or are elderly, you should obtain your doctor's permission before beginning this or any other reduced-calorie diet.

Additional information
Food charts show the composition of foods and there are question-and-answer sessions to help you analyse your weight loss, metabolism profile, fitness level and so on.

The height/weight charts show the minimum and maximum acceptable weights for a woman of 5 ft 4 in (1.63 m) as 8 st 2 lb (51.7 kg) and 9 st 12 lb (62.6 kg), corresponding to BMIs of 19 to 24, which is in line with current medical opinion.

Guidance is given on the World Health Organization's recommended daily intake of fat, carbohydrate and so forth, and you use the book's food charts to plan your future eating accordingly. Judith Wills believes that you should never forbid yourself anything, because feeling deprived makes people want what they can't have even more, and then they are more likely to eat it.

Expected weight loss

Judith Wills feels that it isn't possible to predict how much weight you will lose on the diet, but suggests that you could lose 5–7 lb (2.3–3.2 kg) in the first week and 3–4 lb (1.4–1.8 kg) in subsequent weeks. This is a higher rate of weight loss than medical opinion would recommend.

Keeping off the pounds

Once you have reached your target weight, Judith Wills believes that you will be able to maintain it for the rest of your life, if you stick with your new eating habits and don't go back to your old sedentary ways. When you have attained the shape and weight you want to be, you start with a transition phase, where you gradually begin to eat more over 12 days. You then work backwards through the diets, from Diet 4 to Diet 1, spending a few days on each. Finally you plan your own diet, on a maintenance level for women of 2000 calories per day. However, you don't have to count calories if you keep on eating plenty of carbohydrate, restrict fats and keep up your exercise levels. You are to do the fat-burning routine at least three times a week and the body-shaping routine twice a week, or more if you wish.

Judith Wills says

'Lose weight fast . . . a beautiful body for people in a hurry.'

You say

'I thought being allowed six snacks or meals a day would make this easy to stick to, but the food was pretty boring.'

'The recipes were easy to follow, and the advice was good – I lost 5 lb (2.3 kg) in six weeks. But I drank as well, which you shouldn't.'

We say

The diet itself follows all good nutritional advice, and the exercise section is excellent. The 'transition' period idea is excellent too, because coming off the diet is often the dieter's downfall. Judith Wills has devised a model system so that adapting to life after the diet means that weight gain is gradual and is counterbalanced by plenty of low-fat foods. There are just a few niggles:

- Judith Wills claims that aerobic exercise can keep your metabolism running faster for 24 hours afterwards. Unfortunately the latest scientific findings indicate that this isn't so.
- It is suggested that eating spicy, cold or raw foods can alter your metabolism. Although this is correct, the effect on weight loss would be minuscule.
- Simply being happy won't increase your metabolic rate, although depressed people sometimes have low metabolic rates, which may be associated with chemical imbalances. It isn't known which is cause and which effect.

Calorie counting	✕	Suitable for vegetarians	✓
Weighing of food required	✓	Less than £10 to start	✓
Forbidden foods	✕	Detailed 'who can't use'	✓
Suit single person	✓	Emphasizes fluid intake	✓

Diet type

A low-fat diet high in vegetables combined with an exercise plan.

What is it?

Leslie Kenton believes that although reducing your calorie intake will eventually make you thin, being thin doesn't mean being healthy. A *thin* body is wimpish and soft; it lacks power and energy. To be healthy you must be *lean*. A lean body is muscular and lacking in fat; it is powerful, has good tone, needs more calories than a thin body and is resistant to ageing and illness. You will gain in energy, discover a sense of control over your life, your health will improve and you will look years younger if you follow this diet, she says.

Her 192-page book has chapters on 'Let Diets Die', 'Drink Yourself Lean', 'Liberate Your Energy' and 'Go Primitive'. There is nutritional advice, suggestions for eating out, even tips on useful kitchen equipment. First published in 1994, *Lean Revolution* has sold 40 000 copies to date. It is published by Ebury Press at £5.99.

How does it work?

Research has shown that the high-fat, high-sugar and high-protein diet now eaten in the West is responsible for degenerative diseases such as obesity, Leslie Kenton maintains. She suggests that changing to a diet high in grains, fruits, legumes (pulses) and vegetables will help to avoid these problems or, if you suffer from them already, reverse their effects.

The diet

Calorie counting is an ineffective and dangerous way to lose weight, Leslie Kenton believes. In her view, dieting makes you gain weight — because every time you diet you lose muscle and fat, but when you put weight back on again it's only as fat. Eating satisfying, wholesome food is the real way to control your weight. The first step to revolutionizing your life is to stop dieting, using slimmer foods, counting calories and so on. She

347

suggests that you re-read the chapter in the book which tells you how useless dieting is, every three weeks.

Her Go Primitive Diet is in two phases. You begin with Quickstart, essentially a very low-fat, high-fibre vegan diet. You are allowed to eat as much as you like of vegetables, fruits and complex carbohydrates. You can stay on Quickstart for the rest of your life or move on to Living Lean, where you are allowed small quantities of avocados, olives, nuts and seeds, all of which are high in fat and calories.

On neither phase of the diet should you drink coffee. Alcohol is permitted only occasionally, and sugar, honey, white bread and white flour are absolutely forbidden. The only fat or oil you are allowed is a little olive oil. Meat, fish and dairy products such as milk or cheese are only to be eaten very occasionally, if you must, and in very small quantities. If you have to eat meat, it should be venison or wild boar. It's very important to drink a great deal of water, says Leslie Kenton – it will help you to lose weight by diminishing hunger. An average would be about eight big glasses per day, and if you can afford it this should be best quality spring-bottled mineral water.

The other change you are to make to your diet is to eat less frequently. If you eat too frequently, Leslie Kenton believes, you end up thinking about food all the time, your digestion is upset and you aren't allowing the body time between meals to detoxify. Eating less frequently gives you more energy. Ideally you should eat only twice a day: in the morning have a large breakfast within two or three hours of getting up, and have another, lighter meal by four o'clock in the afternoon. At both you are to eat slowly and chew thoroughly. The idea is to assimilate the Go Primitive Diet into your life gradually and carefully.

You don't have to weigh things exactly or count calories on this diet, but if you buy prepared foods you must make sure that, of your total daily calories, no more than 15 per cent on Quickstart or 25 per cent on Living Lean come from fat. Leslie Kenton believes that after several weeks of this diet you will lose your taste for fat and salt.

A Go Primitive weekly checklist is provided, which you can photocopy and use again. For the first 6–8 weeks of the diet you should check this off daily, to make sure that you are making the right changes to your diet.

A typical day's diet

Throughout the day	8 glasses of water, preferably spring-bottled mineral water	
Breakfast	*Munchy-crunchy granola, made with $\frac{1}{6}$th cup rolled oats, $\frac{1}{30}$th cup each of oat bran, barley flakes, wheat flakes, raisins, $\frac{1}{60}$th cup rye flakes, $\frac{1}{15}$th cup each of shredded coconut and pitted dates, and small quantities of cinnamon, nutmeg, coriander and salt, with $\frac{1}{20}$th cup unsweetened fruit juice concentrate*	*350*
	Soya milk	*50*
	Rye toast with fruit spread	*70*
	1 peach	*50*
	1 cup herb tea	
Main meal	*Easy vegetable curry, made with 1 large onion, 1 tsp olive oil, 3 tsp curry powder, 3 large carrots, 1 medium turnip, 2 potatoes, low salt stock powder, spring water, grated coconut*	*400*
	Sprout salad, made with $\frac{1}{4}$ cup each of lentil, fenugreek, alfalfa sprouts, $\frac{1}{4}$ cup Chinese leaves, 1 carrot, 1 tomato, with balsamic dressing of tomato juice, lemon juice, mustard, soy sauce, garlic, stock	*120*
	Melon	*100*
	Calories (approx)	1100
	Cost	£3.57

Sample meal plans for a fortnight and recipe ideas are given. The recipes mostly serve four, but the granola is made up in servings of 30. Ingredients include some unusual foods – cashew butter, fenugreek sprouts, lima beans – but you are given advice on buying these cheaply, or growing them, and storing them properly.

Exercise
You are advised to take aerobic exercise for at least three and preferably four 20–45 minute periods each week. Aerobic exercise enhances fat-burning for hours afterwards, Leslie Kenton claims. In addition, you should aim to do two weight-training sessions per week, each using ten different exercises, to maximize lean body mass and minimize fat.

Who shouldn't use it?
You are advised that you should always consult a doctor if you are attempting to treat a medical condition.

Expected weight loss
If you lose more than half a pound (225 g) a week you aren't eating enough food, and must increase intake.

Keeping off the pounds
This diet is a total change which you can use for the rest of your life. Every few weeks or so you should start to keep the weekly checklist again, in case you are becoming careless about what you are eating.

Leslie Kenton says
'Let diets die . . . *Lean Revolution* lets you eat more, shed fat, regenerate and rejuvenate your body while feasting on natural, wholesome, *comfort* foods.'

You say
'I kidded myself I was doing it for health when I was doing it for weight – it's really not a sustainable plan.'

'I lost 12 lb (5.4 kg) in three weeks. It is time-consuming and it's quite expensive.'

350

'If you stick to it, it works – I love vegetables and you can do it for a bit, not for always, and have a life.'

We say

Leslie Kenton's work is clearly written and explains complex nutritional issues well, but some of her theories are open to question.

- She states that you can buy the appetite suppressant phenyl-propanolamine (PPA) over the counter. You can, but not in Britain as an appetite suppressant – it's in cough medicine.
- It isn't correct that repeated dieting means you put on more fat each time you gain weight.
- Repeated dieting does not make it harder to lose weight, or easier to put it on. The next time you diet, your body will respond as if you have never dieted before.
- Calorie-reduced diets do not unbalance your metabolism; the new metabolic rate after dieting is right for the new, thinner body.
- There is no scientific evidence that organically grown foods provide more trace elements and minerals than convention-ally grown ones, nor that drinking a lot of water helps you to lose weight.
- The latest research indicates that exercise does not elevate metabolic rate afterwards to any significant degree.

This is a tough-minded diet, and it can be dour. Leslie Kenton says that 'not eating an evening meal can actually become a pleasure'. Such self-denial would never be a pleasure for me, and it's not perhaps very realistic for those who have to cook for a partner or family. Eating the last meal of the day by 4 p.m. could be a problem for many people, too. I don't think I could face telling my boss that I was shoving off early every day to get down to the supermarket for some wild boar meat which I'd need to cook and eat by teatime.

With the addition of the skimmed milk on this diet you could be short of vitamin B12, and it's only the enormous quantities of vegetables that otherwise ensure an adequate intake of minerals and vitamins. If you lost weight on this diet it would be because you were eating fewer calories; changing to a vegan diet would not, in itself, make you slimmer.

Calorie counting	×	Suitable for vegetarians	√
Weighing of food required	√	Less than £10 to start	√
Forbidden foods	√	Detailed 'who can't use'	×
Suit single person	√	Emphasizes fluid intake	√

Food Fact File

They call a spade a spade in Norway; 'liposuction' is *fetsugging*.

Treatment type
Surgical fat removal.

What is it?
Under general anaesthesia, a thin metal tube attached to a suction machine is inserted into the fat deposits to be removed. Three to four pints (up to 2.3 l) of fat are in most cases sucked away by moving the tubes around the area.

Liposuction has been used as a fat reduction technique since the 1970s. Today it is estimated that 10 000 such operations are carried out in Britain each year. Although liposuction is available under the National Health Service, in practice it would be extremely difficult to get it. In any case not many NHS surgeons have the necessary experience.

At present any doctor, trained in surgery or not, can practise cosmetic surgery, and it has been reported that people without any qualifications whatsoever have operated in private clinics. You can find a qualified surgeon by asking for a referral through your doctor or by sending a large SAE with a first-class stamp to the British Association of Aesthetic Plastic Surgeons, at the Royal College of Surgeons, 35–43 Lincoln's Inn Fields, London, WC2A 3PN.

If you become a member of the Cosmetic Surgery Network, Cindy Jackson, who organizes it, will provide you with a consumer report which contains a digest of her own and thousands of other people's experiences with plastic surgery. It includes details of the latest medical findings, and she advises members personally on controversial treatments, the qualifications of surgeons and so forth. Call 0181 983 3567 for details; membership costs £75. Most often people contact private surgeons through advertisements in newspapers and women's magazines, or simply walk into clinics off the street.

To have fat removed from both thighs would cost approximately £1200–2500 using conventional liposuction and about the same for liposculpture (see below).

How does it work?
By removing fat cells the body can be contoured to the desired shape. To avoid obvious scarring, if the fat is removed from the **353**

stomach, the tube is inserted through the navel, and if the fat is being removed from the hips and thighs the incision will be made on the crease of the buttocks.

Variations
You can have an abdominoplasty, where fat and skin are removed from the stomach area. Two other procedures can be performed under local anaesthesia, and so no overnight stay is required. The first is liposculpture, and clinics offering this service are springing up everywhere. Fat is removed with a syringe under local anaesthesia. It has been claimed that 3–4 pt (up to 2.3 l) of fat can be removed in one session by repeated syringing. Ultrasonic liposuction involves the fat being liquefied before removal, using ultrasound waves, and does sometimes require an overnight stay.

Who shouldn't use it?
This technique is not a treatment for people who are overweight all over. Very overweight people are considered to be particularly at risk of complications in general anaesthesia, and anyone with a history of cardiovascular disease or other serious medical problems would probably not be considered suitable for this procedure. Most surgeons would prefer not to treat people who aren't close to their ideal weight.

The best results are achieved with younger people, under the age of 40, because their skin is more elastic than that of older people.

Side-effects
Bruising and swelling of the area is normal, and a lack of sensation in the area may last for some weeks. There may be a permanent scar at the site of the incision.

A survey of American and Canadian surgeons' reported rates for complications following liposuction showed that only one person in a thousand suffered a major complication, such as death, heart attacks or thrombosis, and it was concluded that the procedure is generally safe. (These operations were all carried out by properly qualified surgeons in properly equipped hospitals.) There is no evidence that having fat sucked out alters your metabolism.

The most usual post-operative complication is irregularity in the skin, with some areas sticking up as bumps and others showing as depressions. These problems can generally be cleared up by further operations, where fat is re-injected under the skin or more taken out, depending on the size of the problem area.

Some doctors have been criticized for removing too much fat in one session of liposculpture and then allowing people who were obviously in shock to return home alone. There has been concern over whether ultrasonic liposuction could let fat enter the bloodstream, a potentially fatal side-effect, but there have been no reported cases of this so far.

In older people the skin has lost much of its elasticity, and so after the operation your skin may hang in folds. If this persists it may be necessary for further plastic surgery to remove some of the excess skin.

Additional information
You would be given advice about how best to look after the site of your operation on your return home. Most reputable surgeons would suggest a sensible diet to be followed after the operation.

Expected weight loss
You would immediately lose the amount of fat which had been withdrawn, usually about 4–5 lb (1.8–2.3 kg) in total.

Keeping off the pounds
The problem with liposuction is that so far there is no definite evidence that the weight loss is permanent. The fat can build up again, although there isn't usually as much fat in the same areas as before.

Cosmetic surgeons say
'Simply, safely, effectively, we can reshape your body – completely confidentially.'

You say
'I'm very unhappy about how it's turned out. My skin is lumpy and uneven.'

355

'I have had both traditional and ultrasonic types of liposuction, and although I weigh about the same as when I started, my shape has changed and I am very pleased.'

We say
This is not a way to lose weight permanently.

Some doctors believe that liposculpture and ultrasonic liposuction are potentially dangerous procedures, even when carried out by qualified personnel, and despite the statistics. The chances of anything going wrong are much increased if you are operated on by an inexperienced and unqualified person. It's your money, so you are entitled to buy the best possible treatment, and that includes being operated on by someone who knows what they're doing.

'Trust me, I'm a doctor' is not something to rely on when potentially unqualified people are allowed to practise cosmetic surgery. Make sure that your surgeon is a Fellow of the Royal College of Surgeons who has long and extensive experience of liposuction. It's better not to go to a clinic which doesn't guarantee to give you post-operative care or to correct any problems which may arise after surgery.

Many women complain they can't get rid of saddlebag thighs, or that repeated child-bearing has left them with stomachs half-way to their knees. If you've got the money, and you don't mind the post-operative pain and the risk that you may end up looking worse than you did before, this could be for you.

Calorie counting	✕	Suitable for vegetarians	✓
Weighing of food required	✕	Less than £10 to start	✕
Forbidden foods	✕	Detailed 'who can't use'.	✓
Suit single person	✓		

Diet type
A low-fat, reduced-calorie diet combined with an exercise plan.

What is it?
It is a 176-page book by Rosemary Conley, describing how in a month you can look significantly slimmer and in better shape by following a diet and exercise plan. Ten stages are described, from advice on shopping for low-fat products to food preparation, the diet and weight maintenance. In addition the book contains recipes, record charts, an exercise plan and hints on what to do if your new beach body puts on weight on holiday. Rosemary Conley's *Beach Body Plan* was first published in 1994, since when it has sold more than 100 000 copies. It is published by Arrow at £5.99.

How does it work?
You can increase your metabolic rate and lose weight, Rosemary Conley suggests, by eating normal-sized meals at regular intervals, and taking regular exercise.

The diet
The daily eating plans cover each of the 28 days individually. For each day there are menus, and for each meal you are given a choice of two dishes; there's also a daily tip, many of which are about healthy cooking methods.

There is a daily allowance of skimmed milk, orange juice and one alcoholic drink. All the dishes are very low in fat. You don't have to count calories, but you do have to measure ingredients exactly. All kinds of fatty foods are absolutely banned – butter, oil, cakes, sweets and fatty sauces, for example. You are allowed unlimited green vegetables plainly prepared and salad.

The recipes are given within each day's plan, and are for four servings of the main meal. There's an easy option each day. Most contain meat or fish, and so vegetarians would not be able to follow the daily plans. Simple instructions are given for preparing other dishes.

A typical day's diet

Throughout the day	½ pt (285 ml) skimmed milk	95
	5 fl oz (140 ml) orange juice	50
	1 alcoholic drink	100
Breakfast	2 oz (56 g) muesli with milk from allowance	220
Lunch	2 oz (56 g) wholemeal bread roll, spread with mustard, 1 oz (28 g) ham, and unlimited salad	200
Evening meal	1 serving of coronation chicken, made with 1 skinned chicken portion, 4 oz (110 g new potatoes, 1 fl oz (30 ml) sherry, 1 fl oz (30 ml) low-fat fromage frais, ¾ oz (20 g) low-fat cheddar cheese, parsley and garlic	400
	1 small banana with 4 oz (110 g) strawberries and 2 tsp low-fat fromage frais	140
	Calories (approx)	1200
	Cost	£3.57

Rosemary Conley has some general advice about making shopping lists before going to the shops, and some of her daily tips are designed to increase your motivation to lose weight.

Variations
Men are allowed an extra alcoholic drink each day.

Exercise
Rosemary Conley suggests taking the exercise plans easily at first. You must aim to be moderately active for 20 minutes on five days per week, not counting the warming-up and cooling-

358

down periods. On two days a week you do the toning exercises which are shown, but one day a week you have a rest day.

There are a number of different categories of exercise, with different activities. You can either do one activity all the way through the 28 days, or you can do as many different ones as you like. They include all kinds of games, workouts, walking and so on.

Who shouldn't use it?
No one who is pregnant or has a medical condition should follow the diet or do the exercises described in the book.

Additional information
A chart to record how much and what kind of exercise was done is included in each day's plan.

Keeping off the pounds
There isn't a specific plan, but you are given advice. Essentially this is gradually to increase the amounts of higher-calorie foods you enjoy, while sticking to low-fat cooking methods, but if you find that you have gained more than 2 lb (900 g) you are to go back on the diet.

Rosemary Conley says
'The easiest, most effective way to a beautiful beach body.'

You say
'You have to cut out all fat and you can eat as many vegetables as you like. It was fine and I did well – until I went on holiday.'

We say
This is a well-balanced diet and a sensible exercise plan. Rosemary Conley believes that your metabolic rate can be increased post-exercise and that eating a higher volume of food will also increase it, but I can't find any firm evidence for this and the latest scientific research suggests that metabolic rate drops back to normal very soon after exercise is finished. However, there is no doubt of the value of exercise in preventing a *fall* in metabolic rate.

Calorie counting	×	Suitable for vegetarians	×
Weighing of food required	√	Less than £10 to start	√
Forbidden foods	√	Detailed 'who can't use'	√
Suit single person	√	Emphasizes fluid intake	√

Food Fact File

For six hundred years men railed at women's vanity in squashing their insides by wearing tight-laced corsets to achieve a narrow waist, while admiring the results. The wearing of corsets was supposed to lead to every imaginable illness and disease, and suspected of being used as a means of avoiding pregnancy and procuring abortion.

Diet type
A low-fat, reduced-calorie diet combined with an exercise plan.

What is it?
One of the best-selling diet books of all time, this was first published in 1988 as *The Hip and Thigh Diet*, since when it has been updated and has sold more than 2 million copies worldwide.

The diet came about when Rosemary Conley was diagnosed as suffering from gallstones, but couldn't afford time off to have an operation. She went on a very-low-fat diet and found that by happy accident the diet caused her to lose weight from her hips and thighs. Rosemary Conley described the diet she had devised in this book, after testing it on 120 volunteers, who stuck to the diet rigidly and who also lost weight.

This 408-page book includes 'The Tum and Bum Diet for Men', measurement record charts, fat charts showing the fat in grams per ounce of common foods and special advice for vegetarians and on nutritional requirements for everyone. Rosemary Conley provides statistics throughout the book. These come from questionnaires completed by people who have used the diet. She claims that an average of $1\frac{3}{4}$ in (4.4 cm) is lost from the bust, 3 in (7.6 cm) each from waist and hips, and 2 in (5.1 cm) from each thigh.

Rosemary Conley's Complete Hip and Thigh Diet is published by Arrow at £4.99.

How does it work?
You will lose inches on this diet from the hips and thighs without losing them from the bust, it is claimed. Rosemary Conley thinks that the greatest cause of excess weight is bingeing, which occurs when you feel hungry and deprived. Calorie counting leads to bingeing, and so there is no calorie counting in her diet plans. There are no stipulated portion sizes of, for example, jacket potatoes; she believes that as you use the diet you will learn to prefer smaller portions.

The diet

You should eat three meals per day, although the dinner menus
allow you to break up the courses into snacks for later, if you

A typical day's diet

Throughout the day	½ pt (285 ml) skimmed milk	95
	1 alcoholic drink	100
	4 fl oz (110 ml) fruit juice	40
	1 multivitamin pill	
Breakfast	1 oz (28 g) porridge oats made with water	100
	2 tsp honey	40
Lunch	Pineapple boat, made with ½ fresh pineapple,	60
	4 oz (110 g) fruit of choice,	70
	5 oz (140 g) diet yoghurt,	75
	cherry to decorate	1
Evening meal	Crudités, made with cucumber, carrots, celery, cauliflower, peppers and a dip of 5 oz (140 g) natural yoghurt, 4 oz (110 g) cottage cheese, and herbs	150
	Stir-fried chicken and vegetables, made with 4 oz (110 g) chicken, 1½ (40 g) brown rice, 1 stick celery, ½ carrot, ½ onion, ¼ pepper, 1 oz (28 g) mushrooms, 4 oz (110 g) bean sprouts, stock, spices	300
	Meringue basket, filled with raspberries and topped with raspberry yoghurt	120
	Calories (approx)	1250
	Cost	£3.57

wish. Yoghurt, cheese and milk must be of the low-fat variety, and red meat is limited to twice a week. Where a recipe indicates unlimited vegetables, these can include potatoes, but all must be plainly prepared without fat. Salad vegetables can be eaten as snacks. Vegetarian options are indicated. All kinds of fatty foods are forbidden – butter, oil, cakes, sweets and fatty sauces, for example.

There are plenty of different meals to choose from – a cooked or fruit breakfast, packed or hot lunches, starters, main courses and desserts for dinner. All the dishes are very low in fat.

There is a daily allowance of some items, including alcohol, and you can have three extra alcoholic drinks a week. You should also take a multivitamin pill each day, because a very-low-fat diet could lead to a vitamin deficiency if followed for too long.

The recipes serve one, two or three people and include vegetarian options.

Variations
Men can have an extra alcoholic drink each day.

Exercise
A variety of exercises that Rosemary Conley designed specifically to contour the hips and thighs are fully illustrated. You are reminded to warm up before starting the aerobic workout and to practise the stretch exercises afterwards. It is suggested that you try to do the exercises each day.

Learning new habits
There isn't a specific plan, but in a chapter Rosemary Conley encourages you to develop self-confidence.

Who shouldn't use it?
You are advised that you must always check with your doctor first before embarking on any diet during pregnancy. You should also check with your doctor before starting the Hip and Thigh Diet if you have a thyroid disorder.

Additional information
Throughout the book there are readers' life histories and testimonials. Rosemary Conley has letters from readers showing that people who have benefited from the Hip and Thigh Diet include those with eating disorders, arthritis, backache, coeliac disease, constipation, epilepsy and other diseases.

An exercise video, 'Rosemary Conley's Hip and Thigh Workout', will be on sale from spring 1995 for £10.99 in video shops, or you can write to Rosemary Conley at Quorn House, Meeting Street, Quorn, Loughborough LE12 8EX. The video will be sent to you for £10.99 including post and packing.

Expected weight loss
Results from a questionnaire Rosemary Conley analysed show that dieters who followed the plan for approximately ten weeks lost an average of 2 lb (900 g) a week during that time, which is in line with current medical opinion on the recommended rate of weight loss.

Keeping off the pounds
Rosemary Conley recommends that when you have reached your target weight you continue to eat the same healthy diet, but increase the amount you eat and add new foods if you like, though you shouldn't get into the habit of eating fatty foods again. If you find your weight increasing, go back on to the diet.

Rosemary Conley says
'The proven, no-fuss, no calorie-counting way that sheds those inches other diets leave behind!'

You say
'It's a sensible diet and it's fine if you're cooking all your own meals.'

'I lost 10 lb (4.5 kg) and I thought it was expensive at first, but I cut out chocolate and it's not really.'

'My enthusiasm just wasn't there. There were a lot of things I wouldn't eat like cottage cheese, and there were no dressings I liked. But the video was very good and it got me started.'

'I read the book — it was great — but I couldn't stick the diet.'

'It was the best I tried.'

We say

There is no doubt that this is one of the most successful diets ever devised, as sales show, but there are a few points to bear in mind:

- Unfortunately, experts do not believe that it is possible to shed fat from some parts of your body but not others (see page 330). During the dieting fat is lost from all over the body, and not only from the hips and thighs.
- Medical professionals would be concerned if anyone with an eating disorder went on this diet. Rosemary Conley tells me that she always discourages anyone with an eating disorder from dieting; healthy eating is what she recommends.
- Rosemary Conley says that regular exercise can help to reduce 'cellulite', a fat of dimpled appearance found on the thighs, and that her readers have found that her diet reduced the incidence of cellulite. But doctors absolutely disagree that there is anything special about cellulite — medical opinion holds that fat is fat wherever it occurs on the body.
- I am sure that the readers who wrote to Rosemary Conley did lose as much weight and as many inches as they said, but people who didn't lose weight would be unlikely to write to Rosemary Conley and tell her.

Otherwise this diet is excellent. It is very low in fat, but Rosemary Conley recommends taking a multivitamin pill each day, in line with nutritionists' recommendations for women on low-calorie diets.

Calorie counting	×	Suitable for vegetarians	√
Weighing of food required	√	Less than £10 to start	√
Forbidden foods	√	Detailed 'who can't use'	√
Suit single person	√	Emphasizes fluid intake	×

Rosemary Conley's Flat Stomach Plan

Diet type
A very-low-fat, reduced-calorie diet combined with an exercise plan.

What is it?
A 28-day eating, exercise and positive thinking programme, by Rosemary Conley, contained in a 192-page, large-format book. There are fat content charts which show you how many grams of fat there are per oz (28 g) of common foods, weight and inch-loss record charts, tips for weight maintenance and recipes.

Rosemary Conley's *Flat Stomach Plan* was first published by Arrow in 1994 at £7.99.

How does it work?
Rosemary Conley suggests that you can't get rid of a fat stomach just by doing sit-ups – you can't turn fat into muscle. But you can burn fat, she claims, through aerobic exercise and lose weight by following a low-fat diet.

The diet
Before you begin the programme you are to weigh and measure yourself and enter the details in the chart provided. You are also advised to take a photograph of yourself which you can look at from time to time to remind yourself of your progress, and compare it with a photograph which you should take at the end of the programme. Try on too tight a dress or trousers before beginning the programme and do so again every few days thereafter, Rosemary Conley suggests, so that you can see how the inches are being lost.

Each day you select one breakfast, one lunch and one evening meal. The evening meal is three courses, and you can save the starter or the dessert to have as a treat later. There are two choices of breakfast, three for lunch and three for in the evening. Menus are given for each day, but you can swap the meals about – have the main meal at lunchtime, choose a menu from another day and so on. Snacking between meals is strongly

A typical day's diet

Daily allowance	½ pt (285 ml) skimmed milk	95
	5 fl oz (125 ml) orange juice	50
	1 alcoholic drink	100
Breakfast	5 fl oz (140 ml) orange juice	50
	1 oz (28 g) branflakes, with additional 4 fl oz (110 ml) skimmed milk, with 1 banana chopped in and 1 tsp sugar	250
Lunch	Tuna salad, made with 2 slices wholewheat bread, spread with reduced-oil salad dressing, 3 oz (85 g) tuna, 1 tsp reduced-oil salad dressing and unlimited salad	250
Evening meal	6 oz (170 g) grapefruit segments in natural juice	40
	Apricot-glazed chicken, made with 2 oz (56 g) apricot preserve, 1 chicken breast, 1 oz (28 g) water chestnuts, ½ oz (15 g) Bran Buds, ½ oz (15 g) onions, with celery, mushrooms, tomato paste, margarine, mustard, stock and spices	450
	Low-fat trifle, made with ¼ packet jelly, ½ a banana, 5 fl oz (140 ml) skimmed milk	50
Calories (approx)		1300
Cost		£3.57

discouraged; if you must, you may have raw carrots, cucumber and the like.

There is a list of foods that are forbidden during the course of the programme. These include all kinds of fatty items. There is **367** a daily allowance of skimmed milk, fruit juice and alcohol, and you are always allowed to eat as many vegetables as you like, plainly prepared; potato quantities are unlimited, but pasta and rice quantities are stipulated. You can have as many low-cal drinks as you want.

You don't have to count calories, because this has been done for you, but you do have to weigh items, and the amounts of some high-calorie carbohydrate items such as rice and pasta are more tightly controlled than on Rosemary Conley's Complete Hip and Thigh Diet (see page 361), although only for the duration of the programme. Oily fish was not recommended on the first version of that diet, but is included here, in line with current nutritional thinking. The alcohol allowance is smaller than in some of Rosemary Conley's other diets, which means more calories available for extra courses.

Recipes are included, mostly for four servings but some serve one and some six people. For every lunch, there are packed, regular and quick and easy options (the last two include ready-meals and canned soups). For every dinner, there are regular, quick and easy and vegetarian options; the recipes for these include ready-made dishes, tinned foods, commercial desserts and cook-in sauces.

Variations
Men over 5 ft 8 in (1.73 m) or who do hard physical work are advised to increase all quantities of food by 25 per cent. Men are allowed two alcoholic drinks per day.

Exercise
With the menu plan for each day come detailed descriptions, illustrated with photographs, of the exercises you are to do on that day. You can do these as often as you like, though precise recommendations are given. For each day there are warm-up exercises, stretches, aerobic and toning exercises, and cool-down stretches afterwards. I calculate that the exercises would take 20–30 minutes, depending on the speed at which you moved from one to another.

If you can, you should exercise to music because it is more motivational, according to Rosemary Conley. If you miss a day, you must do that day's exercise before continuing to the next set, because the programme is designed to be followed step-by-step and becomes more strenuous as you move through it. If you find any day's exercise too difficult, you stay with the previous day's exercises until your strength and fitness improve.

Learning new habits

There is a Positive Thought for each day which emphasizes the importance of replacing negative ideas with positive ones. Rosemary Conley believes that you can take control of your eating and of your life in general, and that by thinking positively and setting goals for the future you can improve your self-esteem and make it more likely that you will achieve those goals. There are also practical tips about not drinking too much, not eating between meals and so on.

Who shouldn't use it?

You are advised that if you have a medical condition or are pregnant you shouldn't follow the diet and exercises without first consulting a doctor. Rosemary Conley says that her book is not intended for people who are overweight and happy about being so.

Additional information

You can buy 'The Flat Stomach Plan Workout Video' for £10.99 from video shops. This shows you how to do the exercises, and you can follow three complete workouts set to music. Fitness equipment is also available; contact Rosemary Conley's Fitness Equipment, Quorn House, Meeting Street, Quorn, Loughborough LE12 8EX.

Expected weight loss

No expected weight loss is given, and you are warned to be realistic about what can be achieved in 28 days. Thinness is not the aim; the removal of excess inches from the stomach and other areas, if necessary, is.

Keeping off the pounds

Among tips for keeping off the pounds in the long term is advice about low-fat cooking methods, continuing to exercise and **369** eating regular meals. If you do gain more than 2 lb (900 g), you are to go back on to the programme.

Rosemary Conley says
'The plan is . . . simple, safe and effective. Reduce fat from your stomach – for good.'

You say
'It's good because on some days you can eat as much fruit and vegetables as you like. I lost 6 lb (2.7 kg) in four weeks.'

We say
This is a nutritionally well-balanced diet, with good exercise routines and advice on ways to stay motivated and think positively. Experts do not believe that it is possible to shed fat from some parts of your body but not others, but Rosemary Conley makes it clear that if you're fat all over on this diet, you'll lose fat all over; and if you've got a large stomach as well, you will lose fat from there too. Combined with the exercises to tone your tum, this programme could well be effective.

Calorie counting	✕	Suitable for vegetarians	✓
Weighing of food required	✓	Less than £10 to start	✓
Forbidden foods	✓	Detailed 'who can't use'	✓
Suit single person	✓	Emphasizes fluid intake	✓

Diet type
A low-fat, reduced-calorie diet combined with an exercise plan.

What is it?
This is Rosemary Conley's 28-day eating, exercise and positive thinking programme for women. There are question-and-answer sections, readers' comments, a maintenance plan, fat content tables, weight and inch-loss charts and diet record sheets for each day.

First published in 1990, this 208-page, large-format book has since sold nearly a million copies. Rosemary Conley wrote it in response to comments from readers of *The Hip and Thigh Diet* (see page 361); in this book she aims to combine appetite satisfaction *and* gastronomic appeal.

Rosemary Conley's *Inch Loss Plan* is published by Arrow at £7.99.

How does it work?
Most diets work but willpower fails, Rosemary Conley believes. Encouragement through positive thinking, and real results through looking and feeling slimmer, will nurture adequate supplies of willpower. This programme is designed to make you believe that you *can* change your shape in a short time through diet and exercise.

The diet
Before you begin the programme you are to weigh and measure yourself and enter the details in the record chart provided. You are also advised to take three photographs of yourself, showing front, back and side views. At the end of the programme you take the measurements and photos again, to see how much slimmer you look.

Each day of the programme has a menu with exactly what you are supposed to eat for each of three meals. There is an alternative for every course if you don't like something and there is always a vegetarian option. Some foods – mainly all kinds of fatty items – are forbidden. There is a daily allowance of skimmed milk, fruit juice and alcohol, and you are allowed to

371

A typical day's diet

Daily allowance	10 fl oz (285 ml) skimmed milk	95
	4 fl oz (110 ml) fruit juice	40
	2 alcoholic drinks	200
Breakfast	1 oz (28 g) bran flakes with milk from allowance	100
	1 banana	90
	1 tsp brown sugar	15
Lunch	Sandwich, made with 2 slices wholemeal bread, reduced-fat spread, 2 oz (56 g) chicken breast, unlimited lettuce, tomatoes and cucumber	300
	5 oz (140 g) diet yoghurt	50
Evening meal	6 oz (170 g) chicken joint (no skin)	200
	Unlimited vegetables, including potatoes	200
	Melon surprise, made with 8 oz (225 g) melon and 5 oz (140 g) diet yoghurt	125
	Calories (approx)	1400
	Cost	£3.57

eat as many vegetables as you like, plainly prepared. You can also have as many low-cal drinks as you want.

You don't have to count calories, because this has been done for you, but you do have to weigh items, and some high-calorie carbohydrate items such as potatoes and rice are more tightly controlled than on Rosemary Conley's Complete Hip and Thigh Diet, although only for the duration of the programme. Another difference between the two diets is that on this one the occasional egg is allowed, there are two courses at every meal and the alcohol allowance is higher – you can have two drinks a day.

You are strongly discouraged from eating between meals, or from dividing up your meals so that you can eat more than three times a day. Rosemary Conley believes that eating between meals is the cause of most weight gain. If you *must* eat, you are to stick to raw carrots, celery or other salad vegetables.

The recipes mostly serve one, two or four people, but some are for six servings.

Exercise

Each day's menu plan is accompanied by illustrated descriptions of the exercises you are to do for at least 15 minutes on that day. These were designed by Rosemary Conley – she calls them the Intensive Stretching and Aerobic Programme – and are a combination of isometrics, aerobics, callanetics and yoga.

Warm-up and cool-down routines are explained, and if possible you should exercise to music because it is more motivational, according to Rosemary Conley. If you miss a day you must do that day's exercise before continuing the course, because the programme is designed to be followed step-by-step and becomes more strenuous as you move through it.

Learning new habits

The Positive Thought for each day emphasizes the importance of replacing negative thoughts like 'I can't diet' with positive thoughts – 'I can and I will'. Rosemary Conley believes that you can take control of your eating *and* of your life in general, and that through positive thoughts and visualization of a better future you can improve your self-esteem and achieve your goals.

Who shouldn't use it?

You are advised that in the interests of good health it is always important to consult your doctor before commencing any diet or exercise routine.

Expected weight loss

No expected weight loss is given, although Rosemary Conley says that most women want to reduce by at least one dress size if not two, and that this will be possible over the course of the programme.

Keeping off the pounds

Rosemary Conley says that after finishing the diet people find that they have lost their taste for very fatty foods, so you can follow the basic principles of the programme for the rest of your life. If you still have a significant amount of weight to lose at the end of the programme, you should continue on this diet or move to the Complete Hip and Thigh Diet (see page 361).

If you are nearly at your target weight, you can follow the maintenance programme included in the book. You are advised to avoid fatty foods, but you can have dishes prepared in a low-fat way, such as milk puddings made with skimmed milk. Guidance is given on how to construct your own healthy eating plans, using the fat content tables and lists of recommended daily minimums of essential nutrients. You should also keep up your exercise, ideally three times per week.

Rosemary Conley says

'You have got absolutely nothing to lose except your inches.'

You say

'It was good and I lost weight, but I do think you need some oil or fat in your diet – how does your skin manage otherwise?'

'I kept the weight off for over a year.'

'I'm an aerobics instructor. I lost 5 in (12.7 cm) off my waist and dropped two dress sizes.'

We say

This is a nutritionally well-balanced diet, with a good exercise plan and advice on ways to change negative thinking, in line with psychologists' views on how to alter behaviour.

Calorie counting	✗	Suitable for vegetarians	✓
Weighing of food required	✓	Less than £10 to start	✓
Forbidden foods	✓	Detailed 'who can't use'	✗
Suit single person	✓	Emphasizes fluid intake	✗

Food Fact File

A quarter-pound burger, with medium fries, milkshake, medium cola and a fruit pie is 1400 calories.

Rosemary Conley's Metabolism Booster Diet

Diet type
A low-fat, reduced-calorie diet with an exercise plan.

What is it?
Eight 30-day diet plans which are high in carbohydrate, moderate in protein and low in fat. They are contained in a 336-page book by Rosemary Conley, which has tables showing the fat content of common foods, photographs of an exercise workout, a chapter on maintaining weight loss, and readers' testimonials about the health benefits they discovered while following the diet.

First published in 1992, Rosemary Conley's *Metabolism Booster Diet* has since sold more than 200 000 copies. It is published by Arrow and costs £4.99.

How does it work?
Most diets work but the weight is often regained because dieting slows your metabolism, Rosemary Conley thinks. Age and lack of exercise also contribute to a slowing of metabolic rate. The idea here is to increase your metabolic rate by eating more food and being physically active.

The diet
The diet plans are the Six Meals-a-Day Diet, the Freedom Diet, the Four Meals-a-Day Diet, the Eat Yourself Slim Diet (which is based on the Complete Hip and Thigh Diet; see page 361), the Three Two-Course-Meals-a-Day Diet (based on the Inch Loss Plan; see page 371), the Vegetarian Diet, the Gourmet Diet and the Lazy Cook's Diet. You choose whichever one complements your preferences and lifestyle.

You are advised not to follow any one plan for longer than four weeks. There are seasonal menu plans, covering occasions such as Christmas lunch, Valentine's Day dinner for two and summer barbecues, with advice on accompanying drinks.

You do not have to count calories, but you do have to weigh portions of high-calorie foods. There are forbidden items –

376

mainly all kinds of fatty foods – though not on all the diets in the book. You are allowed an alcoholic drink and are advised to take a multivitamin pill each day. The book includes recipes, mostly for one, two or four servings (some of the recipes are the same as the ones in the *Rosemary Conley Hip and Thigh Cookbook*).

A typical day's diet from the Six Meals-a-Day Diet

Daily Allowance	½ pt (285 ml) skimmed milk	95
	3 fl oz (85 ml) orange juice	30
	1 alcoholic drink	100
Breakfast	½ oz (15 g) porridge oats made with water	50
	Milk from allowance	
	1 tsp honey	20
Mid-morning	5 oz (140 g) diet yoghurt	50
Lunch	2 oz (56 g) chicken	100
	Mixed salad with oil-free vinaigrette	60
Tea	1 banana	90
Evening meal	3 oz (85 g) meat, with gravy and unlimited vegetables	350
Supper	5 fl oz (140 ml) mixed vegetable soup, made with 1 oz (28 g) each of potato, carrot, onion, leek, ½ stick celery, stock, flavouring, herbs	60
	Calories (approx)	1000
	Cost	£3.57

Variations

Men may have an extra unit of alcohol a day on the diet detailed above.

377

Exercise

The exercise workouts suggest that you aim for at least three 15-minute periods of low-impact aerobics each week. There are tables from which you can calculate your personal optimal heart rate while exercising and your exercise level, depending on your age. In addition, Rosemary Conley runs through various activities (washing the car, golf, shopping and so on) and rates their effectiveness in boosting your metabolism. She warns readers not to try too much too soon.

Who shouldn't use it?

You are advised that it is always important to consult your doctor before beginning any diet or exercise programme.

Keeping off the pounds

When you have achieved your desired weight loss, you may not be able to exercise as regularly and intensively as while you were dieting, so Rosemary Conley includes guidelines on foods that you can eat on a low-fat diet, which she recommends that you follow for the rest of your life if you wish to maintain your new figure. She provides a list of foods which you may eat – they are all low fat – and those which you should avoid.

Rosemary Conley says

'By following a varied and flexible eating plan containing freedom of choice, we can boost our metabolism and achieve dieting success.'

You say

'You can put this diet into your lifestyle. If you look at the fat content, you can see a big difference between things. I hate counting calories, it's a lot easier cutting down on fat.'

We say

These plans are well thought-out and nutritionally adequate, and there is tremendous variety. Rosemary Conley states quite specifically that she is not suggesting that her diets can help people with similar medical conditions to those her readers describe as being eased by the diet. I haven't the slightest doubt that the letters she receives are genuine, and that low-fat diets may have particular benefits for some physical problems. But disorders like agoraphobia, anorexia nervosa and bulimia nervosa (reported by some of Rosemary Conley's correspondents) need specialist help, and professionals concerned with treating them would prefer sufferers to seek advice rather than attempt to treat themselves, and so would Rosemary Conley.

Rosemary Conley should specify who shouldn't go on this diet.

As I have discussed before, neither eating a larger volume of food nor exercise is known to have metabolism-boosting effects, but increased activity will slow down the inevitable fall in metabolic rate which occurs on a reduced-calorie diet.

Calorie counting	✗	Suitable for vegetarians	✓
Weighing of food required	✓	Less than £10 to start	✓
Forbidden foods	✓*	Detailed 'who can't use'.	✗
Suit single person	✓	Emphasizes fluid intake	✗

* On some diets.

Rosemary Conley's Shape Up for Summer

Diet type
A low-fat, reduced-calorie diet combined with an exercise plan.

What is it?
A 14-day diet and exercise plan described in a 288-page book by Rosemary Conley. There are chapters on body care – beauty tips for holidays and advice on suntanning – and on planning your packing, as well as advice on first-aid items, insurance, securing your home while away and so on. This book has more on exercise routines than Rosemary Conley's *Beach Body Plan* (see page 357).

First published in 1993, Rosemary Conley's *Shape Up for Summer* has sold more than 100 000 copies to date. It is published by Arrow at £3.99.

How does it work?
Rosemary Conley doesn't say why or how this diet and exercise plan might work.

The diet
You shouldn't wait until your holiday is only a couple of weeks off before dieting; you should start at least a month before, Rosemary Conley thinks. And before beginning the book's 14-Day Diet and Fat-Burner Fitness Programme you must be certain that you are committed to following it through, or you will fail.

Each day of the diet is described separately. You do not have to count calories, but you do have to weigh portions of high-calorie foods. The diet is high in carbohydrate and protein but low in fat. You must not cheat, you must not eat between meals and you must not eat anything from the forbidden list of fatty foods. Vegetables that you can eat as much as you like of include potatoes, but all vegetables must be plainly prepared without fat of any kind. You are advised to use wholemeal rather than white pasta, rice and bread.

380 You must drink at least eight cups of liquid each day, including low-calorie and diet drinks, and tea and coffee with milk from the daily allowance. You can drink as much water as you like. There is a daily allowance of fruit juice, skimmed milk and for women one alcoholic drink.

The diet comes in two versions. On the first, you eat exactly what is shown for each day: a breakfast, lunch and evening meal with dessert. On the Free Choice Diet, you choose which dish you want to eat from a selection of breakfasts, lunches, evening meals and desserts.

A typical day's diet

Daily allowance	½ pt (285 ml) skimmed milk	95
	5 fl oz (140 ml) fruit juice	50
	1 alcoholic drink	100
Breakfast	1 oz (28 g) muesli	100
	5 oz (140 g) diet yoghurt	50
	1 tsp sugar	15
Lunch	Sandwich, made with 2 slices bread, reduced-oil salad dressing, 3 oz (85 g) tuna in brine, unlimited salad	250
Evening meal	Fish curry, made with ½ apple, ¼ onion, ¼ tin tomatoes, ½ tbsp oil-free pickle, tomato purée, curry powder, 1½ tbsp tomato juice, 8 oz (225 g) haddock, garlic, herbs	350
	Melon and yoghurt salad, made with ¼ melon, 2½ oz (70 g) natural yoghurt, sugar, mint	40
	2 pieces of fruit	100
	Calories (approx)	1150
	Cost	£3.57

There are recipes for all the diet-plan dishes and meals. They are mainly for four people, but there are dishes for one, two and even 6–8 servings. Most main dishes contain fish or meat, but Rosemary Conley has vegetarian dishes in all sections.

You follow the diet day by day, doing the appropriate exercises at the same time.

Variations
Men are allowed two alcoholic drinks per day.

Exercise
The exercises for each day are illustrated and the instructions tell you what to do and exactly how many times to do it, including warm-up and cool-down routines.

Learning new habits
Each day's menu and exercise plan begins with encouragement designed to help you stick to the diet and keep up with the exercises.

Who shouldn't use it?
You are not to follow the diet and exercise plan without consulting your doctor if you have a medical condition or are pregnant.

Additional information
There is plenty of advice on foods to choose while away from home. For those in hotels and bed and breakfasts, there are lists of Green foods, to be eaten by dieters in moderation and by healthy eaters freely; Amber foods, which dieters should restrict but healthy eaters can have in moderation; and Red foods which dieters should avoid and healthy eaters should eat sparingly. For those in self-catering accommodation there are tips on low-fat, healthy eating. A five-minute beach workout is illustrated, designed so that you can practise discreetly while lying in the sun.

There is also a Three-Day Post-Holiday Corrector Diet, in case you have put on extra pounds while away, which is not to be followed for more than three days.

Keeping off the pounds

If you still have weight to lose after the diet and exercise programme, you are advised to stick with both until you have shed the required pounds.

Rosemary Conley says

'We can transform you from being tired and listless, flabby, overweight and lacking in confidence, into a *happy new you!*'

You say

'It's organized and easy to follow. I did the exercises every day. The way she goes about it makes you more motivated, because of her whole attitude.'

'I left it a bit late and started the week before I was going away, but still lost a couple of pounds and that made me feel better.'

We say

The exercises are carefully thought-out and the menu plans are well-balanced nutritionally. However, because you have to stick so closely to the diet it wouldn't be feasible to use the ordinary 14-day plan unless you intend to prepare your own lunches – this wouldn't be necessary on the Free Choice Diet.

Some of the exercises involving a beach ball might be difficult to do discreetly while you're on the beach. Anyone who saw you placing a beach ball on your inner thigh, holding it firmly against your bottom with your free hand and then raising and lowering your leg repeatedly while pressing on the ball might wonder what kind of exercises you were doing.

Calorie counting	×	Suitable for vegetarians	√
Weighing of food required	√	Less than £10 to start	√
Forbidden foods	√	Detailed 'who can't use'	√
Suit single person	√	Emphasizes fluid intake	√

Rosemary Conley's Whole Body Programme

Diet type
A low-fat, reduced-calorie diet with an exercise plan.

What is it?
A diet programme that is low in fat, moderate in protein and high in carbohydrate, and exercises designed to lose the maximum possible weight in a healthy way, in the shortest time. This 192-page, large-format book by Rosemary Conley also has exercise plans for pregnant women and post-natal routines to help regain your figure after your baby is born. Dieting vegetarians are offered advice on healthy eating, and people who have tried the diet describe their experiences.

First published in 1992, Rosemary Conley's *Whole Body Programme* has sold more than 200 000 copies to date. It is published by Arrow at £9.

How does it work?
Because your metabolic rate falls as food consumption is reduced, it is important to keep up food intake when trying to lose weight, Rosemary Conley believes. The idea is that if you increase your carbohydrate intake at the same time as you decrease the amount of fat you eat, then you can consume more food and still lose weight. Taking more exercise will use up even more calories and increase weight loss.

The diet
The Whole Body Programme is divided into one-week sections for four weeks in total. For each week there are daily menu plans and an illustrated guide to that week's exercises. There are ten basic rules to the diet, among them not nibbling between meals, only eating fruit with meals, restricting alcoholic drinks to one per day, eating more unrefined foods and stopping cooking with fat. Although potatoes are allowed freely, you should eat pasta and rice in moderation, and fill up with extra vegetables.

To help you when shopping, Rosemary Conley has lists of
384 almost fat-free foods which are ideal for everyone; foods mod-

erately high in fat which are fine for the rest of the family but only an occasional treat for the dieter; and foods high in fat which should be kept to a minimum in family eating (dieters should not eat them for the duration of the programme and should eat them only very occasionally when maintaining weight

A typical day's diet

Daily allowance	½ pt (285 ml) skimmed milk	95
	5 fl oz (140 ml) fruit juice	50
	1 alcoholic drink	100
Breakfast	1 rasher of bacon, grilled	90
	3 tomatoes, grilled	30
	1 slice wholemeal toast	60
Lunch	Cucumber boat with tuna, made with ¼ cucumber, ½ egg white, 2 oz (56 g) tuna canned in brine, 1 oz (28 g) Quark, ¼ tbsp lemon juice, parsley, chives, ¼ tsp mustard, lettuce	150
	Salad	20
Evening meal	Chicken and mushroom soup, made with ¼ onion, ¼ of a carrot, ¼ of a stock cube, chicken bones, herbs, etc.	80
	Prawn pilaff, made with 4 oz (110 g) prawns, 2 oz (56 g) rice, ¼ onion, ¼ pepper, 1 fl oz (28 ml) white wine, 1 oz (28 g) peas, 3 oz (85 g) canned sweet corn, water	475
	½ a melon	100
	Calories (approx)	1300
	Cost	£3.57

385

loss). You are advised to take a multivitamin pill each day. Some foods are forbidden during the course of the programme, mainly fatty ones. You can have a daily allowance of skimmed milk, fruit juice and alcohol, and as many vegetables as you like, plainly prepared, with the main meal of the day.

There are Regular, Budget and Vegetarian options for all recipes for all meals. There's also an eating plan for those who can't be bothered to cook recipe dishes: the Quick and Easy Basic Diet. Each day you are allowed a starter and a dessert with your evening meal from lists you are given.

Rosemary Conley provides recipes for vegetarian meals, lunches, main meals, side dishes, vegetables and desserts; some are illustrated in colour. Most are for two or four servings, but some are for from one to eight people. She also includes Christmas, Boxing Day and New Year's Eve party recipes.

Variations
Men can have three alcoholic drinks per day.

Exercise
Full-colour illustrations show you exactly what to do and how often on each week of the diet. The plan includes warm-up and stretch routines, aerobic, muscular-strength and endurance exercises. There is advice on using machines, and a special set of exercises designed for the elderly or disabled, which can be done sitting on a chair. There is also advice on exercising during and after pregnancy.

Who shouldn't use it?
You are advised that in the interests of good health it is always important to consult your doctor before commencing a diet or exercise programme.

Additional information
Videos of the Whole Body Programme and of the pregnancy and postnatal exercises are available at £10.99 including postage and packing from Rosemary Conley Enterprises, Quorn House, Meeting Street, Quorn, Loughborough LE12 8EX.

Keeping off the pounds

When you have got down to the weight you want to be, the idea is gradually to increase the amount of carbohydrate you eat. In addition, you can stick to low-fat foods or increase the amount of fat you eat by a small amount.

Rosemary Conley says

'A great new shape in just 28 days . . . how to lose the maximum weight in the minimum time.'

You say

'It's good because I'm in my seventies. She has special exercises that I can do sitting down.'

'The video is OK, but you get bored after a while. I couldn't at first, but now I can go right through it. You feel a bit of an idiot prancing round by yourself, but I've got more energy now.'

We say

This is another sound and well-balanced diet, and Rosemary Conley suggests taking a multivitamin tablet each day to ensure adequate nutrition. The exercise plans are easy to understand, the vegetarian advice sensible and helpful. The colour photographs of the food look wonderful. However, there aren't any guidelines on who shouldn't use this diet.

Calorie counting	×	Suitable for vegetarians	√
Weighing of food required	√	Less than £10 to start	√
Forbidden foods	√	Detailed 'who can't use'	×
Suit single person	√	Emphasizes fluid intake	×

Diet type
A reduced-calorie diet combined with an exercise plan.

What is it?
A 21-day plan by Judith Wills which aims to produce rapid improvements through diet and exercise. This plan, it is claimed, can help to improve your skin, nails and hair, alleviate PMT, fluid retention, digestive problems and constipation, and help you to overcome bingeing, while making the transition to a maintenance diet easier. Topics covered include body contouring, spot reduction and fat burning.

First issued in 1993, this 256-page book is published by Arrow at £3.99 and has sold 100 000 copies to date.

How does it work?
Women don't want to be thin, Judith Wills believes. They want to be shapely, with a bust, a waist, hips and a bottom. They want to be size 12, not a certain weight, and through diet and exercise she suggests this can be achieved.

The diet
The diet starts off with two days on a 'tough' allowance of 600 calories a day, moving up to 1100 for four days, then 950 per day for seven days and 800 calories for the last week. You must eat all you are allowed and not miss any meals, and you should drink as much water as you can. You don't have to count calories, but you do have to weigh ingredients.

All the recipes serve two and the plan is suitable for vegetarians. Each recipe is part of the daily plan.

Judith Wills suggests that to look an inch slimmer instantly, you should follow the book's body awareness and realignment programme, which is to do with posture.

Exercise
There are three components. The Body Contouring Programme calls for 20 minutes per day five times a week; the Spot Reducing Programme for five minutes on specified days; and the Fat

A typical day's diet from the highest calorie group, days 3 through 7

Breakfast	5 fl oz (140 ml) orange juice	50
Snack	1 apple	60
Lunch	Egg and salad sandwich, made with 1 boiled egg, unlimited green salad, a tomato, 2 slices wholemeal bread, with low-fat spread and 1 tbsp reduced-calorie mayonnaise	350
Snack	1 sachet low-cal instant soup 1 Ryvita (dark rye or oat bran variety)	40 25
Evening meal	Thai chicken and noodle stir-fry, made with 4 oz (110 g) chicken breast, ½ tbsp each of honey, sherry, corn oil, ½ tsp each of sugar, soy sauce, Thai 7-spice, cornflour, 2 fl oz (56 ml) each of chicken stock, bean sprouts, noodles, ½ each of red pepper, garlic clove, onion, 1 tsp lemon juice	500
	Calories (approx)	1100
	Cost	£3.57

Burning Programme for 20 minutes and more per day five days a week. All the exercises are fully illustrated and described.

Who shouldn't use it?
If you are already on a diet plan given to you by a doctor, or suffer from a particular medical condition, you must get your doctor's permission before you start the programme.

Expected weight loss
You could lose 6 lb (2.7 kg) in the first week of the diet. In the second week you could lose up to 5 lb (2.3 kg). You can be up **389**

to two dress-sizes smaller in 21 days, which is given as about 1 st (6.3 kg) in weight. This is well above medically recommended rates of weight loss.

Keeping off the pounds

The maintenance plan allows you to build up to eating approximately 2000 calories per day. Judith Wills believes that a gradual increase in the number of calories consumed is the best way to avoid the kinds of post-diet overeating that can come about because people think, 'Oh, the diet's finished now so I can reward myself', or because they feel that all their efforts have been wasted when the inevitable return of glycogen stores makes it seem they have put on weight.

She suggests that you follow the basic diet described earlier, but with additions from the lists given of 150-calorie items, for five days. Then you move on to a 1500 calorie diet for two days; then up to 2000 calories per day for a week. Subsequently you are to plan your own diet, repeating previous plans, or making up your own, or using the charts given, and adjusting the amount you eat depending on whether you gain or lose weight.

Judith Wills says

'Instant slimming . . . how to stay size 12 for ever.'

You say

'It was terribly hard. You really do cut down because the calories are very, very low and you do feel hungry, but if you stick at it the diet works'.

We say

Although this diet is well-balanced nutritionally, doctors don't advise that anyone diets on less than 1000 calories per day. The diet plan has been criticized for suggesting that you can lose 1 st (6.3 kg) in a month, which is a considerably higher rate of weight loss than medical opinion recommends.

You would have to be very careful to eat all that you were supposed to, if you tried this diet, in order to maintain good
390 health.

Calorie counting	×	Suitable for vegetarians	√
Weighing of food required	√	Less than £10 to start	√
Forbidden foods	×	Detailed 'who can't use'	√
Suit single person	√	Emphasizes fluid intake	√

Food Fact File

Thirty-seven per cent of schoolchildren aged 12–13 years living in a socially deprived area of East London were found to have eaten no fresh fruit during the week they kept a diary, and only 19 per cent had eaten vegetables (fresh or frozen), other than potatoes, on a daily basis. Their main sources of energy were chips, bread and confectionery.

Diet type
A low-fat, high-carbohydrate diet combined with an exercise plan.

What is it?
Susan Powter's personal odyssey in search of a solution to being fat is told in this 324-page book. She was a housewife who weighed 18 st 7 lb (118 kg) until, she says, she realized that the boys in the medical, diet and fitness industries had her fooled.

In her racy and amusing book, she tells us of the uselessness of dieting compared to the benefits of healthy eating and exercise. Many of her problems arose, she says, because of 'The Prince', her first husband, whose affairs with other women made her start overeating in the first place. She eventually came to realize that it wasn't (her by now ex-) husband's fault she was fat; it was because she couldn't take control of her life.

Learning how to take control of your life is what this book is all about. After endless pills and starvation diets, Susan Powter gave up dieting and started to walk for half an hour a day, carrying her children. She also decided to eat plenty of low-fat high-quality food. After a week she felt less tired, and better physically and, gradually, she got her weight down to normal.

The book is illustrated with photographs of the author as she shed 9 st 7 lb (60.4 kg). It was published by Orion in 1994 and is available for £5.99.

How does it work?
If you are fat and unhappy, you are unwell. Most fat people, in Susan Powter's view, are like the living dead — deprived of oxygen, their metabolic rates gone awry, lugging round useless flab. If you are fat, you don't need your self-esteem improving, you need to get well, she says. To do that you have to take control of your life and decide to eat, breathe and move properly.

The diet
Susan Powter believes that you can eat a greater volume of food

if it is low in fat and high in carbohydrate; and, if you take more exercise, you will still lose weight. She points out that the energy requirement of a 10 st 10 lb (68.1 kg) woman walking or cycling four or five times a week is 1600 calories a day, much more than people usually eat on a diet. It's not food that makes you fat, she feels, it's fat that makes you fat. She shows how to calculate the real percentage of fat in so-called low-fat foods. There are comparison charts to show you that, for example, 4½ lb (2 kg) of rice contains the same amount of fat as one chocolate-chip biscuit.

This diet is essentially a very-low-fat, high-carbohydrate regime. Fruit is not something that Susan Powter recommends you eat often; oils, milk, cheese and eggs are out; you are strongly discouraged from eating red meat and oily fish, and she thinks it best to eat as little white meat as possible. There are no menu plans: you can eat as much as you like until you are full. There are no recipes either, so the diet can be as varied as you want it to be.

While on the diet you are encouraged to stick up for yourself. Susan Powter admits that she has had plastic surgery – a tummy tuck, something done to her ear – and fully intends to have a face-lift. She says she tells anyone who says that she is betraying women and trying to live up to an impossible ideal by having surgery to go to hell.

Exercise
Susan Powter believes very strongly in learning the art of correct breathing, after which you can begin to improve your fitness level no matter what your age or weight. Walking is sufficient to start with, but as fitness improves you can move on to more strenuous activities. There are illustrated exercises covering correct movement, strength, flexibility and resistance, and she advises 30–60 minutes of aerobic exercise a day for six days a week.

Learning new habits
Although there isn't a formal plan for a change of lifestyle, Susan Powter believes that mind modification – meditation and visualization, for example – will help you to achieve your goals. Don't wait around for an increase in self-esteem before you start living your life, she says. Start living it *now*.

393

Who shouldn't use it?
There are no warnings against anyone using this diet.

Additional information
An exercise video, 'Lean, Strong and Healthy' is available in the shops for £11.99.

Keeping off the pounds
To maintain your new lean body you will probably have to keep exercising three or four times per week, and of course stick to your new eating plan.

Susan Powter says
'Change the way you look and feel for ever.'

You say
'The main thing about it is that she says to start where you are and "do something". You don't have to start by running a mile; maybe just walking up a flight of stairs would be a great accomplishment. What she had to say was nothing I hadn't heard before, but I think it worked for her because it was *her idea*. For something to work for most of us, it *must be* our idea. I don't think any of us follows the commercial programmes exactly as they are written. We do something to make them our own.'

'One woman's biography of her struggle. It was interesting – I couldn't believe the photos were of her, she looks like a different person now. The diet was like all low-calorie diets, very boring after a while.'

'The video was simply inspirational – I've never seen fat people on an exercise video before – but the routines are boring.'

We say
An uplifting book, but Susan Powter doesn't give enough details of what the diet actually is. If you do eat as much as you like, even of high-quality, low-fat foods, you will certainly have to increase your exercise level significantly or you may well find that you are putting on weight, not taking it off. As with all very-low-fat diets, it's important not to take things to extremes – some fat is essential to good health.

Susan Powter's criticism of the diet industry rings a little hollow when as it has been pointed out sales of her diets, audiotapes, videos, books and so forth have grossed millions of dollars. She's a one-woman diet industry all by herself.

Calorie counting	×	Suitable for vegetarians	√
Weighing of food required	×	Less than £10 to start	×
Forbidden foods	√	Detailed 'who can't use'	×
Suit single person	√	Emphasizes fluid intake	×

Food Fact File

Weekly shopping list for a poor working-class family of three in the 1930s:

2 lb (900 g) butter	2 lb (900 g) onions
2 lb (900 g) sugar	½ lb (225 g) bacon
½ lb (225 g) tea	½ lb (225 g) prunes
1 tin cocoa	l lb (450 g) peas
12 lb (5.4 kg) potatoes	2 lb (900 g) marmalade
2 lb (900 g) carrots	8 loaves of bread

Ultratone

Diet type
A reduced-calorie diet combined with electrical stimulation.

What is it?
Ultratone equipment consists of a box containing a micro-processor which regulates the flow of electric current. Soft rubber pads are attached by leads to the unit. It is battery or mains-operated and has an electronic timer. Users who want to lose weight as well as tone the body can apply to the makers for a Nutritional Plan.

Ultratone began in Britain in 1989, since when the makers have sold thousands of units worldwide. They advertise their products for home use in the press, and the system is used in many beauty salons. You can have a free demonstration at Ultratone's London headquarters – call 0171 935 0631 for details. The basic home model costs £296. In a salon, treatment would last between 30 and 45 minutes and cost from about £15 to £20 per session. You can also buy smaller Ultratone units, battery-operated, designed for use on the face.

How does it work?
The theory is that electrical stimulation of the muscles, combined with a nutritional programme, will help you both to lose weight and tone your body. Electrical stimulation of the muscles is carried out by applying the rubber pads, wetted with water, to your thighs, hips, bust, stomach or waist. The pads are attached to your body with fabric straps or you can buy disposable pads impregnated with an adhesive gel.

The basic unit has eight pads and the exercise cycle is preset at two seconds on and two seconds off, with variable strength of stimulation. This means that the pulse is transmitted 15 times a minute, causing your muscles to expand and contract, so your muscles are stimulated 450 times in half an hour.

More expensive units have ten pads each and allow you more variation in the timing of the impulse. You don't have to do anything while you are being stimulated; you are advised to relax, read, watch TV or listen to music.

The machines used in salons are much more complex and can

stimulate up to 20 areas at a time with varying intensities and frequencies.

The diet
If you want to lose weight and not only tone your body, you apply to the makers for the Nutritional Plan. First you must complete a questionnaire which asks about your medical and

A typical day's diet

Throughout the day	1 pt (570 ml) skimmed milk	190
	2 small diet yoghurts	100
Breakfast	1 small glass orange juice	50
	1 oz (28 g) porridge oats	100
	5 fl oz (140 ml) skimmed milk (extra to allowance)	40
Light meal	2 crispbreads	50
	1 oz (28 g) lean ham	30
	2 oz (56 g) low-fat cottage cheese	50
	Large mixed salad, no dressing	20
	1 peach	50
Snack	1 white chocolate log	155
Main meal	6 oz (170 g) grilled gammon rasher	260
	1 ring of drained pineapple in natural juice	20
	2 oz (56 g) sweet corn	70
	Boiled green beans	30
	4 oz (110 g) blackberries, fresh or frozen, with artificial sweetener	30
	2 tbsp low-fat yoghurt	20
	Calories (approx)	1250
	Cost	£3.57

dieting history, your current measurements and level of exercise, what you normally eat for different meals and how much snacking you do, and so on. Then you are sent a diet plan devised by a *Slimming* magazine nutritional expert.

The plan allows three meals per day – a breakfast, a light meal and a main meal – plus one or more snacks depending on how much weight you have to lose. The snacks are listed and you make up your own daily plan.

You can have as many low-calorie vegetable nibbles and low-calorie drinks as you like. In addition, there is a daily allowance of diet yoghurt and skimmed milk, which you can use for coffee or tea. Portions should be weighed where a weight is stated, but you don't have to count calories. The diet plan includes convenience foods, and vegetarian diets are available.

Who shouldn't use it?

You cannot use Ultratone electrical equipment if you have multiple sclerosis, unless approved by a doctor. Anyone with a heart pacemaker, a serious medical problem or diabetes, or who is pregnant or has had a major operation, would not be allowed to use the system.

Side-effects

Occasional problems with skin irritation are reported by people with allergies to rubber. Putting gauze between the pads and the skin will prevent this problem, according to the makers.

Additional information

An audiotape and a fully illustrated, step-by-step colour guide which come with the unit explain how to use the system. Consultants are always available to answer queries by telephone.

If you apply for the Nutritional Plan, complete the questionnaire and return it within 14 days, fill in and return a progress report every month for three months, use the Ultratone unit daily and don't put on any weight, and your measurements still haven't changed, your money will be fully refunded.

The height/weight chart included with the diet plan gives the acceptable weight range for a 5 ft 4 in (1.63 m) person of small
to above average build as 8 st 3 lb (52.5 kg) to 9 st 5 lb

(59.5 kg). These represent BMIs of about 20–22 and are in line with current medical opinion.

Expected weight loss

Promotional literature included with the product doesn't give any indication of expected weight loss, but you are told that one user lost 19 lb (8.6 kg) in three months, which would be within the medically recommended rates.

They say

'The best way to lose weight is to combine Ultratone exercise with a good diet plan, thus avoiding the sagging and flabbiness which is often a penalty of just dieting alone.'

You say

'It's a bit weird at first because you don't expect to see your body move without you telling it to, but you get used to it. The diet was just the same as all the others – low in fat – so if you did it, I suppose you would lose weight. I just couldn't be bothered.'

'I just like the pampering that goes with it at the salon.'

We say

If you followed the diet plan, which is well-balanced nutritionally, then you would lose weight. Whether electrical stimulation improves body tone has never been scientifically established, but it certainly won't lead to weight loss.

The directors of Ultratone assure me that they have never had any incidents reported to them where people have been burned or electrocuted when using the unit. Nevertheless you should always follow the instructions carefully, as when using any electrical equipment.

Calorie counting	×	Suitable for vegetarians	√
Weighing of food required	√	Less than £10 to start	×
Forbidden foods	×	Detailed 'who can't use'	×
Suit single person	√	Emphasizes fluid intake	×

Diet type
A reduced-calorie diet combined with an exercise plan.

What is it?
A 30-day, low-fat, high-fibre diet plan. Les Snowdon and Maggie Humphreys were overweight and unfit until they took up regular walking and a low-fat diet. The book they then wrote, *The Walking Diet*, was published in Britain in 1991 and has since sold more than 100 000 copies worldwide. This was followed by *Walk Slim*, first published in 1994. The authors wanted to expand their concept of health and fitness to include aerobic walking for the whole family – for all ages and levels of fitness. *Walk Slim*'s topics include fitness for all the family, dealing with stress and living healthily for longer, and there are also readers' testimonials, the diet plan and an aerobic fitness plan. The 192-page book is published by Mainstream at £5.99.

How does it work?
Brisk aerobic walking is the easiest and most effective way to lose weight, when combined with a healthy diet, *Walk Slim* maintains, as aerobic walking burns off 400 calories per hour. At first, you just stick to walking. The authors believe that it is easier to start dieting once you have seen your energy levels rise as a result of your increased activity.

The diet
The Walk Slim Diet is a 30-day plan of light meals and main meals using a pyramid system. Foods at the 'top' of the pyramid, like fat, you can only eat a little of; foods at the 'bottom', like green vegetables, can be eaten in larger quantities. You don't have to follow the menu plans; if you prefer, you can substitute other foods from the recipes given. Nothing is forbidden, but you are advised to stick to fresh foods and to reduce your intake of sugar, fats, sweets and the like.

You don't have to count calories, but you do have to weigh foods to make up the recipes. There isn't a specific recommendation for breakfasts, but guidelines are given. With each meal you are to serve additional vegetables or a salad, and you can have wholemeal bread and fruit as well, within the guidelines of the pyramid. The recipes are divided into light meals and main meals. They are for two servings and include pasta and rice, vegetarian, fish and meat dishes.

The calorie count on this diet would depend on how many additional foods you ate. The sample menu below allows for three extra pieces of fruit and four slices of bread, and for a serving of baked potato with the main meal.

A typical day's diet

Throughout the day	*Extra bread and fruit*	*500*
Breakfast	*Porridge and semi-skimmed milk*	*150*
Light meal	*Garden salad, made with 1 carrot, 1 tomato, ½ stick celery, ½ a pear, cucumber, lemon juice, pepper Vegetables/salad*	*200*
Main meal	*Chicken Provençal, made with 1 chicken breast, ½ tin chopped tomatoes, ½ onion, ½ aubergine, 2 oz (56 g) courgettes, 1 oz (28 g) mushrooms, ½ red pepper, 1 oz (28 g) olives, garlic, herbs Vegetables/salad*	*400*
	Calories (approx depending on added vegetables)	1250
	Cost	£3.57

Exercise

There are two parts, the 30-Day Walkout and the Whole Body Workout. Illustrations show you how to warm up before beginning to walk and what cool-down stretches should be done **401** afterwards. There is guidance on equipment, steps per minute, stepping routines and how and when to increase your rate.

In the first week of the 30-Day Walkout you walk for 30 minutes, covering 1.9 miles (3 km) on each of five days; by the last week of the plan you should be up to 50–60 minutes per day, covering 3.1 to 3.75 miles (5–6 km). For the development of stamina, strength and suppleness you must follow the Whole Body Workout as well, three times a week.

The authors claim that exercise increases metabolic rate even when the exercise period is over.

Variations
Walk Slim explains the benefits of walking for children, for the over-50s, and for people with backache, arthritis or diabetes.

Who shouldn't use it?
The unfit, pregnant women and those with a medical problem that exercise might affect should not start the programme without first consulting a doctor.

Additional information
The height/weight chart gives the ideal weight for a 5 ft 4 in (1.63 m) woman of medium build as 9 st (57.2 kg), representing a BMI of 22, which is in line with current medical opinion. In addition, the book has a 'Fat and Fibre Facts' section which details the fat and fibre content of ingredients used in the recipes and for other common foodstuffs.

You can buy the 'Walk Slim' video from video shops for £10.99. This includes details of the 30-Day Walkout and the Whole Body Walkout. There is also an audiotape that you can listen to as you walk; one side has instructions on how to increase your pace gradually, the other side has music. It costs £9.99.

Expected weight loss
You are expected to lose 1 st (6.3 kg) in a month, which would be about 3–4 lb (1.4–1.8 kg) per week. This is above medically recommended rates.

Keeping off the pounds
There is no formal programme, but you should continue to follow the rules of healthy eating and walk a minimum of four times a week for 30 minutes at a time.

They say
'Say goodbye to failure and hello to sweet, glorious success. The Walk Slim Diet Plan will shift those unwanted pounds, tone and trim you.'

You say
'It's the kind of thing I go for anyway, as I'm a keen walker. The food was good, but the plan was very strict – you get to feel obsessed about doing your allotted hours, and there's pressure to speed up all the time.'

'I couldn't do the diet – you're not allowed puddings.'

We say
The benefits of walking are stressed in every study about improving your health. Walking is easy, it costs nothing and you can involve the whole family, all of which make it the best and most accessible form of exercise. It would be great if there was evidence of psychological benefits from increased exercise too, but so far the evidence is not clear-cut.

It's unfortunately not the case that your metabolic rate increases for any significant period after exercising, as *Walk Slim* claims. A less important point is that the diet could be more clearly laid out, because when following meal plans and choosing from the meat or fish recipes you must refer back to the healthy eating pyramid every time, to make sure that you are getting sufficient carbohydrate.

Calorie counting	×	Suitable for vegetarians	√
Weighing of food required	√	Less than £10 to start	√
Forbidden foods	×	Detailed 'who can't use'	√
Suit single person	√	Emphasizes fluid intake	×

I haven't given any of the diets in this chapter a tick for promoting long-term healthy eating if they forbid certain foods and don't suggest a gradual introduction of these high-fat, high-calorie items *in moderation* after you have reached your target weight. Nutritionists always recommend a wide range of foods in any diet; and although we are all supposed to cut down on fat consumption, some fat is essential to good health.

If a programme maintains that your metabolic rate is increased for a period after exercising – which it isn't, except slightly and for a short time – I have still given the programme a tick for 'Theory scientifically proven' if the diet is a sensible one, because this was received wisdom until relatively recently. I can't do the same for diets claiming spot reduction (i.e., that you can lose fat from some parts of your body but not others), because this has never been established scientifically, nor for any diet that claims you can eat as much as you like and still lose weight.

Key features of spot reduction, body shaping and exercise programmes

Name	Theory scientifically proven	Promotes long-term healthy eating	Suggests new habits	Exercise plan	Weight-loss maintenance programme
Exercise	✓	—	—	✓	—
A Flat Stomach in 15 Days	✗	✓	✗	✓	✓
Judith Wills' Complete Speed Slimming System	✓	✓	✓	✓	✓
Lean Revolution	✗	✗	✗	✓	✗
Liposuction	✓	✗	✗	✗	✗
Rosemary Conley's Beach Body Plan	✓	✓	✗	✓	✗

Rosemary Conley's Complete Hip and Thigh Diet	✕	✓	✕	✓	✓
Rosemary Conley's Flat Stomach Plan	✓	✓	✓	✓	✓
Rosemary Conley's Inch Loss Plan	✓	✓	✓	✓	✓
Rosemary Conley's Metabolism Booster Diet	✓	✓	✕	✓	✓
Rosemary Conley's Shape Up for Summer	No theory stated	✓	✓	✓	✕
Rosemary Conley's Whole Body Programme	✓	✓	✕	✓	✓
Size 12 in 21 Days	✕	✓	✕	✓	✓
Stop the Insanity!	✕	✕	✓	✓	✕
Ultratone	✓*	✓	✕	✕	✕
Walk Slim	✓	✓	✕	✓	✓

* For the diet, not the electrical treatment.

Chapter 17

Weight Loss Methods Not to Try

I'm not awarding any marks for these methods, because potentially they are all extremely dangerous to health. The financial cost is irrelevant because the personal costs are so high. None is effective in the long term.

Fasting – giving up food altogether for periods of time – has been practised for thousands of years, not as a means of reducing weight but of increasing holiness. All the major religions of the world have advised their followers to fast for periods of time, and each year millions of people do.

Gluttony is a vice, but fasting has been seen as a virtue. The Christian Church, like others, has asked its adherents to fast regularly as a way of pleasing God and asking Him to grant forgiveness and mercy. Being able to ignore the body's demands for food and deny the flesh has always been a proof of spirituality. Many of the early Christian saints seem to have taken this too seriously and became positively anorexic in their fasting for religious reward.

Strictures on fasting were almost always relaxed for vulnerable people – nursing mothers, the elderly, children – because it was realized that they could suffer ill-effects from an overzealous regime. Psychologists know that in states of physical weakness people are often more susceptible to emotional pressure: the steps to cathedrals are carefully designed to make you breathless before you enter, for example; and the sustained breath control required for hymn-singing combined with the effects of not having eaten for some time gave medieval worshippers a heightened sense of spirituality.

Bear in mind, though, that fasting is not always used to mean eating nothing or very little. Muslims 'fast' during Ramadan, but only in the sense that they may not eat or drink between sunrise and sunset (after sunset, they can eat their fill). Likewise, Christians traditionally fast during Lent, but this does not mean they give up eating altogether.

In recent times, fasting has become a possible method of weight reduction for extremely heavy people, but it has usually been carried out under medical supervision. However, in the 1970s fasting became extremely popular as a method of dieting for ordinary overweight people. It was bound up with all sorts of spiritual nonsense about improving mental health. Even as a short-term measure fasting can be harmful, but continued for any length of time it becomes extremely dangerous.

Eating almost nothing doesn't just mean that your body won't **407** get the nutrients necessary for good health or that you will feel hungry. Losing weight too quickly – and you will certainly lose weight if you don't eat – means that you can lose too much muscle and bone as well as fat. The side-effects of fasting include dizziness, nausea, dehydration, fatigue, loss of minerals such as potassium, calcium and magnesium, possible liver and kidney damage, and sudden death (usually from heart failure, especially if prolonged fasting has caused the heart muscles to waste away).

It is possible to fast without fully realizing what you are doing. When a diet specifies that you may only eat a small number of foodstuffs, what often happens is that one item – say, for example, pineapple – is so expensive that the dieter cuts out the others to the point where he or she might as well be fasting. The Beverly Hills Diet, for example, allowed only exotic fruits, for their supposed fat-burning qualities (which they don't have). This became known as the 'Diarrhoea Diet' and many would consider it one of the worst diets ever devised; all the symptoms associated with fasting were experienced by people who tried it, except death; no one could stand it for that long. So if you come across a diet that promises dramatic results from eating only one type of food, have nothing to do with it.

You say

'I've tried not eating anything for days on end and then I just go berserk and eat everything. It's a waste of time.'

We say

Don't do it.

Purging means the use of laxatives, enemas ('colonic irrigation'), diuretics (drugs that make you pee more), emetics (drugs that make you sick) and simply making yourself sick. For hundreds of years, people dosed themselves with strong purgatives that often had them writhing in agony in attempts to control their weight, at a time when the right dosage of any medicine couldn't be calculated. Herbal treatments contained differing quantities of the active ingredients, depending on the season, the way they were prepared, how long ago they had been picked and so forth.

Even today some people use laxatives, enemas and diuretics to try to lose weight. Purging is most common in people who suffer from eating disorders, but is also practised by ordinary dieters and by slim non-dieters who feel that their stomachs are sticking out too much, or because they feel bloated, particularly at menstruation, or because they want to rid themselves of food they feel they shouldn't have eaten. Very occasional use of purging is probably harmless even if completely unnecessary, and there's no need to think that you've got an eating disorder if you've ever tried any of these methods.

Diuretics work by causing the kidneys to expel mineral salts, especially potassium chloride, but also zinc and magnesium. To flush out the salts water must be used, and as 1 pt (570 ml) of water weighs about 1 lb (450 g), the result is a slight weight loss. This is completely temporary. Within a few hours the weight will have returned. With repeated use, the body becomes used to these drugs, so higher and higher doses are needed to achieve the desired effects. All too soon people can become diuretic or laxative abusers, taking more than the recommended dose – often many times more. Serious side-effects of abuse include fits, coma, paralysis and death through heart failure. This is all a complete waste of time because taking laxatives or diuretics even in enormous quantities does not lead to weight loss.

One problem that occurs with laxative abusers who have been taking laxatives for a long time in high doses is that if they do stop abruptly they may become constipated, puff up horribly and immediately put on a lot of weight. People are often so frightened that they go straight back to using laxatives again. **409**

Diuretics abusers experience similar problems if they stop taking the tablets. The best thing to do is to tell your doctor and seek help while you *gradually* cut down on the dose. Sudden withdrawal of diuretics can cause extreme water retention, but that's all it is – it isn't a permanent weight gain.

Making yourself sick is something a lot of people do occasionally, although taking drugs or medicines to make yourself sick is more unusual. Regular use of either of these methods is very dangerous. As with the abuse of laxatives and diuretics, the metabolic balance of the body is disturbed, as essential minerals are lost. Dizziness and fatigue are common; tooth enamel can be rotted off through the action of acids in the vomit; heart irregularities may occur; and in any case as a long-term method of weight control making yourself sick is *completely useless*.

Most of the physical ill-effects of purging are completely reversed once the practice is given up. Often the person feels happier, too – knowing that you are really messing up your body really messes up your mind.

You say

'I was on 10 or 12 laxatives twice a day for ages, then I started to have blackouts. God knows what it's done. I can never go to the toilet normally but I can't tell the doctor.'

'I've been making myself sick for years, and I'm the same weight as I was when I started. I feel guilty and depressed all the time, because if people knew what I was doing they'd be disgusted. I'm disgusted.'

We say

If you are worried because you are abusing purgatives, go and see your doctor. If you really can't face doing that, call one of the numbers listed on page 415–16 and ask for help.

In 1971 the British Medical Association recommended that so far as possible amphetamines should not be prescribed. This was because amphetamines can be addictive, and in any case their appetite-suppressing effects wear off quite quickly unless the dose is continually increased. Slimming-pill abusers – people who take drugs not prescribed for them – tend to increase the number of tablets they take to the extent that they may be taking 10 or 20 times the correct dose. They buy illegally made pills, which are often amphetamines, or they persuade their friends to get standard appetite-suppressant drugs prescribed by gullible or irresponsible doctors, and then take the tablets themselves.

The side-effects of abusing amphetamines in large doses include fits, coma and death, and in smaller doses dizziness, insomnia, depression, hallucinations, fatigue, nausea and vomiting. The drugs prescribed by doctors are generally safe at the recommended dose – at higher doses anxiety, nervousness and irritability are common. Problems can arise when you stop taking these tablets. It's important to seek a doctor's advice if that happens to you.

Even with legally prescribed drugs there's very little evidence of long-term weight loss, and there's no evidence that ones taken illegally are any better.

You say

'I was taking 30 or 40 a day – I got my pals to get them from the doctor. I only ate half a slice of bread a day. I was nervy and panicking all the time. I was so light-headed I felt I was walking in the air. I was so thin I lost my bust, I was all bone. I couldn't sit in the bath it was so sore and my husband and I nearly broke up over it, he was so fed up with me.'

'I felt terrible, on edge and hyped-up all the time, and I didn't even lose any weight.'

We say

If you are abusing slimming pills, do seek your doctor's advice. You won't get into trouble for taking the pills, and your doctor **411** will help you to stop taking them gradually – This is important because sudden withdrawal from these drugs can be physically and mentally very distressing.

Food Fact File

By 1936, 100 000 people in the USA were taking the metabolism-boosting drug dinitrophenol to lose weight. It caused appalling skin rashes; many people went blind and others died. It was suppressed in 1938.

Smoking Cigarettes

Smoking has been marketed as a slimming aid for years. Sometimes the tobacco barons have been blatant about it, as in the 1920s advertisements which promoted 'Smoking – the modern way to diet'; at other times they have taken a more subtle approach to addiction. For years, advertising copy was full of words like 'slim' and 'thin', in case you hadn't got the message.

Smoking does have effects on weight. These may be because smoking affects metabolism in the same way as food – it has been calculated that smoking 20 cigarettes uses up 70 calories per day. But there's also evidence that smokers tend to eat different things from non-smokers. Men smokers eat more white bread, sugar and butter, but less fruit, protein, carbohydrate, polyunsaturated fat and fibre than non-smokers. It doesn't seem to be true that smoking actually makes you *feel* less hungry, but it may change the way you taste food. This may also be affected by the fact that smoking alters your sense of smell, and how foods taste is actually a combination of how we both taste *and* smell what we eat.

Everyone believes that smokers weigh less than non-smokers, so it's easy to suppose that smoking must make you thin. A recent survey showed that 37 per cent of young girls who smoked had taken up cigarettes in the forlorn hope it would control their weight. This is *not* always true! Recently it has been shown that British women who smoke weigh *exactly the same* as those who don't. (There is a slight difference for men – male smokers are a few pounds lighter than non-smokers.) The proportion of smokers and non-smokers who are very seriously overweight is the same.

The main side-effect of smoking is, of course, death from lung cancer. Smoking also increases your chances of heart disease and stroke, as well as highly unpleasant respiratory complaints like emphysema.

Another popular myth is that giving up smoking means instantly becoming a fatty. This need not happen at all. Most of any weight gain is the result of ex-smokers rewarding themselves for being good by scoffing sweets and chocolates, and eating more overall because as their sense of smell improves they enjoy their food more. Most ex-smokers who gain weight return to their previous weight within a couple of years. This may seem a long time, but if you know what to expect when you stop smoking you can reward yourself with special non-food treats such as clothes or evenings out with all the money you've saved. You can also congratulate yourself on depriving the cigarette companies of fat profits and the government of hundreds of pounds per year in tax.

You say
'I just wish I'd never started.'

We say
Your doctor can prescribe tablets, patches or gum which will help you to stop smoking, or you can simply buy them in the shops. In addition, there may be stop-smoking clinics at your local hospital or community centre. For advice and help, call the QUITLINE on 0171 487 3000 if you live in England or on 01232 663281 if you live in Northern Ireland, or 01222 641888 in Wales. In Scotland, calls to The Smokeline, on 0800 848484, are free of charge.

Are you being realistic?

You don't have to diet if you don't want to. Don't diet to please anyone else; it's not effective. Doctors recommend a BMI of between 20 and 25, but it's not until BMI reaches 27 that being overweight may become a risk to health. So long as you are eating healthily, you needn't be concerned.

Keeping off the pounds

The methods you employ when losing weight are *not* the same as those needed to keep the weight off in the long term. People tend to avoid very tempting foods when dieting, but not many can or want to avoid them for the rest of their lives, so they must learn to eat these foods in a controlled manner, without starting to overeat.

Diets tend to last for a short time, but maintaining weight loss long-term involves making healthy food choices that you can make into part of your lifestyle.

You don't have to exercise to lose weight, but exercising is associated with keeping to your new weight in the long term.

If things get out of hand . . .

If you have or think you have an eating disorder, or simply feel that you are losing control of your eating habits, call these two organizations. Either one will advise you and recommend professional help:

Eating Disorders Association
39 Sackville Place
44 Magdalen Street
Norwich
Norfolk NR3 1JE

Tel: 01603 621414

National Centre for Eating Disorders
54 New Road
Esher
Surrey KT10 9NU

Tel: 01372 469493

Feel good about yourself!
If you are very overweight then losing some of it will greatly benefit your health. But don't sit at home reading articles about slimming or watching videos about dieting and worrying about losing weight. Go out and have a good time, enjoy yourself! Life is too short to care about a few pounds either way.

Write to me
I would welcome comments from anyone who has read this book and tried any of the dietary methods described in it, or from anyone who feels that I have missed out a diet that should be included in the next edition. Write to:

Jane Dunkeld
Department of Psychology
University of Edinburgh
7 George Square
Edinburgh EH8 9JZ
Scotland

Alternatively, you can contact me by e-mail at:
jane dunkeld@ed.ac.uk

Estimated Average Requirements (EAR) and Reference Nutrient Intake (RNI) Tables

Estimated Average Requirements (EAR)

These figures are the British government's Estimated Average Requirements per day for adult men and women's intake of protein, fat, fibre and carbohydrate. The figures are only averages; a taller or shorter, large-framed or small-framed person would need more or less of them. Figures are given in grams.

	Men	Women
Protein (g)	45	36
Fat (g*)	85	65
Carbohydrate (g)	319	243
Calories	2550	1940
Fibre (g)	18	18

* You don't really need fat except for essential fatty acids, so this is calculated at 30 per cent of total calorie intake, the recommended amount.

Reference Nutrient Intake (RNI)

These figures show what the British government calls the Reference Nutrient Intake (RNI), the daily amount of a vitamin or mineral which is estimated to be enough for 97 per cent of the population. That is more than enough for most people. Figures are given in milligrams and micrograms.

Average Requirements and Reference Nutrient Intake Tables

Vitamins	Men	Women	Minerals	Men	Women
Vitamin A (μg)	700	600	Calcium (mg)	700	700
Vitamin B1 (thiamin) (mg)	1.0	0.8	Copper (mg)	1.2	1.2
Vitamin B2 (riboflavin) (mg)	1.3	1.1	Iodine (μg)	140	140
Vitamin B3 (niacin) (mg)	17	13	Iron (mg)	9	15
Vitamin B6 (pyridoxine) (mg)	1.4	1.2	Potassium (mg)	3500	3500
Vitamin B12 (cobalamin) (μg)	1.5	1.5	Phosphorus (mg)	550	550
Folate (μg) (Folic acid)	200	200	Magnesium (mg)	300	270
Pantothenic acid (mg)*	3–7	3–7	Selenium (μg)	75	60
Biotin (μg)*	10–200	10–200	Sodium (mg)	1600	1600
Vitamin C (mg)	40	40	Zinc (mg)	10	7
Vitamin D (μg)**	0	0			
Vitamin E (mg)	7	5			
Vitamin K (μg)***	1	1			

* This is considered adequate, although the exact amount is not yet known.

** So long as you expose your skin to the sun in summer, you don't need additional vitamin D.

*** The recommended amount is 1μg per kilo of body weight.

Food Labelling

Major ingredients in diet products and slimming supplements

Name	What is it?	Effect or supposed effect
Aspartame	artificial sweetener	sweetener
Barley flour	flour	thickener
Bearberry	herb	diuretic
Beeswax	animal product	stiffening agent
Beta fibre	plant fibre	thickener
Boldo	herb	diuretic
Buchu	herb	diuretic
Calcium carbonate	chalk	anti-caking agent
Caraway	herb	flatulence reducer
Carrageenan	seaweed extract	stabilizer, thickener
Cellulose	additive	stabilizer, thickener and emulsifier
Chickweed	herb	laxative
Chromium picolinate	chemical	metabolism booster
Cinnamon	herb	flatulence and diarrhoea reducer, flavouring
Clove	herb	flavouring
Corn bran	plant extract	bulker
Couch grass	herb	diuretic

Food Labelling

Name	What is it?	Effect or supposed effect
Dextrose	type of sugar	sweetener
Dicalcium phosphate	additive	mineral supplement
Disodium orthophosphate	additive	anti-caking agent
Echinacea	herb	laxative and emetic
Fennel	herb	diuretic
Fenugreek	herb	flavouring
Fructose	type of sugar	sweetener
Gelatine	animal extract	thickener
Glucose syrup	type of sugar	sweetener
Guar gum	additive	thickener
Guarana	herb	metabolism booster
Gum arabic	additive	stabilizer, thickener and emulsifier
Hawthorn	herb	digestive aid
Honey powder	type of sugar	sweetener
Invert sugar syrup	type of sugar	sweetener
Juniper	herb	diuretic
Karaya gum (sterculia gum; Indian tragacanth)	additive	stabilizer, thickener and emulsifier
Kelp	seaweed	metabolism booster
L-arginine hypochloride, arginine	amino acid	appetite suppressant
L-ornithine hypochloride, ornithine	amino acid	appetite suppressant

Name	What is it?	Effect or supposed effect
Lactose	type of sugar	sweetener
Lecithin	additive	emulsifier
Liquorice	herb	laxative
Magnesium bicarbonate	additive	anti-caking agent
Magnesium oxide	additive	anti-caking agent
Magnesium stearate	additive	anti-caking agent, emulsifier
Maltodextrin	type of sugar	sweetener
Maltose	type of sugar	sweetener
Meadowsweet	herb	diuretic
Methylcellulose	additive	stabilizer, thickener and emulsifier
Monocalcium phosphate	additive	anti-oxidant
Papain	fruit	diuretic
Pectin	additive	stabilizer and emulsifier; laxative
Phaseolamin	plant extract	starch blocker
Potassium chloride	additive	gelling agent; salt substitute
Potassium phosphate	additive	acidity regulator
Propylene glycol alginate	chemical	used as a vehicle for drugs insoluble in water
Psyllium husks psyllium seeds	plant extracts	laxative
Rosehip	herb	laxative
Safflower oil	herb extract	metabolism booster

Food Labelling

Name	What is it?	Effect or supposed effect
Sodium benzoate	additive	preservative
Stearic acid	additive	anti-caking agent; lubricant
Sucrose	type of sugar	sweetener
Tri-calcium phosphate, tri-calcium orthophosphate	additive	anti-caking agent
Tri-potassium orthophosphate	additive	emulsifier, anti-oxidant
Tri-sodium citrate	additive	anti-oxidant
Verbena	herb	flatulence reducer, flavouring
Walnut	nut	laxative
Wheatgerm	plant extract	thickener
Xanthan gum (corn sugar gum)	plant extract	stabilizer, thickener and emulsifier

Body Mass Index (BMI) Tables

To find your BMI, consult one of the charts on the following pages. Look up the number that matches your height in inches and your weight in pounds (pages 424–5) or alternatively your height in centimetres and your weight in kilograms (pages 426–7).

Imperial

Weight in pounds	Height in inches														
	58	59	60	61	62	63	64	65	66	67	68	69	70	71	72
90	19	18	18	17	17	16	15	15	15	14	14	13	13	13	12
92	19	19	18	17	17	16	16	15	15	14	14	14	13	13	13
94	20	19	18	18	17	17	16	16	15	15	14	14	14	13	13
96	20	19	19	18	18	17	17	16	16	15	15	14	14	13	13
98	21	20	19	19	18	17	17	16	16	15	15	15	14	14	13
100	21	20	20	19	18	18	17	17	16	16	15	15	14	14	14
102	21	21	20	19	19	18	18	17	17	16	16	15	15	14	14
104	22	21	20	20	19	18	18	17	17	16	16	15	15	14	14
106	22	21	21	20	19	19	18	18	17	17	16	16	15	15	14
108	23	22	21	20	20	19	19	18	17	17	16	16	15	15	15
110	23	22	21	21	20	19	19	18	18	17	17	16	16	15	15
112	23	23	22	21	20	20	19	19	18	18	17	16	16	16	15
114	24	23	22	22	21	20	19	19	18	18	17	17	16	16	16
116	24	23	23	22	21	21	20	19	19	18	18	17	17	16	16
118	25	24	23	22	22	21	20	20	19	18	18	17	17	17	16
120	25	24	23	23	22	21	21	20	19	19	18	18	17	17	16
122	26	25	24	23	22	22	21	20	20	19	18	18	18	17	17
124	26	25	24	23	23	22	21	21	20	19	19	18	18	17	17
126	26	25	25	24	23	22	22	21	20	20	19	19	18	18	17
128	26	26	25	24	23	23	22	21	21	20	19	19	18	18	17
130	27	26	25	25	24	23	22	22	21	20	20	19	19	18	18
132	27	26	26	25	24	23	23	22	21	21	20	19	19	18	18
134	28	27	26	25	25	24	23	22	22	21	20	20	19	18	18
136	28	27	26	26	25	24	23	23	22	21	21	20	19	19	18
138	29	28	27	26	25	25	24	23	22	22	21	20	20	19	19
140	29	28	27	26	26	25	24	23	23	22	21	21	20	20	19
142	29	28	27	27	26	25	24	24	23	22	21	21	20	20	19
144	30	29	28	27	26	26	25	24	23	23	22	21	21	20	20
146	30	29	28	27	27	26	25	24	24	23	22	22	21	20	20
148	31	30	29	28	27	26	25	25	24	23	23	22	21	21	20
150	31	30	29	28	28	27	26	25	24	24	23	22	22	21	20

152	154	156	158	160	162	164	166	168	170	172	174	176	178	180	182	184	186	188	190	192	194	196	198	200	202	204	206	208	210	212	214	216	218	220
21	21	21	21	22	22	23	23	23	23	24	24	24	25	25	25	26	26	26	27	27	27	28	28	29	29	29	29	30						
21	22	22	22	22	23	23	23	24	24	25	25	25	26	26	27	27	27	27	28	28	28	29	29	29	30	30	30	31						
22	22	22	23	23	23	24	24	24	25	25	25	26	26	26	27	27	27	28	28	28	29	29	29	30	30	31	31	31	31	32				
23	23	23	24	24	24	25	25	25	25	26	26	27	27	27	28	28	28	29	29	29	30	30	31	31	31	31	32	32	33					
23	23	24	24	24	25	25	25	26	26	26	27	27	27	28	28	29	29	29	30	30	30	31	31	32	32	32	33	33	33	34				
24	24	24	25	25	25	26	26	27	27	27	28	28	29	29	29	30	30	30	31	31	31	32	32	33	33	33	34	34	34	35				
25	25	25	26	26	26	27	27	28	28	28	29	29	29	30	30	31	31	31	32	32	33	33	33	34	34	35	35	35	36					
25	26	26	26	27	27	28	28	28	29	29	30	30	30	31	31	31	32	32	33	33	33	34	34	35	35	36	36	37						
26	27	27	27	28	28	29	29	29	30	30	30	31	31	32	32	32	33	33	34	34	34	35	35	36	36	36	37	37	38	38				
27	27	28	28	28	29	29	30	30	31	31	31	32	32	32	33	33	33	34	34	35	35	36	36	37	37	37	38	38	38	39	39			
28	28	29	29	29	30	30	30	31	31	32	32	32	33	33	33	34	34	35	35	36	36	36	37	37	38	38	39	39	39	40	40			
29	29	30	30	30	31	31	31	32	32	33	33	34	34	34	35	35	36	36	37	37	38	38	38	39	39	39	40	40	41	41	41	42		
30	30	31	31	31	32	32	33	33	33	34	34	34	35	35	36	36	36	37	37	38	38	39	39	40	40	40	41	41	42	42	42	43	43	
31	31	32	32	32	33	33	34	34	34	35	35	36	36	36	37	37	38	38	38	39	39	40	40	41	41	41	42	42	43	43	43	44	44	45
32	32	33	33	34	34	34	35	35	36	36	36	37	37	38	38	39	39	39	40	40	41	41	41	42	42	43	43	43	44	44	45	45	46	46

Metric

Weight in kilograms	Height in centimetres																
	150	152.5	155	157.5	160	162.5	165	167.5	170	172.5	175	177.5	180	182.5	185	187.5	190
40	18	17	17	16	16	15	15	14	14	13	13	13	12	12	12	11	11
41	18	18	17	17	16	16	15	15	14	14	13	13	13	12	12	12	11
42	19	18	17	17	16	16	15	15	15	14	14	13	13	13	12	12	12
43	19	18	18	17	17	16	16	15	15	14	14	14	13	13	13	12	12
44	20	19	18	18	17	17	16	16	15	15	14	14	14	13	13	13	12
45	20	19	19	18	18	17	17	16	16	15	15	14	14	14	13	13	13
46	20	20	19	19	18	17	17	16	16	15	15	15	14	14	13	13	13
47	21	20	20	19	18	18	17	17	16	16	15	15	15	14	14	13	13
48	21	21	20	19	19	18	18	17	17	16	16	15	15	14	14	14	13
49	22	21	20	20	19	19	18	17	17	16	16	16	15	15	14	14	14
50	22	21	21	20	20	19	18	18	17	17	16	16	15	15	15	14	14
51	23	22	21	21	20	19	19	18	18	17	17	16	16	15	15	15	14
52	23	22	22	21	20	20	19	19	18	17	17	17	16	16	15	15	14
53	24	23	22	21	21	20	19	19	18	18	17	17	16	16	15	15	15
54	24	23	22	22	21	20	20	19	19	18	18	17	17	16	16	15	15
55	24	24	23	22	21	21	20	19	19	18	18	17	17	16	16	15	15
56	25	24	23	23	22	21	21	20	19	19	18	18	17	17	16	16	16
57	25	25	24	23	22	22	21	20	20	19	19	18	18	17	17	16	16
58	26	25	24	23	23	22	21	21	20	19	19	18	18	17	17	16	16
59	26	25	25	24	23	22	22	21	20	20	19	19	18	18	17	17	16
60	27	26	25	24	23	23	22	21	21	20	20	19	19	18	18	17	17
61	27	26	25	25	24	23	22	22	21	21	20	19	19	18	18	17	17
62	28	27	26	25	24	24	23	22	21	21	20	20	19	19	18	18	17
63	28	27	26	25	25	24	23	22	22	21	21	20	19	19	18	18	18
64	28	28	27	26	25	24	24	23	22	22	21	20	20	19	19	18	18
65	29	28	27	26	25	25	24	23	22	22	21	21	20	19	19	18	18
66	29	28	27	27	26	25	24	24	23	22	22	21	20	20	19	19	18
67	30	29	28	27	26	25	25	24	23	23	22	21	21	20	19	19	19
68	30	29	28	27	27	26	25	24	24	23	22	22	21	20	20	19	19

69	70	71	72	73	74	75	76	77	78	79	80	81	82	83	84	85	86	87	88	89	90	91	92	93	94	95	96	97	98	99	100
19	19	20	20	20	21	21	21	22	22	22	22	23	23	23	24	24	24	24	25	25	25	25	26	26	26	26	27	27	27	27	28
20	20	20	21	21	21	21	22	22	22	23	23	23	24	24	24	25	25	25	25	26	26	26	26	27	27	27	27	28	28	28	28
20	20	21	21	21	22	22	22	23	23	23	23	24	24	24	25	25	25	25	26	26	26	27	27	27	27	28	28	28	29	29	29
21	21	21	22	22	22	23	23	23	23	24	24	24	25	25	25	26	26	26	27	27	27	28	28	28	28	29	29	29	29	30	30
21	22	22	22	23	23	23	23	24	24	24	25	25	25	26	26	26	27	27	27	27	28	28	29	29	29	30	30	30	31	31	31
22	22	23	23	23	23	24	24	25	25	25	26	26	26	27	27	27	27	28	28	28	29	29	29	30	30	30	31	31	31	32	32
23	23	23	24	24	24	24	25	25	26	26	26	27	27	28	28	28	29	29	29	30	30	30	31	31	31	32	32	32	33	33	33
23	23	24	24	25	25	25	25	26	26	27	27	27	28	28	28	29	29	29	30	30	31	31	31	32	32	32	33	33	33	33	34
24	24	25	25	25	26	26	26	27	27	27	28	28	28	29	29	29	30	30	30	31	31	31	32	32	33	33	33	34	34	34	35
25	25	25	26	26	27	27	27	28	28	28	29	29	30	30	30	31	31	31	32	32	33	33	34	34	34	35	35	35	36	36	36
25	26	26	26	27	27	28	28	28	29	29	29	30	30	30	31	32	32	32	33	33	33	34	34	35	35	35	36	36	36	36	37
26	26	27	27	28	28	29	29	29	30	30	31	31	31	32	34	33	33	33	34	34	35	35	36	36	36	37	37	37	37	37	38
27	27	28	28	29	29	29	30	30	31	31	32	32	33	33	34	34	34	35	35	36	36	36	37	37	38	38	38	38	39	39	39
28	28	29	29	30	30	31	31	31	32	32	33	33	33	34	34	35	35	35	36	36	37	37	37	38	38	39	39	39	40	40	40
29	29	30	30	30	31	31	32	32	32	33	33	34	34	35	35	35	36	36	37	37	38	38	38	39	39	39	40	40	41	41	42
30	30	31	31	31	32	32	33	34	34	34	35	35	36	37	37	37	38	38	39	39	39	40	40	40	41	41	42	42	43	43	43
31	31	32	32	33	33	34	35	35	36	36	36	37	37	38	39	39	40	40	41	41	42	42	43	43	44	44	44	44	44	44	44

Index of Diets

(*Note*: Individual diets are in ordinary type, categories are shown in bold.)